A Garland Series

The English Stage
Attack and Defense 1577 - 1730

A collection of 90 important works
reprinted in photo-facsimile in 50 volumes

edited by
Arthur Freeman
Boston University

The Touch-Stone

by

James Ralph

with a preface
for the Garland Edition by

Arthur Freeman

Garland Publishing, Inc., New York & London

1973

Copyright © 1973

by Garland Publishing, Inc.

All Rights Reserved

Library of Congress Cataloging in Publication Data

Ralph, James, d. 1762.
  The touch-stone.

  (The English stage: attack and defense, 1577-1730)
  Reprint of the 1728 ed. printed by the booksellers
of London and Westminister in London.
  1. London--Amusements. I. Title. II. Series.
DA688.R17 1973   790'.09421   78-170491
ISBN 0-8240-0630-5

Printed in the United States of America

Preface

James Ralph (?1705-1762) is one of the more interesting and well-traveled miscellaneous writers of his splendid era — boyhood friend of Franklin, enemy of Pope, hack poet, distinguished historian, schoolteacher, dramatist, dramatic critic, editor, and journalist for diametrically opposing factions. He was born probably in Philadelphia, about a year before Franklin, with whom he formed a great friendship; Franklin dedicated his precocious Dissertation on Liberty and Necessity, Pleasure and Pain *(1725, largely burned by its nineteen-year-old author) to Ralph, and praises him for eloquence, manners, and vivacity in his* Memoirs: "*I never knew a prettier talker.*" *In 1724 Ralph accompanied Franklin to England, where he remained for the rest of his life; penniless at first, he took a schoolteaching position in a Berkshire village, assumed — apparently with Franklin's consent — Franklin's own name, and remained a rather expensive intimate, until a breach, involving Ralph's*

PREFACE

village mistress and Franklin's "improper advances" to her, duly rejected, parted the two permanently. This would have been in 1728, at which time Ralph returned to London and set up as a hack writer, now aged about twenty-three.

The Touch-Stone, *with its madcap title and facetious preface, is probably the "first fruits" of its pseudonymous author, although in the same year appeared three individual poems,* Night *(dedicated to Chesterfield and later ridiculed by Pope),* The Muse's Address to the King: an Ode, *and* The Tempest, or the Terrors of Death. *In 1731* The Touch-Stone *was reissued with a cancel title as* The Taste of the Town *(Lowe-Arnott-Robinson 870), still pseudonymous, the dedication signed "A. Primcock." The book is by no means as zany as its title suggests, being instead a rather sober examination of playgoing habits and other forms of entertainment, the Prynne-Collier-Bedford-Law axis, a serious suggestion to revive religious drama for playing on Sundays and holidays, and critiques of audience behavior, practices of dancing, masquerades, puppet shows, cockfighting, "antient" athletic sports, and even the pulpit performance of "Orator" John Henley.*

Ralph's career after 1728 followed the familiar

PREFACE

*route of pasquil, poem, literary infighting (espe-
cially with Pope), playwriting (notably
unsuccessful, even in collaboration with Henry
Fielding), journalism, editing newspapers both for
and against the ministerial establishment, and
finally to the "serious" semi-contemporary history
for which he remains best known. Besides Fielding,
his friends and associates included Bolingbroke,
William Beckford, Garrick, and George Hogarth; he
was predictably an enemy of Sir Robert Walpole,
scorned by Horace, and an activist in the pursuit of
authors' rights to their own works. We reprint* The
Touch-Stone *from a copy of the 1728 first edition
in the Yale University Library (Franklin Collection
421 1728r), collating π 1 [half title / a-h*b* c*²* B-X*b* / X6
blank]. Lowe-Arnott-Robinson 869.*

February, 1973   A.F.

THE

TOUCH-STONE:

O R,

Hiftorical, Critical, Political, Moral,
Philofophical and Theological

E S S A Y S

Upon the reigning Diverfions of
the T o w n.

THE
TOUCH-STONE:
OR,

Hiftorical, Critical, Political, Philofophical,
and Theological

ESSAYS

On the reigning Diverfions of the Town.

Defign'd for the Improvement of all AUTHORS,
SPECTATORS, and ACTORS of OPERAS,
PLAYS, and MASQUERADES.

In which every thing antique, or modern, relating
to MUSICK, POETRY, DANCING, PAN-
TOMIMES, CHORUSSES, CAT-CALLS,
AUDIENCES, JUDGES, CRITICKS,
BALLS, RIDOTTOS, ASSEMBLIES, NEW
ORATORY, CIRCUS, BEAR-GARDEN,
GLADIATORS, PRIZE-FIGHTERS, ITA-
LIAN STROLERS, MOUNTEBANK STA-
GES, COCK-PITS, PUPPET-SHEWS,
FAIRS, and PUBLICK AUCTIONS, is oc-
cafionally handled.

By a Perfon of fome Tafte and fome Quality.

With a PREFACE, giving an Account of
the AUTHOR and the WORK.

——— Ridiculum Acri
Fortiùs & meliùs magnas plerumque fecat res.
Horat. Sat. Lib. i. Sat. x.

Non hic Centauros, non Gorgonas, Harpyiafque
Invenies : Hominem pagina noftra fapit.
Martial Ep. iv. Lib. x.

LONDON:
Printed, and fold by the Bookfellers of London and Weftminfter.
MDCCXXVIII.

EPISTLE DEDICATORY.

To the Right Notable

---- *PAYNE*, Efq;

*Supervifor General of the Mall,
Political Cenfor of Great-Britain,
and Heir ExpeElant of a very
great* POST.

Wonderful SIR !

SHOULD ESSAYS of this publick, private, general, particular, grave, merry *Nature*, appear under the Protection of any Name but the illuftrious 'Squire *Payne*, the World would fo far refent my Choice of a *Patron*, as not even to read my

Preface: But when the Town is
aſſur'd that your Approbation was
Midwife, as your Perſon ſtands *God-
father* to this Infant; without Heſi-
tation, or Peruſal, they'll of courſe
allow it all the *Quantums* and *Quales*
of your Body and Mind.

Your Solemnity of Countenance
prognoſticates its Wiſdom, and your
Air of Inſinuating Addreſs its Penetration; your laughing at great People,
and little People's laughing at you,
are manifeſt Tokens of its Humour
and facetious Diſpoſition. From your
good Breeding they depend upon its
Politeneſs; from your eaſy Conver-
ſation, its being the Standard of ſheer
Wit; and from your picquant Reflections, they expect in it the ſharp-
eſt but juſteſt *Satyr.*

To you then, Sir, the *Criterion*
(to the Vulgar, the *Touch-Stone*)
flies for Refuge. Point out to the
ignorant World its Beauties, and ex-
cuſe to the Learned its Errors. Shield
it from the piercing Tongue, and
blaſting

blaſting Breath of the Malicious and Envious. Let it retreat under the Shelter of your Eye-Brows, and cover it with the Wings of your Authority; ſo ſhall it remain as ſnug and ſafe as a Murderer in a Catholick Church.

Pardon, dear Sir, my being thus buſy about my Book, that I have forgot you: In this widely differing from moſt modern Dedicators, who deſignedly neglect themſelves, in order to have an Opportunity of talking more largely in Praiſe of their Patrons. But not to be quite dead to the Faſhion—— I muſt have a Touch at your Honour; though I fear, that even in this Caſe, I ſhall prove the Reverſe of our preſent Set of Authors; for they generally attribute to their Patrons a Rag-man-roll Liſt of Virtues, poſitively in the Affirmative, tho' uncertain in every Point; whilſt I ſhall, in the Negative, abſolutely ſuppoſe you adorn'd with all Perfections that I ought to know, or can deſire you capable of.

a 3 As

A s to your noble Family, it may be of older Date than History it self can go back to; nor can any Man say, but that every illustrious Branch of it may have been loaded with prime Ministers, Generals, Admirals, Bishops, and Judges; tho' some spiteful Persons have falsely advanc'd, that you never had any *Ancestors,* because you are universally acknowledg'd to be an *Original.* As to your Parts and Prudence, we cannot deny, but you might have shone out a *Wolsey,* or *Richlieu,* had any Prince put the same Confidence in you, and brought your Capacity to the Test. If our publick Papers are silent, as to any remarkable Proofs of your Courage, yet who's the Man that ever worsted you in the Field, or dares affirm, that he saw you fly from Danger? This we may modestly assert, That let your Family be ever so eminent, you are undoubtedly the most extraordinary Person of it; which few modern *Panegyrists*

can

can plead in Favour of their Patrons, without ſtretching the Truth on too large a Laſt.

L E T not my Forgetfulneſs oblite-rate the Wonders of your Hand, as made apparent in thoſe valuable Sen-tences, wiſe Apopthegms, and im-mortal Maxims, ſo long and learned-ly carry'd on in Behalf of our Con-ſtitution, to the Honour of our Coun-try, and to the utter Ruin of its and your Foes. Theſe fine Precepts are the moſt curious Medley of Zeal, publick Spirit, Learning, Wit, Hu-mour, Politicks, Religion and neceſ-ſary Nonſenſe, prudently adapted to the *Britiſh* Taſte. What Pity it is, that like the Prophecies of the *Sybils*, they are only deliver'd to us on the Leaves of Trees, or the Sides of the *Mall!*

T H E mentioning of which warns me, not to incroach upon thoſe Mo-ments, the leaſt of which is of the utmoſt Conſequence to the Nation, and gives me an Opportunity of
wiſhing,

wiſhing, that you may long live to enjoy (at leaſt in Imagination) thoſe Poſts you are certainly capable of a-dorning.

S I R,

I am, with the profoundeſt

Reſpect, your moſt

Devoted humble Servant,

A. Primcock.

THE

THE

PREFACE:

OR,

INTRODUCTION.

Giving a particular Account of the
AUTHOR and the WORK.

OST Books have a PREFACE,
and every Thing of Moment
should have a proper Introduction; the first being customa-
ry, and the other necessary,
I could not distinguish which is most to my
Purpose; therefore give the World both in
one. This the Criticks may fall upon, either
as an Absurdity, or Innovation: But my Writings

tings are as far out of the Power of their Criticifms, as my Fortune is of their Ill-Nature. It is fufficient for me to let them know, that I write for the univerfal Benefit of my Country; that is, to improve one Part, and get the other Bread. But if thefe learned Snarlers bite their Nails at this Beginning, they may chance to eat their Fingers before they come to the laft Page.

As the Generality of Readers would willingly pry into the moft material Secrets relating to an Author (being very inquifitive about his Birth, Life, Circumftances and Converfation) fo on the other hand, he is very often as much upon the Guard, to fcreen himfelf in all thofe Particulars, from their curious Search. But in order to gratify both my felf and them at the fame Time, I fhall vary from the common Method of proceeding; and by telling pofitively who I am, keep my felf, as hitherto, abfolutely conceal'd from the whole World.

I am lineally fprang, by my Father's Side, from Adam's *chief Root, the Family of the* Cocks; *and, by my Mother's, from the firft* Welfh *Kings: So that the Antiquity and Gentility that run in my Veins, admit of no Difpute, or Rival, in Heraldry. I am the only Son of a younger Brother, of the Branch*

of

of the Primcocks; *which is noted for producing very fine* Gentlemen, *and generally great Favourites with the* Ladies. *The* Laycocks *are very numerous, and most commonly Females: They bear the Character of being* Romps *of the first Magnitude, and were the Inventors of the Game of* Hot-cockles. *The* Allcocks *are of an amorous Disposition; and though but low of Stature very often, yet by standing on Tip-toe, and other Devices, they exceed those who seem larger, by several Inches. The* Stopcocks *are altogether given to the Study of* Physick *and* Surgery; *their Knowledge in these Sciences, is of manifest Advantage in most Diseases particularly incident to the Family of the* Cocks. *The* Handcocks *are their nearest Relations, and are employ'd in those Affairs, under them, which require manual* Operation. *Several of these last, who are settled abroad, give mightily into a monastick Life. The* Halfcocks *enjoy the greatest Fortunes, and are allow'd to be the best dress'd Branch of the Family. We have but few* Nococks *in* England, *and they are generally esteem'd for their fine Voices, and acknowledg'd by us all to be the best Singers. The* Smartcocks *have naturally a fierce Air, and a strong Inclination to a military Life; tho' they often affect a lac'd Hat and*
red

red *Coat*, *when they do not belong to the
Army. The* Lobcocks *are thoroughly vers'd
in Multiplication, and breed so fast, that they
exceed all the other Tribes in Numbers: They
are as fond of an Ecclesiastical State, as their
Cousin-Germans the* Woodcocks *are of a
Country Life; few of whom rise higher in
Power, or Title, than a Justice of Peace, or
an Esquire. Most of these two last Branches
are got upon Hay-cocks. As for the* Cock-
a-Hoops *and* Cockneys, *they are at best but
Bastards of our Family; nor could their
Wealth, or pretended Courage, ever prevail
upon us to call Tradesmen and Bullies the le-
gitimate Issue of the* Cocks. *In short, our
Family has spread so wonderfully, that in
some Respect we are allied to every Man in*
Europe; *from* L—s *of* B—n *to* Tom Tram.

*Being descended from Parents more illu-
strious than rich, my Education was becoming a Gentleman's Son, but conducted in a
Method rather learned than polite. Losing,
when at School, both Father and Mother, I
was left to the Care of an Uncle, who soon
after died, and bequeath'd me a small Estate
in* Wales. *Having by this Time attain'd my
Eighteenth Year, a strong Inclination to seeing
the World seiz'd me: Upon which I sold my
little Fortune in the Country, and came up to*
Town

Town with a borrow'd Name, under which I purchas'd a moderate Annuity, and after a short Stay in London, *went abroad. In about the Space of five Years, I made the Tour of those Parts of* Europe *which are most worthy a Traveller's Curiosity. This I performed in a manner as reasonable as agreeable. My Genius (encourag'd by what I saw in other Countries) prompted me to an Improvement in my Travels, which may seem too trifling in one who was brought up to severer Studies. I div'd not into the political Principles of any State, but knew to a Tittle, what City had the most elegant Buildings, the best judg'd Amusements, or the finest Women. I troubled not my Head about the endless Controversies in Religion, nor enquir'd where I came, which flourish'd, which was tolerated, or which oppress'd: But I narrowly inspected the Architecture and Ornaments of their Churches; observ'd how the Rules of the Antients and Moderns agreed, and compar'd the Beauties and Proportions of the several Orders. I never sought the Conversation of their Divines, Philosophers, or Astrologers; but became intimate with every Poet, Critick, Painter and Statuary, each different Country call'd eminent. In short, I principally study'd the Fundamentals of the publick Amusements*

b

most

most follow'd, *wherever I came* ; *I judi-*
ciously weigh'd the minutest Particulars in
all Entertainments exhibited in OPERA
or PLAY-HOUSES ; *both on this, and*
t'other Side the Alps.   *I read attentively*
all the French *and* Italian *Criticks* : *I could*
repeat the greatest Part of three hundred
and thirteen German *Commentators* ; *and*
went to the Bottom of all the Low-Dutch
Authors who commented upon them.   Then
considering that Speculation is but barely
a Foundation in every thing, which Pra-
ctice can only compleat,   I sung the chief
Part of an OPERA, *at* Paris, *a whole Win-*
ter, and with equal Applause appear'd as
the Hero of a Tragedy, at Amsterdam.
Thus loaded with critical Learning, and
cloath'd with necessary Experience, I re-
turn'd to my native Country, and have,
since that Time, liv'd in publick, yet un-
known, making my Studies my Amuse-
ments, always pleasing and improving my
Mind by the noted Entertainments of the
Town. I am now near my grand Climacte-
rick,   and have for above thirty Years,
thus play'd Hide and Seek with the World :
I am rarely known to two Persons by the
same Name, and to no body, by my true
one.   I frequently change my Lodgings,
                                        and

*and in them all, go generally by the Title
of the strange Gentleman.*

*Tho' I seldom quit the Bills of Mortality, yet I rarely go into a Tavern: My
Evenings are devoted to the publick Amusements ; nor do I ever miss* OPERAS *or*
PLAYS, *that are good, or new. My Daylight is divided betwixt the Booksellers
Shops (where I am welcome to pick out the
Learning I cannot purchase, in Return of
the little I buy) and those Coffee-Houses,
where all critical Affairs are bandy'd* pro
and con *; there I am oftener a Hearer than
Speaker. I make frequent Visits to* Fleet-Ditch, Moor-Fields Rails, *and* Holborn-Bars, *where I spend many agreeable Hours,
in meeting with Wit, Truth and Reason,
conceal'd from that Part of Mankind, who
scorn to look for them there ; and unknown
to that Part, who condescend to look, but
cannot find them out. Having for so long
a Space, nicely canvass'd, and maturely
consider'd all things premis'd in my Title-Page, I cannot but look upon my self as a
Person every way adequate to the Undertaking ; and may, without Vanity affirm,
that by Genius, Study and Experience, I
am sufficiently qualify'd to inspect, criticise, and determine upon the reigning Di-*

versions

versions of the TOWN. *I blush not to own, that I was the famous* Trunk-Maker, *of whom the* TATLER *so often made just and honourable Mention* : *As I then gave Laws to the Realms of both* THEATRES, *I am now the only Body that can awe the Footmens* GALLERY *into any tolerable Degree of Order* ; *nor am I less noted for being universally call'd upon, as an infallible Umpire, in all Disputes that happen betwixt Men or Brutes, at the* BEAR-GARDEN.

I thought it would be proper to inform the World of every Circumstance in my past Life, that was preparatory to my being an Author. I shall next, in the Out-lines of the following Work, give them a general Idea of the various Parts that compose the whole, so conclude this necessary Introduction.

My Manner of Criticizing, as observ'd in these ESSAYS, *differs widely from any thing that has yet appear'd under that Name* : *Both Censure and Panegyrick are introduc'd after a Method entirely new. I could never give into the slovenly, canting Reflections of* Pryn, *the arbitrary malicious Learning of* Collier, *the enthusiastick, insipid Arguments of* L----w, *or the severe, tho'*

tho' juſtifiable Rules of Rymer *and* Dennis. *I hope my Animadverſions upon all polite Entertainments, will be allow'd more agreeably juſt, if not ſo deeply Learned. Were we to be regulated by theſe Reformers and Criticks, we muſt with one Party demoliſh all Stage-Entertainments, upon account of ſome few bold Licences, which no Man will pretend to countenance; and, with the others, cramp every enterprizing Genius within the narrow Bounds of Art; blind to the Charms of the moſt beautiful Irregularities. The firſt would remedy ſome Diſorders in our Stage-Plays; as if a Surgeon ſhould cure a Mortification in a poor Fellows great Toe, by cutting off his Head; and the laſt are reſolv'd to allow no Coin to be current but what comes from their own Mint. But I ſhall place theſe Affairs in another Light, and by ſome Hints tolerably uncommon, point out to the World, what I judge perfect, and what wants Amendment in theſe Amuſements; at the ſame time propoſing the moſt probable Remedies.*

I am ſo far perſwaded of the Innocence and Uſe of all our publick Diverſions, taking them either in a moral, or religious Senſe, that I ſhall endeavour to remove all Prejudices rais'd againſt them by unthink-

ing

ing Zealots.   This I hope to accomplish, either by giving pertinent and satisfactory Answers to the most material Objections of Consciences truly scrupulous, or by well-judg'd Alterations and Abolitions, bring about that Reformation in our Pleasures, as must of Course silence the specious Cavils of the most Inveterate.

As we cannot reasonably expect to be ever all of a Mind, as to the Principles of Religion or Politicks, I should be glad, we might in some Respect, be look'd upon as an united People ; that we may at least agree in Singing and Dancing, since we cannot in Preaching and Praying.

My Lucubrations being principally confin'd to the most taking Diversions of the Town, *no* POETRY *comes under my Consideration, but* Dramatick ; *nor any* MUSICK, *but the* Royal Academick. *I flatter my self, that the Method observ'd in the following* ESSAYS, *will be thought pretty exact in the Point of* Decorum ; *tho' I have ventur'd to introduce* Sounds *before* Wit.   *'Tis true, as a Scholar, I must maintain, that* POETRY *is the Head of all the fine Arts that ever were, or can be ; the utmost Perfection that human Nature can excel in : But then as a Man of the* Town, *and one that has seen the World, and*

and all that, I muſt give MUSICK *the right Hand, becauſe fine Gentlemen, and fine Ladies, always allow it the firſt Place; they both liking and underſtanding it beſt. Thus in my firſt* ESSAY *I ſhew my good Breeding, and in the ſecond, my good Senſe.*

The OPERAS *therefore being look'd upon as the Centre of the* Beau Monde, *I begin with them; in an hiſtorical Manner trace them to their firſt Riſe: I make manifeſt their Beauties; how ſhocking the* Italian *Performance and Language are to ſome* Engliſh *Ears; ſhew what is wanting, what ſuperfluous, and what Alterations or Additions are requiſite to ſuit them to all Capacities, and adapt them to the Taſte of this Nation in general.*

In the ſecond ESSAY, *I conſider the Inſtruction and Delight given by* Dramatick *Poetry, its great Merit, and the Eſteem paid it by the Antients; why degenerated and deſpis'd in the preſent Age: That the Stage has ſo many Enemies, imputed to Poets, Actors and Auditors; the moſt reaſonable Remedies propos'd for all Diſorders in the Conſtitution of this fine Art, as occaſion'd by the Writers, Managers, or Spectators of Plays.*

I then naturally ſlide into a third, but not contemptible, Theatrical Entertainment,

ment, viz. Grotesque, *or* Dramatical Dancing; *in which I introduce an historical Account of the old* Mimes *and* Pantomimes; *with a just Comparison betwixt them, and their modern Imitators, the Race of* Arlequins, Scaramouches *and* Punchinellos. *I endeavour to shew how far this Art may be render'd of general Use, from what has been done in it; then conclude with some necessary Reflections and Documents of a publick and private Nature, tending to form a compleat Dancer.*

I next proceed to take Notice of our total Neglect of the most beautiful Appendix to the foregoing Entertainments, viz. *A* Grand Chorus, *always judg'd of the greatest Importance to the Stage, by Antiquity; their Magnificence and Use in* Operas, Plays, *and* Dances, *explain'd; as approv'd of by the most learned of the Moderns:* To which is added, a short Chronology, with the Nature, Use and Design *of the* British Chorus *of* Cat-calls.

In the Fifth Essay *I enter into that Part of the Second, which relates to the Decay of* Dramatick Poetry, *being occasion'd by its Spectators and Readers: I there animadvert upon our* Audiences, *as to the Articles of Behaviour and Judgment, both within Doors and without.*

out. After having properly diftinguifh'd the feveral Orders and Degrees that form a regular Audience, I throw in fome Hints and Rules for their Conduct, neceffary to their future Amendment ; then conclude with an Examination of Criticifm in General, and a full Account of the feveral Kinds of Judges and Criticks.

I next vary my Subject, without quitting the Stage, by enquiring into the Original, Ufe, and Danger of Masquerades *in General; I there demonftrate their great Antiquity, their pernicious Confequences, as now practis'd, and how far capable of being render'd as beneficial as agreeable : Several Arguments advanc'd and fupported, to prove their Importance to the publick Welfare, if turn'd into a right Channel. To this Amufement, I tack fome fmall Remarks upon that of going to* C——h, *ending with a modeft Propofal in Behalf of the* O—ry *in* N————t M——t.

In my laft Essay, *I run over concifely, the Rife, Progrefs, Studies and Exercifes of the Old* Grecian Games; *their* Gymnasia, Stadia, &c. *fet apart for training their Youth up to thefe Martial Amufements. In the next Place, I fhew, that from them fprung the* Circus,

CIRCUS, NAUMACHIÆ, AMPHI-
THEATRES, *and* CAMPUS MAR-
TIUS *of the* Romans, *being of a-piece,
in Design, Sports, and Improvement.*

Upon a Parallel with the antient CIR-
CUS, *I fix the* BEAR-GARDEN, *being a finish'd Copy of that great Original;
or rather being descended from the same
Illustrious Family: Its present Conduct
defended with a Demonstration of a farther Improvement, if properly encourag'd.
To this is annex'd a just Comparison betwixt the* PRIZE-FIGHTERS *and*
GLADIATORS; *the* Italian Strolers
and Mountebank-Stages: *The Whole con-
cluding with some particular Observations
upon* COCK-PITS, FAIRS, PUP-
PET-SHEWS, *and Publick* Auctions.

*It is probable, that my Method of
Writing will not be sufficiently surprizing, or out of the Way, to take with the*
English *Nation. I would rectify their
Errors, and make even their Pleasures
advantageous, by rational Courses; I
speak to them as Men, and hope for a
Man-like Reformation. I suppose no flying Islands, enchanted Castles, or fancy'd
Regions, to amuse them. I bring home
no Pygmies of six Inches, or Giants of
sixty Foot, to moralize and talk Politicks*
to

to them ; nor *speaking Brutes to preach
to them. Every Fool can furnish us with
Countries and Chimæras hatch'd in his
own Brain, and form a Speech out of my-
sterious Nothingness, and a Jargon not
even to be pronounc'd ; luckily judging,
that by the Majority of Readers (who
only skim the Surface of a Work, and are
fond of strange Monsters) he must be held
wise, who is unintelligible. My Remarks upon the Errors in our Conduct, my
Reasons for Amendment, and my Method
for attaining it, are drawn from Nature
and Experience. Happy if I can but point
out one wrong Step to be avoided ; or that
my rude Scheme may serve as a Hint to a
brighter Genius, equally willing with me
to promote the publick Good.*

Some Politicians, Informers, Reformers, and small Wits, may be very inquisitive about my half Blanks, whole
Blanks, or mutilated Sentences : But I
can assure my Readers, they need not
dread any Scandal, Treason, or Impiety
being couch'd in them. I am sensible
most People love to meet with such Gaps,
in order to fill them up. If every Thing
was set down plain, and at full Length
in any Work ; no Words to be guess'd at,
or no Obscurity in the Sense, it would be
thought

thought only proper for the perusal of a
School-boy, and argue an Author's Assurance, in his giving no fair Play to a
Reader's Penetration. Many dull Things,
in suitable Expressions, have been admir'd,
for the sake of those which were left out,
and of course suppos'd to be very witty:
The first and last Letters of Words, no
Words at all, a Dash, or an Asterism,
may contain more Merit than any Thing
the whole Alphabet can produce in a regular Way. To this End were design'd
the Mysteries, Hieroglyphicks, and Ænig-
mas of the Antients, to sharpen the
Imagination, imploy idle People, and en-
hance the Value of any Thing discover'd.
Moreover, as no Author can pretend, in
Writing, to please the various Humours
and Desires of Mankind ; let him but
leave some Parts of his Work imperfect,
and every Man, in finding out the Meaning, will undoubtedly strive to please himself. In short, to ride Post thro' any
Treatise, without Stop, Guess-work, scratch-
ing the Noddle, or grope in the Dark, is
as insipid as a Fox-chace without Fatigue, a Victory without Danger, or a
Wedding-night without a M--n---d.

THE

THE

CONTENTS.

c　　　　　puted

ESSAY

E S S A Y VII.

E S S A Y

ESSAY I.

OF MUSICK;

Particularly DRAMATICK.

The Original of OPERAS *look'd into. An Historical Account of their Progress in this Nation. The Objection to the* ITALIAN OPERAS *answer'd; and some Rules proposed for adapting them to the* ENGLISH TASTE *in general.*

F all the fine ARTS, (excepting POETRY) none has exceeded MUSICK, or shewn a great *Genius* in a more distinguished way.

POETRY has the Advantage of delivering to its Readers or Hearers the finest Precepts of Morality, nay, Religion it self, in the most insinuating Manner; so, by pleasing, it instructs; as, some Dis-

cases

eafes are cured by being tickled. It is indeed the utmost Perfection human Nature can arrive at, to give or receive what is truly profitable with Delight. This is the happy Talent of POETRY, either *Epick* or *Dramatick*: And certainly of all other Arts a compleat OPERA comes nearest that perfect State of POETRY; becaufe you may there enjoy a finished regular *Fable*, accompanied with the moft exquifite *Harmony*.

As to the Antiquity of thefe Half-Sifters, I fhall not here prefume to make any Parallel. By all Accounts, facred and profane, both are very ancient; though moft People feem inclined to give *Mufick* the Preference; and amongft others, for the following weighty Reafon. The Foundation of our publick Entertainments of all kinds, is undeniably owing to fome Part of the Religious Worfhip of the firft Ages; this is notorious beyond any Ground for a Difpute, in MUSICK, POETRY, DANCING, and even all the Diverfions of the *Bear-Garden*, which we have certainly borrowed from the Ancients.

Now the earlieft Accounts we have of any Adoration paid to a fupreme Being, either in facred or profane Hiftory, inftructs us; That the Performance was mufical, either in Hymns or Songs, or by the Sounds of Inftruments; and as the Notions of a Divinity were naturally implanted in the Minds of Men, fo their Expreffions of that Knowledge firft employed their leifure Hours, and it is probable, by MUSICK: And I am apt to think, that the Meafures of that Art firft gave the Hint and Model for the Numbers of POETRY.

This we are certain of, that in all Ages of the World, nothing has fhewn a greater Power over the Paffions in general, than MUSICK: It commands the Soul, and moulds the Heart at Will; it forces Mankind to be gay or grave; a-
morous

morous or religious; effeminate or brave; according to its Beauty, Juftnefs or Variety: The Mafter's Skill infpiring us with Sentiments artfully thrown into our Minds, and all over our Bodies, by thrilling Notes, and captivating Sounds.

Now fince a compleat OPERA is a regular mufical DRAMMA, and approaching very near to the Excellency of POETRY, (becaufe Virtue may be there inculcated by a proper Fable) I fhall in this *Effay* confine my felf to OPERAS alone; all other kinds of MUSICK, which are not perfect theatrical Entertainments, being entirely foreign to my Defign.

BUT before I proceed any farther in canvaffing our prefent harmonious Amufements, I believe it will be neceffary to look back a little into the Original of OPERAS, which will be at beft but Guefs-Work, or a Grope in the Dark, without the Affiftance of the fmalleft Star to guide us; then I will prefent my Readers with a more regular Sketch of the Rife and Progrefs of OPERAS in this Ifland, from their firft rude Eftablifhment, to that State of Perfection we now enjoy them in.

IT will prove a difficult Task to form any true Judgment of the Original of OPERAS; efpecially how far the *Italians* (where certainly they firft arrived to any tolerable Degree of Perfection) are indebted to the Ancients, or other modern Nations for this Mufical *Dramma*. From *Italy* and *France* we have borrowed whatever has appeared on our Stages in that Way: We muft then travel thither in fearch of the Hints which firft gave Life to this Entertainment.

DRYDEN (who was one of our greateft Criticks, as well as Poets, and who has given us three *Englifh* OPERAS in a different Tafte) owns, he could not, by the niceft Scrutiny, get any juft Light, either as to the Time, or the firft Inventers of OPERAS. He imagines *that the* Italians, *observing the Gallantries of the* Spanish Moors, *at their* Zambras, *or* Royal Feasts, (*where* MUSICK, SONGS *and* DANCING *were in Perfection; together with their Machines at their running at the Ring, and other Solemnities*) *might have refined upon those* Moresque *Amusements, and produced this pleasing kind of Dramma, by leaving out the warlike Part, and forming a poetical Design for to introduce more naturally the* MACHINES, MUSICK *and* DANCES. Then he proceeds; *that however the* OPERAS *began,* MUSICK *has for some Centuries flourished principally in* Italy; and he believed, *their* OPERAS *were first intended for the Celebration of the Marriages of their Princes, or the magnificent Triumphs of some general Time of Joy; and accordingly the Expences upon these Occasions were out of the Purse of the Sovereign or Republick, as has been often practised at* Turin, Florence, Venice, &c.

IN this last Point, it is very probable, he is justly exact; but as to the first, he allows it himself to be but conjectural; and, indeed, I think so too; therefore, begging Pardon for dissenting from so great an Authority, and for whose Judgment I have the utmost Deference; I must say, that in my Opinion, the Conjecture is mightily strained, and the Supposition very far fetch'd, and that the *Italians* had not the least Regard to, or Notion of a *Moorish* Solemnity, in bringing OPERAS on the Stage.

LET us thoroughly consider this Entertainment in all its Parts, and we shall readily perceive, they could only have an Eye to Antiquity, in its Invention and Establishment; particularly to the MAGNIFICENCE, MACHINES, MUSICK and DANCING of the old *Grecian* CHORUS; they (allowing for the different Design and Manner of their
being

OF MUSICK. 5

being introduced) anfwering exactly in the moft essential Parts that compose one and the other.

DRYDEN himfelf, in a Poftfcript to the Preface of *Albion* and *Albanius*, recants and owns, *That possibly the* Italians *went not so far as* Spain *for the Invention of their* OPERAS; *they might have taken the Hint at Home, and formed this* Dramma, *by gathering up the Shipwrecks of the* Grecian *and* Roman *Theatres, which were adorned with* MUSICK, SCENES, DANCES, *and* MACHINES, *especially the* Grecian; *adding, that though they are a modern Invention, yet they are built on the Foundation of* Ethnick *Worship.*

Now indeed he fpeaks to the Purpose, and gives us the juftest Idea of their Original; then pray, from what Part of the Shipwreck of the *Grecian* or *Roman* Theatres could the Design of an OPERA be plan'd out, but that of the Chorus? only what was but an Interlude, or a neceffary Part of a Stage-Play with the Ancients, they enlarged, and fwelled into a compleat Entertainment.

But there remain ftill two Points not yet taken Notice of by any Critick, which bear fome Relation to the Birth of OPERAS, and weigh very much with me.

THE firft is, the frequent Mention made in all Authors, (who treat of the Antiquities of *Greece*) of their *Odeum,* or Mufick-Theatre; every one fpeaks of it, and defcribes its Magnificence, efpecially that of *Athens*, which was looked upon as the moft fumptuous Building of that noble City; they mention it feparately from the other Theatres, and call it, in a fignificant way, the *Mufick Theatre*; which certainly muft imply a Theatre where Mufical Entertainments alone were performed: This has a Face of Probability; though none of the Authors who defcribe the Place, let us into the Secret, what the Nature of the Enter-

B 3 tainments

tainments was, that appeared upon that Stage; but I humbly fubmit my private Opinion to be canvaffed, and cenfured, or approved by the learn-ed World.

'T i s true, Mr. *Kennet,* in his *Roman Antiquities,* takes Notice of the *Odeum* at *Rome,* built in the ordinary Form of other Theatres; but (as he fays) *only made ufe of for their Actors and Muficians to exercife themfelves privately in, before they appeared upon the Stage*; a Cuftom parallel to our Rehear-fals. If this was the fole Intent of the *Odeum* at *Rome,* I fhall not pretend to determine; but if we may judge from the imperfect Accounts we have of the *Grecian* Odeum, it is impoffible we fhould believe it defigned for that Purpofe; and, to corroborate my Affertion, I call upon his Quo-tation from *Plutarch*; who fays, " That as to the " Contrivance of the *Odeum,* the Infide was full of " Seats, and Ranges of Pillars; and, on the Outfide, " the Roof or Covering was made from one Point " at top with a great many Bendings, all fhelving " downwards, in Imitation of the King of *Perfia's* " Pavilion." Now if they encouraged this extrava-gant Expence, only that the Actors and Muficians might privately rehearfe the Pieces they were obliged to prefent on the Stage; what glorious Edifices muft the Theatres themfelves be: Or if the Grandeur of thefe fort of Buildings was con-fined to thofe Theatres alone where they rehear-fed, and they publickly performed in wooden Booths, we can only liken them to a Man, who would put on his Shoes and wafh his Hands in a Brocade Night-gown, then drefs himfelf in Rags, in order to go abroad.

T h e other Head (that I would inftance here, and which has been hitherto unobferved) is, that I have fome Grounds to believe, that the *Italians,* in their firft modelling their O p e r a s, had part-

ly

ly in their View the Conduct of the famous Priests of *Cybele*; at least, if we may judge from the Majority of their present Performers, and the Conduct of their Entertainments both in *Italy* and *Britain*. These Priests of *Cybele* bore various Names, but generally were known by the Denomination of the *Galli*.

T h e i r Ceremonies were all performed in Publick, and consisted entirely of M u s i c k, vocal and instrumental, intermixed with portable Machinery and all kinds of Dances; their Performers were all Eunuchs, and positively Foreigners to the *Roman* State, being all *Phrygians*. Whether this Description corresponds with O p e r a s, as shewn abroad, is not my Business to assert; but in most Respects it tallies with what we have at Home.

B u t of all our Variety of Conjectures on this Subject, there is but one we can fix upon with any tolerable Look of Certainty, which is this: The *Italians*, in attempting to restore the Grandeur of the ancient *Grecian* and *Roman* Theatres, instead of the Magnificence of the old Tragedy, with a suitable Chorus, they revived that Part which they imagined would prove most generally entertaining; and being then infected with *Gothick* Whims, Licences, and trifling Ornaments in every thing polite; in place of a musical Chorus, which was the great Embellishment of the old Stage, they trump'd up an Entertainment to consist wholly of M u s i c k, D a n c i n g, and M a c h i n e r y.

W h i l e I am tracing the Original of O p e r a s, it will be expected that I should, at least in a cursory manner, take some Notice of the M u s i c k of the *Ancients*, both Vocal and Instrumental: But, I confess my self altogether at a Loss to produce any thing upon that Head, either in the way of Study or Conversation, that will prove satisfactory to my Readers. I have canvassed many
Authors,

Authors, in order to make fome regular Remarks upon their Compofition, Harmony, and Difference of Inftruments, as ufed fingly, or in Confort; but found the Affair fo puzling, and my Guides fo blind, that, defpairing of Succefs, I quitted the Search. The prodigious Force of Sounds we often meet with in all their Poets, exaggerated to the moft miraculous Degree, and ftretched beyond the Bounds of Probability: But we are fenfible, that with them every thing was envelop'd in myfterious Allegories. Thus moral Inftructions were convey'd to the People in the Fables of *Amphion*'s Lute's building the Walls of *Thebes*; *Orpheus*'s Lyre's taming the moft favage Beafts; and *Arion*'s Harp's charming the Monfters of the Deep into a Tendernefs unknown to Mankind. Yet, fetting all Fiction afide, though inftructive, this we may take for granted, that the trembling Strings, touched by *David*'s artful Hand, calm'd into Gentlenefs the raging Tyranny of froward *Saul*; and the Conqueror of the World was fubdued by *Timotheus*'s Notes, the skilful Mafter raifing and lowering his Spirits, or whirling him from Paffion to Paffion, juft as he pleafed to exert his Power.

V o i c e s were in great Requeft with the Ancients, and were frequently ufed at moft publick Feftivals, or private Feafts, Marriages, Funerals, *&c.* nay, even in War. We find the Names of many Inftrumenss on Record; as Organs, Drums, Trumpets, Tymbrels, Cymbals, Pfalters, Lutes, Harps, Lyres, Sack-buts, Dulcimers, and all forts of Pipes, but particularly the Flute, which was the Inftrument principally made ufe of at all folemn Games, or indeed at all Seafons, where either Grief or Joy required the Relief or Affiftance of M u s i c k. Of Flutes there were many different Kinds, which were varied as the Occafion

demanded,

demanded, the *Phrygian*, the *Lydian*, the *Carian*, or the *Myfian*; fome were right-handed, fome left; fome to be play'd fingly, others doubly. But as this Inftrument in particular has raifed endlefs Difputes in the learned World, which we can enter into with fmall Profpect of Improvement (Authors being ftrangely divided in their Opinions about it, and all leaving us in a blind State of Uncertainty;) I think it will be more effential to the Affair in hand, to pafs on to the paft and prefent State of modern MUSICK; an Article, in which, I believe, we far excel the Ancients: For even the ftrongeft Prejudice muft allow, that in feveral Refpects, they were a Parcel of *dull Dogs,* compared to this more brillant Age.

As to the Rife and Progrefs of OPERAS at Home, I hope my Readers will not be difpleafed with the following concife Chronology of them, it being the moft exact Account my Reading or Obfervation have made me Mafter of.

THE firft regular OPERA (as I take it) that *England* could ever boaft of, was performed in the Time of the great Rebellion; when Hypocrify was called Religion; Anarchy, Government; and Enthufiafm Wit. Sir *William D'avenant*'s poetical Genius being debarr'd from entertaining the Town with the ufual Theatrical Reprefentations; he, under the Notion of an innocent mufical Performance, introduced the Siege of *Rhodes,* in two Parts; the Model of which was rather taken from the *French,* than *Italian* OPERAS: But whether there were any more of this kind prefented during that Scene of Villany, Confufion, and Nonfenfe, I could never difcover; nor is it very material to our Purpofe.

BEFORE I proceed any farther, I beg Leave to obferve, that in the three Reigns preceeding the *Æra* juft now mentioned, there were often performed

formed privately in the Royal Palace, and by the Gentlemen of the Inns of Court, MASQUES; contrived by the greatest *Poets, Musicians* and *Archetects* of that Age, which were in effect a kind of Drammatick Opera, or an Imitation of the old *Chorus*, being composed chiefly of MUSICK, MACHINERY and DANCING; but these will not in Propriety be looked upon as OPERAS.

AFTER the Restoration, we had at different Times several Entertainments, which were then stiled *Drammatick Operas*; which were indeed regular Stage-Plays larded with Pieces of occasional MUSICK, vocal and instrumental, proper to the Fable, and introduced either in the Beginning, Middle, or End of an Act, by single Voices, two or three Part Songs, and Chorus: These were likewise embellished with Scenes, Machines, *French* Dancing-Masters, long Trains, and Plumes of Feathers: Of this sort were the *Fairy Queen and Tempest*, alter'd from *Shakespear*; *Dioclesian* and *Island Princess*, from *Beaumont* and *Fletcher*; *Dryden's Fall of Man*; never acted, and King *Arthur*; *D'avenant's Circe*; *Granville's Brittish Enchanters*; *Dennis's Rinaldo* and *Armida*; and *Durfey's Kingdom of the Birds*. These I believe were the principal, if not the whole that appeared upon our Stages of this Kind of Dramma: and, as I remember, during their Possession of the Stage, nothing was admitted in any other musical Way, excepting *Dryden's Albion* and *Albanius*; which consisted altogether of MUSICK in Recitative and Airs; tho' I believe more after the *French* than *Italian Gou*; being set to Musick by a *Frenchman*. This I look upon as the second Age of OPERAS, as we then stiled them; but I absolutely deny them that Title; that Term implying a regular, compleat musical Entertainment, which they never could arrive at, till they entirely came into a finished

nifhed *Italian* Plan; nor do we beftow the Name of OPERA on any Dramma, but thofe where every Word is fung.

INDEED the only Merit they could boaft of, was their claiming a kind of Refemblance or Relation to the old *Grecian* Tragedy and Chorus; and could they have fupply'd the neceffary Expences effential to the Grandeur of fuch a Defign, I muft own their Performances would have proved no bad Imitation even of the *Grecian* Stage in its greateft Luftre.

HOWEVER, in this State remained our Theatrical MUSICK, or the Shadow of an Opera-Stage for feveral Years; one Houfe ftriving to out-do the other, or ruin Wit by Sound and Shew; till Mr. *Clayton* happily arriving from *Italy*, introducing at once OPERAS after their manner; that is, *Englifh* Words, with *Italian* Airs; true home-fpun *Britifh* Manufacture, cut out in the *Trans-alpina* Fafhion: *Arfinoe, The Temple of Love,* and fome others of that Stamp, pleafed as long as they were a Novelty; but they only inftructed us to have a Relifh for better MUSICK; fo fome Operas of the beft *Italian* Mafters were tranflated into *Englifh*, and the MUSICK preferved, as *Camilla, Thomyris*, &c. Thefe fucceeded tolerably well, till grown too familiar, and that we began to underftand them; then an *Italian* Singer or two crept in by degrees, to charm us with fomething new and unintelligible; and this pretty motly Performance pleafed for fome Time; but fome good Senfe ftill remaining amongft us, the Abfurdity of that Converfation *a la Babel* was fo notorious, that it was look'd upon as more inexcufable, than having the whole Performance in one proper, though foreign, Language: This of Confequence threw us into entire *Italian* OPERAS, both as to Language, Mufick and Performers, which gradually has work'd

them

them up to that high Pitch they now fhine tri-
umphant in; and, we may boldly fay, we excel
any thing *Italy* ever knew, (as to one particular
Stage) both in Compofition and Performance:
For feveral Years they have kept their Ground,
againft all vain Attempts to diflodge them; only
allowing for fome fmall Receffes for breathing
Time: And as an *Italian* Opera can never touch
the Comprehenfion of above one Part in four of
a *Britifh* Audience, it is very probable their Theatre will be crowded as long as we are a Nation.

BUT fince the bare Name of an *Italian* Opera,
as eftablifhed at prefent amongft us, is to the laft
Degree fhocking to the Ears of many honeft Inhabitants of this METROPOLIS. In order to
remove all groundlefs Prejudices, let us briefly
and impartially, as poffible, ftate the Cafe betwixt
the contending Parties, by confidering the moft
material Objections to this Entertainment, and
framing a juft Method of anfwering them: Thus
wipe off, or at leaft compound for, thofe things
they look upon as Abfurdities or Impofitions.

I think the Objections of greateft Weight may
be reduced to four Heads. The firft exclaims a-
gainft an Opera's being performed in a Language
fo little underftood. Its Enemies cry out againft
this as a thing highly unnatural —— *What! be attentive to what is* Gibberifh *to us!* —— *Chatt-
'ring Monkies!* —— *Ridiculous Apes! We fpend our
Money and lofe our Time, and perhaps only to be
curfed or laughed at!* —— The fecond is ftarted by
thofe who are charmed with the MUSICK; particularly the Airs; but naufeate the odious *Recitative:* —— Or that the Whole of an Opera fhould
be fung —— *They die with Laughing to hear a Tyrant rage and ftorm in a vaft Regularity of Sounds;
a General fing at the Head of an Army; or a Lover,
Swan-like, expire at his Miftrefs's Feet; and that*
                                                    there

There is not an imperial Mandate, a Word of Com-
mand, or Billet-doux delivered but in expreſſive Flats
and Sharps. The third bears hard with a moſt
general Out-cry upon the exorbitant Prices we
pay the Performers; eſpecially the Foreigners:
---*Intolerable! --- ſo many Hundreds!--- for a Thing of*
nothing! —— a Voice! — a meer ha, ha! — naſty
Puſſes, odious filthy Things! — Let them ſtay at
home and ſtarve, or ſing at reaſonabls Rates. ————
The fourth is altogether critical, and raiſed by
thoſe Gentlemen who are Maſters of ſo much
good Senſe, and juſt Criticiſm, that they are o-
bliged to be diſpleaſed with every thing that will
not ſtand the Teſt of A R I S T O T L E and R A-
P I N. An Opera throws them into Convulſions;
one Part is ridiculous, another improbable; a third
unnatural; a fourth improper; a fifth irregular, ——
and ſo they run themſelves out of Breath —— *Zounds,*
no Unity in Time, Place or Action obſerved!

L E T me now, as briefly as I ſtated theſe Objections, animadvert upon them, according to
the Sentiments of thoſe who are profeſſed Admirers of our preſent O P E R A S: Then I ſhall
naturally throw in my private Opinion, and,
like a true Critick, point out both Beauties and
Blemiſhes, ſtand up in Defence of what is right,
and propoſe Remedies for what is wrong.

A s to the firſt Objection; The muſical Part of
this and all other modern Nations have agreed, that
the *Italian* is undoubtedly the moſt proper Language
to be joined to Sounds, for Reaſons ſo obvious,
that it would be Impertinence to mention them.
But, not to tire my Reader with Quotations, let
us hear what one of our greateſt Refiners and
Improvers of the *Engliſh* Tongue ſays; and every
Man will allow D R Y D E N to be a Judge: *All,*
ſays he, *who are converſant in that noble Language,*

C
the

the Italian, *cannot but observe, that it is the softeest, sweetest, and most harmonious, not only of any modern Tongue, but even beyond any of the Learned. It seems to have been invented not only for* POETRY, *but* M U S I C K; *the Vowels so abounding in all Words, especially in the Terminations, that, excepting a few Monosyllables, the whole Language ends in them. Then their Pronunciation is so sonorous, that their very Speaking has more* M U S I C K *in it, than* Dutch P O E T R Y *and* S O N G: *And if we must call it barbarous, it is the most beautiful and most learned of any* Barbarism *in the modern Tongues.*

I N the next place we cannot have native Performers for our Mother Tongue, but what will fall far short of the excellent Voices and Taste of those we are supplied with from Abroad: Some Women we boast of, and Boys; but the first generally lose their Voices before they begin to learn, and are then ill taught; as the latter are obliged by Nature to part with theirs, by the time they know any thing of the Matter: A tolerable Bass Voice we may meet with by Chance in an Age: But as we are denied the Liberty of artificially tuning the Pipes of those Performers who are neither Men nor Women, and who are the Foundation of the *Italian* O P E R A S; I do aver, that I think it impossible to form a perfect and compleat Musical Entertainment of our own People, or in our own Language.

N O T to go any farther back than last Winter, the Attempt of introducing *English* Operas at L——n's - Inn - F——ds Theatre, will sufficiently justifie my Assertion. Their Endeavours, though headed by a great Master, and supported by some People of the best Fashion and Interest, in a few Weeks did but expose to the Ridicule of every body, that had any Notion of M U S I C K, their wretched

ed Performance; and even then, those that made the best Figure on their Stage were Foreigners: 'Tis true, that Representation had a Run, (as they term it) and brought several full Houses; but I speak of its Merit, and not its Success; the first was obvious to every Ear; the last was forced by a Party, during the Vacation of the *Italian* OPERAS.

NOTHING but the Wantonness of Plenty from the lowest Necessity, could have thrown People into such an Absurdity, thus profusely to squander away on bad Voices, what was got by clever Heels; and to choose that Season, when the whole of *English* MUSICK was at the lowest Ebb, and the OPERAS at the *H—y-M—t* at that Height, (both as to Composition and Performance) which no ancient Theatre could ever have an Idea of; nay, it is almost unknown to *Italy* it self.

I was so unfortunate, as to be oblig'd once to sit *Ca —— la* out, to the great Disquiet of my Ears; nor have I perfectly got rid of the Head-ach it gave me, yet; and I vow, had it not been for Mrs. B —— *ier*, and my old Friend L —— *dge*, I could have swore the Stage had returned the Favour the Audience sometimes does them, and play'd a full Choir of Cat-calls upon us.

THIS Season they reviv'd *Thomyris* at *L——n's Inn-F——ds*; but that being rather a better OPERA, and more justly performed than the other, the Town would not go near it.

So finding their Finances run very low, by striving to do well, they thought it absolutely necessary to do something very bad, in order to retrieve their undone Affairs.

THIS indeed they have happily effected in Conjunction with a great Poet; and by giving us

　　　　　　　some-fomething more execrable in relation to M u s i c k, than the World ever dreamt of feeing on any Stage, they are Made; and we run mad with Joy in being fo agreeably difappointed.

T h e *Beggar's Opera,* by robbing the Performers at *Pye-corner, Fleet-ditch, Moor-fields* (and other Stations of this Metropolis, famed for travelling Sounds) of their undoubted Properties, has reinftated them in Wealth and Grandeur; and what fhock'd moft Ears, and fet moft Teeth on edge, at turning the Corner of a Street, for half a Moment; when thrown into a regular Entertainment, charms for Hours.

I muft own they never appear'd to that Advantage in any mufical Light as this O p e r a of *Beggars:* Their Rags of P o e t r y and Scraps of M u s i c k joining fo naturally, that in whatever View we confider it as to Character or Circumftance, its Title is the moft *apropos* Thought upon Earth.

T h e fecond Objection, at firft Sight, may appear very plaufible; but, upon Examination, very ill grounded; for it is impoffible to have a perfect mufical *Dramma,* without Recitative: No Ear can fupport the Whole being all-Air; therefore if you take away the Recitative, it is no O p e r a: And the beft Judges value a Mafter as much upon the Merit of one as the other: The Recitative is but a tuneable Method of fpeaking; and in the Article of M u s i c k, but refines upon Speech, as far as polite Comedy excels common Converfation, or Tragedy in Heroicks, the ordinary Stile of the Great. As for the critical Part of the Objection againft Recitative, I defire that our Poets, Criticks, and Fine Gentlemen, banifh firft greater Abfurdities and Inconfiftencies from their Stage-Plays; for I

cannot

cannot imagine, that to sing all the Parts of an OPERA is by half so unnatural, as the sparkling Nonsense, gilded Fustian, and pompous Bombast in most, if not all our Tragedies; nor so improper as the quaint *Double Entendres*, and forc'd Similies, squeez'd out in the midst of Misfortunes, or at the Point of Death: The Heroes there quietly and stupidly sleep over four Acts in a dull regular Way of Life, till by Danger they are rouz'd from their Lethargy into a State of Wit; like the Prince born dumb, whose Tongue was never loosen'd, till the Sword was at his Father's Throat. In short, nothing is ridiculous that executes a regular Design: That of an OPERA, is to represent to us, in the Drammatick Way, some instructive *Fable*, where the Words are all to be deliver'd in MUSICK; therefore a King must rule, a General fight, a Lover sigh, in Harmony: Nor is there wanting in this Art a Variety to touch the different Passions, as justly as any Kind of POETRY: Nor can I observe any thing in singing a Conversation-Piece, more absurd or ridiculous than a familiar Dialogue in Heroick *Rhime*.

THE third Objection indeed carries great Weight with it: Our Prices are immoderately extravagant; and all we can say to justify them is, that we are arrived now to so picquant a *Gou* in MUSICK, that nothing but what is superexcellent will pass. What pleases at *Venice* or *Rome* may chance to be hiss'd at the *H---y-M--t*. If we must have those of the greatest Merit, they will be paid accordingly. If they don't meet with more Encouragement here than at Home, who will run the Hazard of coming near us? Should we pay them double, still the Odds is against them; an English Morning or Evening

may

may ruin them for ever, and a North-East Blast in *July* rob them of their Bread at once: 'Tis but just, that if our Ears demand the best Performers, that our Purses should pay the highest Prices; else 'tis culling the choicest Fruit at *Leaden-Hall* and *Covent-Garden* Markets, and expect it as cheap as the withered Refuse of a blind Alley-Stall.

THE exorbitant Expences occasion'd by introducing an *Italian* OPERA amongst us, may be reduc'd to two Heads: *First*, the vast Salaries given to the Singers by the Academy. *Secondly*, what the Audience pays to the Academy, which is the natural Consequence of the other. As to the first, I think it fully answer'd before, nor is the Academy in the least to blame; our Taste is so refin'd, and our Judgment so solid in relation to all Parts of MUSICK, that such an Entertainment cannot be supported but by the Tip-top Performers of the World; and they will have Prices equal to their Merit. As to the second, it would be highly unreasonable to expect that the Directors of the H——y-M——t Th——re should amuse us at their own private Expence; they run a great Risque to please us, in engaging for vast Sums, whilst it is left to our Choice whether we'll come or no, to ease them of Part of the Burden: Nor can they with the highest Prices be certain of coming off clear one Season, unless they have crowded Houses every Night.

THE fourth Objection is altogether critical, and carry'd on in the stiff pedantick Rules that Tribe have settled, by which they form a Judgment on every thing polite, and of consequence damn all Amusements where Spirit and Life prevail over their unanimated Works of Clay. These merry Gentlemen would reduce OPERAS to the

Standard

Standard of *Aristotle* and *Rapin*. Should these Entertainments in any Point prove Malefactors, they are for bringing them before improper Judges; it is carrying the Cause into as wrong a Court of Judicature, as trying a Pyrate for Murder in *Chancery*, or a Highwayman in *Doctors-Commons*. An OPERA borrows no Helps from their *Poeticks*, is not built upon the Foundation of their Stages, nor must their Rules interfere with any Part of the Superstructure: Were it otherways, why should not this Amusement as well as others, upon Occasion, plead the Benefit of their Clergy; and when it is guilty of what is irregular or unnatural, excuse it, by calling it a bright Thought and bold Beauty. It has ever been granted by those who allow an OPERA any Existence at all, that things wholly super-natural and marvellous are warrantable in this Kind of *Dramma*; though they would be damn'd in a regular Tragedy or Comedy: AN OPERA may be call'd the Tyrant of the Stage; it is subject to no poetical Laws, despises the Power or Limitations of a Parliament of Criticks; and subsists altogether by absolute Sway, and its own uucontroulable Prerogative: It has Liberty to range Heaven, Earth, and Hell; call Gods, Spirits, and Devils to its Assistance; and all this unbounded Freedom is taken for the Probable, or rather what is necessary in this Entertainment.

BUT let me corroborate my Opinion on this Head by the Words of one even of our most eminent Play-Wrights and Criticks; who says, *That an* OPERA *is a poetical Tale or Fiction, represented by Vocal and Instrumental* MUSICK; *that the suppos'd Persons of this* Musical Dramma *are generally supernatural, as* Gods, Goddesses *and* Heroes: *The Subject therefore being extended beyond the Limits*

mits

mits of human Nature, admits of that sort of mar-
vellous and surprizing Conduct, which is rejected in
other Plays: Humane Impossibilities are to be receiv'd
as they are in Faith; because where Gods are in-
troduc'd, a supreme Power is to be understood, and
second Causes are out of Doors: But still Propriety
must be observ'd even here; the Gods must manage
their peculiar Provinces; and what was attributed
by the Heathens to one Power, ought not to be per-
form'd by any other——— This laft Part (which im-
plies a proper Decency) is the only Reftriction
that O P E R A S are laid under.

B u t after this Defence of O p e r a s in general; our mufical Stage is rarely guilty of fuch
Faults as may incur a critical Cenfure: Thofe
Licences and Allowances, in my Mind, are too
fparingly made ufe of in that Theatre; and their
Modefty too great, in rejecting fuch juft and
beautiful Alliances; which I cannot avoid confidering, as Appendixes abfolutely effential to fuch
Entertainments.

I had fome Thoughts of adding to thefe Objections, a fifth, not rais'd by the Oppofers, but
Admirers of O p e r a s; and that is a Complaint
of too great Simplicity or Samenefs in thofe A-
mufements: The Whole being meer M u s i c k,
not diverfify'd with Grand C h o r u s s e s, D a n c i n g,
M a c h i n e r y, and all the other Theatrical Em-
bellifhments, which are look'd upon as the very
Limbs of the Body of an O p e r a; which it not
only allows, but demands; and fo effential are
they to its Nature, that the Neglect of them
fhews us at beft but a lame, imperfect Figure:
But I fhall fpeak more fully to this Point, in
the Effay appropriated to *Choruffes,* where I fhall
obferve how far thefe auxiliary Ornaments are
to be made ufe of in an O p e r a: Therefore I
fhall

ſhall now proceed to conſider theſe Objections in a new Light; and as there may be ſome juſt Grounds for finding Fault, yet let us not raſhly cut down the Tree we ſhould only prune: 'Tis more praiſe-worthy to improve than to deſtroy; nay, if we look upon our Love of MUSICK as an incurable Folly, let us then find out ſome Lenitives to moderate the Malignity of the Diſeaſe we can't entirely eradicate.

I hope none of my courteous Readers will be ſurpriz'd, if I declare that I am ſo far charm'd with our preſent OPERAS, though perform'd in *Italian*; that I look upon them as compleat Entertainments in their way; that is, to the laſt Degree perfect, as to the Article of MUSICK; which is the only Point they aim at.

BUT as I am ſenſible, that their being perform'd in a foreign Tongue diſguſts many of my Countrymen, who (tho' great *Philarmonicks*) yet being *True Britons*, and ſtaunch *Proteſtants*, to ſhew their Love to their Country, and their Zeal for their Religion, are prepoſſeſs'd againſt Singing as well as Praying in an unknown Dialect: I propoſe to remove this ill-grounded Suggeſtion, and help the Academy in this Scene of Diſtreſs, by dividing the Argument. As the Dir——ors of the OPERA can never hope for a Set of Singers, Natives of this Iſland, equal to what we are ſupply'd with from Abroad (as long as our Laws in Relation to Emaſculation confine that ſmall Ceremony to the Bodies of our Brutes;) if they would but allow ſome extraordinary Events either hiſtorical or traditionary (which wholly regard our ſelves) to be tranſlated into *Italian*; I'll engage for my Countrymen they'll reſign the Language for the Hiſtory, that being undoubtedly

edly originally our own, and the *English* Page always leading in the Opera Books, we gain the disputed Punctilio, and bring off our Honour safe, which is dearer to every *True Briton* than Life.

To set this Affair in a true Light, I beg leave to illustrate this Essay with some of our most noted domestick *Fables*, which must please an *English* Audience, and at the same time make a beautiful Appearance on the Stage: These shall be principally borrow'd from a Subject which can boast an inexhaustible Fund of Models for Theatrical Entertainments, particularly O P E R A S; *viz.* *Knight-Errantry*, which has in all Ages produc'd so many valuable Volumes of Romances, Memoirs, Novels and Ballads, either written or oral.

A late eminent ingenious Author propos'd to the then Master of the O P E R A-S T A G E, *Whittington and his Cat*; and went so far in the Design, as to procure a Puss or two, who could pur tolerably in Time and Tune: But the Inconveniencies arising from the Number of Vermin requisite to be destroy'd, in order to keep up to the Truth of the Story, blasted that Project.

M A N Y worthy Patriots amongst us (through the Prejudice of their Infant-Education) would doat upon the Representation of *Valentine and Orson*; but the Scene thro' every memorable Event of that wonderful History being entirely foreign, I cannot approve of its Admission; though I must own the *H——y-M——t* can never hope to shew the World two finer Bears than they can produce at present, which would be no small Addition to a Musical *Dramma*.

T H E Generality of this Nation would likewise imbibe a Fondness for the *Seven Champions of* *Christen-*

Chriſtendom, even from their Nurſery ; but the Ac ——my not being able to furniſh ſo many Heroes at a Time, we muſt drop that Deſign : Though I muſt ſay, our own St. *George*'s Part would equip us with Characters and Incidents for a very beautiful *Dramma* ; in which the whole Hiſtory of the G —— r might be properly and naturally introduc'd ; with a little Epiſode thrown in about the O —— r of the T——le ; then tack to to their Tails a large Troop of the K ——ts of the B——h, with their Eſ —— res, by way of a Grand Chorus : And this Scene would be truly great, and worthy a *Brittiſh* Audience.

But I fear we ſhould find ſome Difficulty in meeting with a proper Dragon ; unleſs the *Af——n* Company could procure us a ſucking one, juſt out of the Neſt, to be brought up tame, and ſkilful Maſters to inſtruct it in the Rudiments of Musick ; or that *Doctor Fauſtus* could be prevail'd upon to part with his artificial one, which really roars out a good tuneable Baſs : Then if Sign^r *B —— chi* would condeſcend to ſing the Part of St. *George's Horſe*, with *S——no* upon his Back ; and Sign^r *Pal——ni* allow himſelf to be clapp'd into the Dragon's Belly : I believe this Plan would ſurprize us not only with a noble Scene of Recitative, but furniſh us with an Opportunity of throwing in the neweſt and fineſt *Duet* that ever was heard, *viz.* betwixt the *Horſe* and the *Dragon*.

'Tis true, I here digreſs from my original Deſign of only celebrating old *Engliſh* Occurrences ; for St. *George*, though our Patron Saint, was by Birth a *Cappadocian*, as this particular Scene of his Life was laid in *Egypt* ; whoſe King's Daughter he freed from that terrible Monſter. But as my mentioning a Dragon may excite the

Curioſity

Curiofity of many *Connoiffeurs* to fee fuch a Creature fly or tread the Stage, and hear him fing; I think we need not go from Home for a Fable, whofe Authority is undifputed, and which can furnifh out as noble a Monfter Scene, as if we had gone to *China* for the Story.

Most of our Countrymen, who are deeply read in the old *Brittifh* Ballads, (which have been fo curioufly and carefully collected lately by a judicious Antiquary, with learned Obfervations and Annotations, by which means many remarkable Tranfactions are preferv'd in thofe Singfong *Annals*, which Hiftory has neglected) will readily imagine, that I hint at the noted Combat betwixt *Moor* of *Moor-hall*, and the Dragon of *Wantcliff*; which for the Beauty of Fable, Variety of Incidents, a Quantity of the Marvellous, and a glorious Cataftrophe, may vie with any Story, ancient or modern.

Indeed this *Dramma* will admit but of two principal Characters; *viz.* 'Squire *Moor* and the *Dragon:* But here is the moft proper Occafion imaginable of introducing a magnificent Chorus in every Act; a Stage-Decoration fo efteem'd by all the Ancients and Learned Moderns, that they thought all Theatrical Entertainments imperfect without one; as I fhall farther explain in a feparate *Effay*.

In the firft Act you have a Chorus of Men, Women, and Children, whofe Bread and Butter, Milk-Pottage or Relations the Dragon had devour'd, accompany'd by a fuitable Noife of Sobs, Sighs and Groans on proper Inftruments; which muft have a fine Effect, as to moving Pity. Thefe Lamentations roufing up the dormant Spirit of *Moor*, he declares for the Combat, which naturally ufhers in the fecond Act a Chorus of

warlike

warlike Inſtruments on his Part, preparative to the Battle, join'd to a compleat Roar on the Part of the Dragon, which muſt exhibit Terror to a vaſt Degree: Then the third Act beginning with the Combat, concludes nobly with the Dragon's Death, and a grand Chorus of the whole Country; where Sounds of Triumph and Joy, mix'd with Bells, Bon-fires and Country - Dances, perform'd by Country - Squires, Shepherds, Milk-Maids, and a Saint or two introduc'd by a Machine; one ſuppos'd to have given *Moor* a Breaſt-Plate and Head - Piece, another more than humane Courage, to atchieve ſo wonderful an Exploit: Thus the Whole ends agreeably, and ſends every Perſon of the Audience Home well pleaſed: In this little Story all the Paſſions are finely expreſs'd.

Robbin Hood and *Little John* cannot fail of charming the *Brittiſh* Nation, being undoubtedly a Domeſtick Matter of Fact; but as no Singer in *Europe* can top the Part of *Little John* but *Ber——dt*, we muſt ſuſpend that Performance till his Return, to bleſs our Eyes.

The *London 'Prentice* would infallibly gain the Hearts of the City, beſides the valuable Incident of a *Lion-Scene*; as the *Abbot* of *Canterbury* would procure the Favour of the Clergy, and then the whole Audience (in Imitation of that polite, agreeable Cuſtom practis'd at *Paris*) might join the Stage; every body beating Time, and ſinging, *Derry down, down, down,* &c.

Tom Thumb would be a beautiful Foundation to build a pretty little Paſtoral on; his Length too being adequate to that of a Summer's Evening, the *Belles* and *Beaus* might arrive Time enough from either Park, and enjoy the whole of his Affair: Nay, it would admit of ſome very

D   new

new Scenes, as furprizing as true: Witnefs the Accident of the Pudding, which would be fomething as uncommon as ever appear'd on any Stage, not excepting even a *Dutch* Tragedy --- *N. B.* Cu——ni *in Breeches would make a delightful* Tom Thumb.

SHOULD this Project of mine fucceed, *Chevy-Chace* will be demanded by every *South* and *North* B——n. I confefs the Beginning is very Theatrical, and will admit of a good Number of *French Horns,* which have been lately receiv'd at the H——y - M——t with tolerable Succefs: But I fear its bloody Cataftrophe will not fo well anfwer our Purpofe: For though we have had fome very handfome noify Skirmifhes on that Stage, and where both Generals and common Soldiers have merited an old *Roman* Triumph; yet I cannot fay, that I ever knew any of the *Virtuofi* concern'd in thofe Engagements, reduc'd to fo low a Pitch, as either to fight or fing on their Stumps; nor would they, I believe, be fond of the Operation.

I know, the fevere deep-read *Criticks* will object to the Simplicity of thefe Subjects, and the Lownefs of moft of the Characters; our prefent OPERAS being generally form'd upon Plans of the greateft Events, and moft celebrated Parts of Hiftory: To this I anfwer, that we are not oblig'd to be always ty'd down to Affairs of that vaft Moment, fome Stories of an inferior Rank allowing as proper Entertainments, as juft Morality, and as tender Sentiments, as where we dwell entirely upon the Fates of Kings and Kingdoms. Let us inftance that famous OPERA, where *Patient Griffel* appear'd in her proper Character, to the entire Satisfaction of feveral Audiences, as polite as crowded: Nay, fome of the
beft

beſt Tragedies belonging to the *Engliſh* Stage, are founded entirely upon the Diſtreſs of low Life, and the Misfortunes of private Families.

Thus *Dryden* allows, *That though the Perſons repreſented in* Operas *are generally Gods, Goddeſſes, and Heroes, who are ſuppos'd to be their peculiar Care: Yet this hinders not, but that meaner Perſons may ſometimes gracefully be introduc'd; eſpecially, if by Reaſon of their Innocence, thoſe happy Mortals were ſuppos'd to have had a more familiar Intercourſe with ſuperior Beings; and therefore Shepherds might reaſonably be admitted, as of all Callings the moſt innocent, the moſt happy; and who, by reaſon of their almoſt idle Employment, had moſt Leiſure to make Verſes, and to be in Love; without which Paſſion no* Opera *can poſſibly ſubſiſt.* This Conceſſion is all I plead for, to make good my Aſſertion.

But at once to ſilence all Cavils of this Nature (without tiring my Readers, by pointing out any more proper Fables, or anticipating their Pleaſure in finding them out for them,) I beg Leave to produce but one Example more, to ſtregthen my Argument, and to knock down all Opponents: This is an *Engliſh* Story, entirely calculated for the preſent Set of Singers, and capable of giving us a vaſt deal of the *Pathetick,* the *Wonderful,* and the *Terrible,* the diſtinguiſhing Characteriſticks of Musick, as well as Poetry; nor will any of my Readers, I hope, ſeem ſtartled, when I ſet full before their Eyes, *The Children in the Wood.*

As to the Drammatical Diſtribution of the ſeveral Characters in this beautiful Fable, I fear we muſt implore the Aſſiſtance of Mr. H——ger, who has always graciouſly condeſcended to act any Part in Life, which could amuſe this Nation in a polite Way: His Countenance (though far different from his Nature) will beſt become the *Uncle's* cruel Part: And ſome of our preſent Compoſers have a few ſavage Songs ready compos'd, adapted to his Face and Character in this O P E R A. As F——*na's* Shake and Graces qualify her to appear the firſt old Woman in *Europe*, I have mark'd her as Nurſe to the two Children; S——*no* and B——*di* will make a couple of chopping Infants; and as they can equally act the Parts of Boys or Girls, the Ac——my ſhall determine which ſhall be Male, which Female: Then I have an original Painting in my Poſſeſſion, which with a little of B———*chi's* Advice and Stitching, will equip them with ſuch Hanging-Sleeve-Coats, Bibs and Aprons, as were worn in thoſe Days; which will add a Luſtre to the Propriety of Dreſs. B——*chi* and P——*ini* may be very happily introduc'd as two Hob-goblins, to frighten the *Uncle* out of his Wits: Nor would it be amiſs, if we could prevail on A——*a* R——*n* to perform the Part of an old Maiden *Aunt*, a Character abſolutely neceſſary in a Country Family; and ſhe, in Conjunction with the lamentable D——*ti*, would move moſt feelingly in a Funeral Chorus. Which laſt Scene, if well manag'd, cannot fail ſhewing true Diſtreſs to a vaſt Height. Then to make the Affair appear more ſolemn, after the Manner of the Ancients, there might be hir'd from *Ireland* (where that Cuſtom is ſtill obſerved) a full Cry of *Burial-Howlers*: And to add ſtill to the Grandeur of that Scene, the Ac——my might agree with their Joiner to dreſs them cheap, a magnificent Wooden Supper, according to that old *Engliſh* Cuſtom. As for our little Warbler C——*ni*, though laſt mention'd, yet neither deſpis'd, nor forgot; we can here fit her with the

fineſt

fineſt Part, ſhe ever ſhone in. As her Size and Voice will furniſh out a mighty pretty Bird, ſhe ſhall ſing the Part of the *Robin-Red-Breaſt*, which covers the dead Children with Leaves : She ſhall be uſher'd in by a *Cock-Sparrow*, and allow'd two *Tom-Titts* to hold up her Tail. N. B. *The Compoſers of* Elpidia, *and ſome other late* OPERAS, *will be the proper Maſters to ſet this* Dramma *to* MUSICK.

As touching and, of Conſequence, improving the Paſſions, is the higheſt Flight that Art, in conjunction with Nature, can ſoar ; we ſee from the Plan of this ſimple neglected Story, to what a Pitch of Inſtruction the muſical Stage may be ſcrew'd ; when all the *Utile Dulci* of POETRY may, even in an OPERA, be exhibited for the Benefit of Mankind.

THE furniſhing our *Muſick-Theatre* with Fables of this Kind will produce another Advantage, perhaps not yet diſcover'd by the Admirers of that Art ; the Simplicity and Lowneſs of the Characters in general adapted to theſe Scenes in Life, will extinguiſh thoſe Fire-brands of Diſſention, and Heart-burning Animoſities, which Grandeur, and natural Love of Empire, have kindled in the Breaſts of ſeveral of our Performers ; eſpecially thoſe of the Fair Sex ; and for the future, prevent the Sparks inherent to the Jealouſy of Power, from being blown up into ſuch Flames.

WE are ſenſible this Thirſt of Royal Sway had almoſt prov'd fatal to the Republick of *Sounds* ; nor have we yet perfectly recover'd what we ſuffer'd and fear'd from thoſe horrid Civil Wars. In theſe Stories I recommend, the principal Parts will be upon the Level : No Room for Conteſt ; no Diſpute who ſhall be Empreſs, Queen, or Princeſs ; no Rivalſhip but in Love, when contend-

D 3   ing

ing Nymphs and Shepherdesses strive and scold,
and sing to gain S——no's Heart.

Not that I would entirely banish from the
Opera-Stage Heroick Deeds, or Characters of the
first Rank: Nor would I confine the *Dramma*
to such alone: Our *English* History is prolifick
of Ground-work for all Theatrical Entertainments.
As our Nation can boast of Persons and Actions
equal in Fame to any Part of Antiquity; so can
we vie with their Golden Age, in *Sylvan* Scenes,
and rural Innocence.

This amusing Variety in the Choice of Subjects for our Operas, will allow a greater Latitude in Composition than we have yet known:
It will employ all our Masters in their different
Talents, and in course destroy that Schism which
at present divides our Lovers of Music, and
turns even Harmony into Discord: The Dispute
will not then be, who is the justest, or brightest
Composer, or which the finest Operas; those
of our own Growth, or those imported from *Italy*?
Every Man would be set to Work, and strive to
excel in his own Way. H——l would furnish
us with Airs expressive of the Rage of Tyrants,
the Passions of Heroes, and the Distresses of Lovers in the Heroick Stile. B——ni sooth us with
sighing Shepherds, bleating Flocks, chirping
Birds, and purling Streams in the *Pastoral*: And
A——o give us good Dungeon Scenes, Marches
for a Battel, or Minuets for a Ball, in the *Mise-
rere*. H——l would warm us in Frost or Snow,
by rousing every Passion with Notes proper to
the Subject: Whilst B——ni would fan us, in
the *Dog-Days*, with an *Italian* Breeze, and lull us
asleep with gentle Whispers: Nay, the pretty
Operas from t'other Side the Water, might
serve to tickle us in the Time of *Christmas-Gam-
bols*,

bols, or mortify us in the Time of *Lent*; so make us very merry, or very sad.

I have made my Remarks on this Head the more full, in hopes that the Hints advanced here, might of themselves accommodate our *Italian* OPERAS to the *British* Taste and Ears; and in some Measure, make a small Recompence for the Defects we find in them, or the Prejudices we have unthinkingly entertain'd against them, in the foregoing Objections: However, I shall lightly touch upon each of the other three, as I go along, so proceed orderly to the second, which would destroy the *Recitative*.

No Criticism upon our OPERAS has prevail'd more universally, nor more unjustly, than that upon the *Recitative*; yet so it happens, that the Generality of our Audiences have a secret distaste to it; and many, even of our Patrons of MUSICK, are shock'd with it: How to remedy this Want of Taste, or how to sacrifice our Recitative to Caprice, I know not: We must therefore find out some moderating Expedient to humour the first; for giving into the latter, would demolish the Design and Nature of an OPERA quite.

I have been inform'd of a Medium propos'd in this Affair by some true *English-men* (who bear a vast Respect for the last Age; and who would have as much of their Country appear in every thing, as possible) which is, to have the Recitative Part of every Character perform'd by an *English* Singer, or Actor; and then at an Air, his *Italian* Counter part slip from behind his Robe, or jump out of his Pocket, and sing the Air: but the Contradictions and Absurdities of this Proposal are so notorious, that I think my self to blame in the bare mentioning of it.

THERE-

THEREFORE to wave Things of this Nature, which are founded on Whim and Chimera, and at once to fix upon something new, pretty and probable; I must acquaint my Readers, that of fourscore and nineteen Expedients I started, I could lay my Finger but upon one to please my self, and that, if rightly understood, will have the desired Effect: My Project is, to have the Singers of the OPERA all thoroughly skill'd in DANCING, and so the whole of the Recitative danc'd, after the expressive Manner of the old *Pantomines*, and our modern *Grotesque Dances*. Every body must be sensible of the Force and Elegance of a Meaning-Dance; and as all Dances are to some Tune, the Musick need never cease, no more than in the accompanying the Recitative; so the OPERA will still appear all of a-piece. This will produce an agreeable Variety, and lead us insensibly into the Beauty of an *Antique Chorus*, which consisted both of DANCING and SINGING: But, in order to explain this Proposition in a more just and regular Method, let us but seriously reflect, that none of the Passions, either in PLAYS or OPERAS, can be agreeably express'd by the Voice, or at least not truly, without some emphatical Motions so order'd, as to support the Meaning by a significant Force, and which are judiciously adapted to every particular Subject and Passion: For as Recitative is not properly either direct MUSICK or SPEECH, but a tuneable Sort of a Medium betwixt both, which makes a juster Alliance betwixt the Words and the Voice: So all proper Actions, which give new Life and Vigour to SPEECH in the Explanation of our Thoughts, are a Kind of DANCING; and every Posture, Attitude, or Motion requisite to that Purpose, is but a different Step of the *Grand Dance*; and where there is a strict and

beautiful

beautiful Union betwixt these two *Sister-Graces*, in the Manner here propos'd, the Expression of the Passions must appear in a more ravishing Point of View, than has been ever known in Modern O P E-R A S or P L A Y S; or even to *Rome* and *Greece* themselves.

F O R Example; ———— Should a Hero make Love to a Princess in Recitative; if he danc'd a little at the same time; I cannot suppose, that an easie Minuet-step, a sprightly Caper, or a strong Bound, would appear ungenteel, unactive, or unnatural; all Members would shew out in full Order and high Vigour, and might perhaps prove as recommendatory Graces with most fine Ladies, as a sweet Voice.

S H O U L D an absolute Monarch, in a Rage, display unlimited Rule; I fancy, that thundering Kicks and Cuffs, those weighty Expressions of Anger by Legs and Arms, laid on in proper Time and Tune, would denote the Tyrant, and Arbitrary Power, in a greater Force of Reasoning, than any Words, or Notes, that ever Poet or Musician produc'd.

O R, if we may be allow'd to borrow a Beauty from the *French* Opera-Stage; what Phrases could be invented, to delineate the Fury of a Mad-man, with that Strength of Meaning, as when *Roland Furieux*, without Saying, or Singing, shews you Madness to the Life, in traversing the Stage with a thousand frantick Capers and Gestures; whilst the expressive Flourishes of a broad Back-sword, hack and hew to pieces an entire Sett of Scenes, as large as the *Bois de Boulogne*.

T H E same Reasons will hold good in every Character in Life; there being as great a Variety and Latitude in D A N C E S, as in the Passions themselves: But I shall proceed no farther on this Head at present, being oblig'd to treat it more at large

in

in the third *Essay*, where the Affair of DANCING
in general, comes upon the *Carpet*: So I shall
step on to the third Objection, *viz.* the High
Prices we pay at an OPERA.

I have already acknowledg'd, that the Clamour
rais'd against our OPERAS in this Objection, is
very near as just, as it is general; and I have likewise made manifest, that as the Majority of our
People of Fashion are willing to have such exquisite Entertainments at any rate; so it is impossible
to remedy the Inconveniencies arising from the
first Part of this Objection, by having the best
Performers at a trifling Expence. Every body
must be satisfy'd with the Reasons already given
on that Point; but as to the second Part, the Price
every Person of the Audience pays, there we may
be readily eas'd, which will answer our Purpose
to the full, as well. I will be bold to say, there is
but one Method can be pursu'd in attaining this
desir'd End; and I at the same time, with all humi-
lity aver, that the original Hint is not my own: For
I have often heard it very publickly whisper'd, that
some great People intended to have a larger *Opera-House* built; but what obstructed so noble and
laudable a Design, I could never learn. Had it
been carried on, and executed, according to the
Plans of some THEATRES in *Italy*, which are
capale of containing an Audience of several Thou-
sands, the Advantages resulting from so great an
Undertaking would prove infinite.

AN *Opera-House* so contriv'd as to allow a Number of Spectators, would admit of several Degrees of Seats, suited in their Prices to all Ranks
of People, from the highest to the lowest Station
of Life: And from an Audience so numerous,
might be rais'd all Sums necessary to defray the
greatest

greateſt Expences; as the heavieſt Taxes are
made eaſy, by being made general.

Such large Sums coming in every *Opera Night*,
would quickly enable the Directors of the *H——y
M——t* to out-bid all *Europe* in the Salaries given to Performers, both Vocal and Inſtrumental;
and fix the beſt Compoſers obedient to their
Call. What Glory would redound to the *Britiſh*
Nation, from ſo ſignal a Triumph! So far ſhould
we then be from grudging the neceſſary Expences of an OPERA, that we might afford
to be profuſe, to Extravagancy, in the moſt trifling Ornaments; and leave no Grounds for Complaint, that the Magnificence of our Muſical Stage,
as to Chorus, Scenes, Machines, and Dancing, is
totally neglected.

How poliſh'd a People ſhould we then prove?
The very Envy of our neighbouring Nations!
When not a Tinker or Cobler ſhould miſs an
OPERA. The Prices being once reduc'd, no
Man ſo profeſs'd a Foe to Muſick, as not to turn
Proſelyte to ſo delicious an Entertainment ——
Happy *Venice!* where every *Gondolier* can whiſtle
his *Opera-Air*, and judge of *Harmony!* Could we
but live to ſee ſuch pleaſant Times in *England*,
I make no Doubt but OPERA-STOCK would
ſoon out-ſell the *Indian* or *South-Sea*. How great
was our Misfortune, that the Foundation of a
capacious, ſplendid *Opera-Houſe* was not laid, the
wonderful Year of Projection! Thence proceeds
my Concern, the Want of a ſpacious Piece of
Ground, and a ſuitable Fund to carry on ſo
publick-ſpirited a Deſign, while People are running mad in ſubſcribing to HISTORY, POETRY,
ROMANCES; nay, SERMONS too; there's no
Subſcription propos'd for what out-weighs them
all: But ſtill I keep cloſe a Project *in petto*, which
can

can effectually do our Bufinefs, and lay no new Burden on the Rich or Poor.

But not to keep my Fellow-Citizens longer in Sufpence, I propofe the feizing the Revenues, Ground, and Buildings of one of our largeft Hofpitals; and by converting them into ready Money, raife a Structure worthy fuch an Entertainment and fuch Audiences: Befides, there will be an Annual Income fufficient to defray thofe neceffary or accidental Charges we can't avoid, fhould a Deficiency at any Time happen.

This Propofal may found very harfh at firft to moft charitable Ears; but I fhall make it evident to all my unprejudic'd Readers, that though I would willingly help the Ac——my in their generous Labours to pleafe Mankind, by feafonable Inftructions how to render the OPERA as reafonable in its Prices, as it is delightful in the Performance; fo that we may agreeably fpend our Time, and fave our Money; yet my Intentions are fo far from defeating the well-meant Defign of any pious Founder of fuch Edifices, that the juft Execution of my Project will infallibly maintain a greater Number of the *Old* and *Infirm*, and yearly educate and difpofe of more young and helplefs Orphans, in a more regular Method, and after a genteeler Manner, than ever was practis'd in any fuch Foundation, either at Home or Abroad.

As to the Aged and Sickly Part of an Hofpital, there are very few of them but might be of vaft Service to the Ac——my; and according to their former Stations in Life, before they were reduced by Age, Difeafes or Misfortunes, they fhould make their Appearance on the Stage. A decay'd Gentleman would furnifh out a Captain of the Guards, a grave Senator, or filent Embaffador:

In

ïn fhort, all Places of Honour, where their Parts require them to march gravely, look wifely, feem thoughtful and be mute; a ftately Step, a graceful Bow, the Coat of Mail, or folemn Robe would become them, as the Scene requir'd it: Orderly Matrons, and unfortunate Widows might commence *Dames of Honour*, drop a Curtfy, flirt a Fan, fhew their Bubbies, fhine in Tinfel, and make F——na's and C——ni's Trains of *State-Virgins* compleat: Others not fo qualify'd for the Grandeur of publick Shew, would ferve as Neceffary-Women to the Stage-Queens and Princeffes behind the Scenes: Men of an inferior Rank fhould form Troops of Guards, a full Senate, Attendants to all Solemnities; in fhort, be ready on all Occafions, where a crowded Stage is requifite, to give an Air of Magnificence to that Part of the Performance; then they might clafh Swords, beat Drums, move Scenes, fnuff Candles, and each, according to his Talent, manage fome Employment in the many that are neceffary in a Theatre.

Thus People need not idle the latter Part of Life away, but do fomething, by Gratitude at leaft to merit a Support; the Day would be fufficient for them to eat, drink, and pray in: Nor would their Labour be more than a genteel Evening's Amufement.

As for the friendlefs Infants belonging to this Hofpital, in order to be fent into the World capable of getting their Bread, particular Regard fhould be fhewn to them by the Managers of the Opera: Yearly out of them fhould be chofen a certain Number of Males and Females, (we being not allow'd to make ufe of the Neuter Gender) who in their tendereft Years fhould be inftructed in the jufteft Notions of Harmony by Mafters, and as it were moulded into a Mufical

E   Form:

Form: Those who succeeded best in that Art, should, when perfect, be brought upon the Stage; and thus we might make the justest Trial of our native Voices; the others dispos'd of as usual, to proper Trades, according to their Governours Judgments: Then the Directors of the OPERA may lay a well-grounded Claim to the Title of an Ac ——my; and we, after the Rules of some of our wisest Neighbours, mix even in our Amusements, something of manifest Advantage to the *Publick Good.*

THIS Project, like many of the utmost Importance, may chance to be approv'd, but never follow'd: I own my self at a Loss by any other Means to contrive an Abatement of the immoderate Expence these Entertainments occasion. This I have supported not by plausible Surmises, but the strongest Matters of Fact. As the Case stands, we must have good OPERAS, or none— If none, how shall we spend our Time? If good—— we must pay for them.

I am now arriv'd at the fourth and last Objection; *viz.* the Absurdities and Irregularities which our Lords the *Criticks* smell out in the OPERAS. This is already so fully answer'd, and shewn in it self so ridiculous, that it shall give me very little Trouble here.

THEIR Criticisms are improper, and their Complaints groundless; therefore I think my self not oblig'd here, as in the others, to study a Redress of Grievances: The former Objections had but too much Weight in them, not to be thoroughly consider'd: Being sensible of their Defects, I made some Overtures in each, towards accommodating the Differences betwixt the Stage and the Audience. In this there is no Medium left, to build a Reconciliation on; their Demands are so monstrous, that giving them the
leaft

leaſt Grains of Allowance, deſtroys the very Being of an OPERA; but all true Judges of this Entertainment have plac'd it out of their Juriſdiction: However, in hopes to pleaſe the froward Infants, and to amuſe their ſower'd Tempers during the Time of the OPERA; we give them Leave to note down in their Books —— Such a Scene is highly unnatural, according to *Ariſtotle* —— *Rapin* would damn that *Simile*; it has no Buſineſs there —— If *Longinus* is to be credited, the Words of this Air are not the true *Sublime* —— Perhaps the Sufferance of theſe little Liberties, might calm the boiling Ferment of their Blood, and ſweeten Spleen it ſelf into good Humour.

As OPERAS are divided into two principal Factions, the *Italian* and the *French*; *England*, ſome Parts of *Germany*, &c. following the firſt; *Holland*, *Flanders*, &c. the latter; it may be expected, that having been very ample in my treating of one, ſome Notice ſhould be taken of the other; at leaſt by Way of Parallel. But though I have been often an Auditor, and ſometimes a Performer in *French* MUSICK, I can neither deſcribe, nor give any Man, that has not heard it, a tolerable Idea of it: 'Tis ſo much an Original, that it neither tallies with, nor imitates any other Sounds that ever were, antique or modern: 'Tis entirely their own Invention, and all of a Piece with itſelf: So I leave it with them, being foreign to my Deſign, and claiming no Place in an Eſſay upon *Harmony*.

SOME clever Adepts in MUSICK will ſhew as unreaſonable a Surprize as the former, that while I am diſcourſing on this Subject, I ſhould paſs over in Silence the pretty harmonious Appendixes to moſt of our publick Diverſions; as the Farcical OPERAS and MASQUES often exhibited

E 2   hibited

hibited at both Play-Houses; the fine Performances of some *Italian* Airs, stole or borrow'd from
the *H———y-M———t*, which so genteely embroider a plain Play; or that new Method of filling
the Vacancies betwixt the Acts with the choicest
Opera - Songs improv'd by the additional Excellencies of a hoarse Hoat - Boy, or a screaming
little Flute, which, by the Strength of Imagination,
we are to belive *S — no* and *C———z———ni*:
But I beg of those Gentlemen to consider, that
introducing such Rabble amongst the Company
we now are in, is dressing in *Monmouth-Street* of
a Birth-Day.   I propos'd in these Essays giving
our publick Diversions some Physick, in order to better their Constitutions; but I intend,
going through the Operation without prescribing
Water-gruel. A Person of nice Judgment in Dress,
may find it reasonable to rectify some small Dis-
orders in a Lady's Hair, Mantua, or Hoop: Is
it therefore necessary he should new - model her
Kitchen-Maids Pinners into a *French* Head, her
Lockram Handkerchief into a Tippet, or stiffen
her dangling doily Tail into a fashionable Rump?
No! parallel to this Case are our Act-tunes, Play-
House Jigs, *Scotch* Songs, *C———y's* Ballads,
and *Beggars Operas.*   The Nakedness of one is
cloath'd with Sounds, which they call MUSICK;
as the Kitchen-Maid is with Gown and Petticoat,
and fancies her self dress'd to go to *Court.*

I flatter my self, that by this Time, every
thinking *Briton* is convinc'd, that an *Italian Opera*
is an innocent and perfect Entertainment, and
may be render'd as improving as agreeable: It
may indeed be disorder'd in some Parts of its Constitution, but labours under no Disease that is incurable.

ESSAY

E S S A Y II.

O F P O E T R Y;

Particularly DRAMATICK.

The Decay of those Entertainments enquir'd into: Imputed to Poets, Actors, and Spectators: Their Mistakes set in a true Light, and some of the most probable Amendments to those Grievances proposed.

O spend Time here in a pompous Dissertation upon the Dignity, Excellence, Use or Pleasure of POETRY in general, would be justly esteem'd absurd and impertinent. All Ages have in some extraordinary Manner shewn their Value for it; and all Men of true Wit and Learning have agreed in its being the noblest and

most

moſt uſeful of the Polite Arts; nay, Barbarity it ſelf has ever had its POETRY.

IT may be thought as trifling and improper to take Notice in this Place of the Conteſt betwixt the *Epick* and *Dramatick Poets* for Preeminence. My Study in POETRY confining me at preſent to the *Dramma* alone, I may be looked upon as too partial to my favourite Lucubrations; therefore ſhall only aſſert, That both are admirable in their different Views; divinely bright are the Virtues they plant in our Souls; and innocently raviſhing, the Amuſements they give us.

I muſt beg Leave tho' to throw in a trifling Hint by way of Obſervation, before I quit this Subject entirely; which is, that in all Nations where POETRY has the leaſt Influence, the *Dramma* muſt be of more general Uſe than the *Epopæia*, as to the improving our Minds, the Reformation of Manners, and as an Academy of Politeneſs; and amongſt others, for the two following Reaſons.

IN the firſt Place, the beſt *Epick Poets* the World can boaſt of, are in the dead Languages; and either read or underſtood by a few *Literati*, or but indifferently tranſlated into the living Languages; ſo can have but very little Influence on the preſent Age: On the other hand, *Drammatick Poets*, are ſeen, read and enter'd into by all Degrees of Stations or Underſtandings; nor are we oblig'd to copy entirely from the Ancients on that Head, ſince we can produce Originals that come up to, if not excel, the beſt of their Stage-Performances.

SECONDLY, the *Dramma* approaching ſo near Nature in Life and Action, every thing appears real; and of conſequence is more apt to ſtir, awake, and improve the Paſſions, than thoſe tedious Narrations, which moſt People read with-

out

out being in the least agreeably mov'd: So that we may venture to affirm, that one Stage-Play, well acted, will have more Power over the politest Audience, in the Articles of Pleasure and Reformation, than all the *Epick Poems* that ever were wrote. Now if the Criticks will not allow the Shadow of a Parallel betwixt them in the Point of Merit, we may claim justly a Superiority in that of Use; and being undoubtedly more beneficial to Mankind.

If *Aristotle* may be appealed to as a competent Judge, he decides very fairly in Favour of *Tragedy* against the *Epopæia*; he impartially examines to the Bottom, which is most excellent; candidly proposes every thing that can be advanced on the Side of the latter; but declares for the first, in shewing the infinite Advantages it has over its Rival: Which 'tis needless to enumerate here, since every body can easily turn to his *Poeticks* in that Language, antique or modern, which he's most Master of.

With us I hope the Stage will subsist, as long as we have the least Remains of Liberty, Virtue, or an elegant Taste; maugre *Prynn*'s Enthusiastick Nonsense; *Collier*'s ill-grounded, dogmatical Zeal; or *Bedford*'s and *Law*'s ignorantly pious Blunders: Nor shall Men, eminent for Sense and Morality, blush to patronize it; the Vicious and Foolish may rail; their Censures leave no Blemishes behind them.

Since then the Antiquity, Rise, Progress, or different Kinds or Poetry, need not be canvass'd here (those Subjects being so copiously handled by the greatest Geniusses, and most learned Pens of the past and present Times;) let us at once strike into, and proceed regularly in the beaten Path of our publick Diversions,

from

from which I have deviated a little; fo change the Scene without quitting the Stage, by a fmall Hop from the *Opera* to the *Play-Houfes*.

But firft it will be highly proper, and prove a material Evidence in explaining the Merits of this Caufe, to inquire into the Deference, and vaft Regard paid by the *Ancients*, to their *Poets, Players* and *Theatres*.

In *Greece* the firft were held almoft facred in their Perfons, Profeffions and Works; particularly the Drammatick Writers: Their Name implied a Kind of Divinity attending their Productions, they being ftil'd *Creators*. The Privileges and Immunities granted to them, were extraordinary and numerous: They were always efteem'd fuperior to the Profeffors of all other Kinds of Literature, Arts and Sciences: Often entrufted with the Management of the State or Army; ftill proving equal in Capacity or Courage, for Court or Camp; nor did they want but the laft Adoration to make them, even in this Life, equal to their Gods. *Plato* himfelf wrote feveral Tragedies, and was protected by *Dion*, who at his private Expence furnifh'd the *Chorus*.

As *Lycurgus* was proud of being a Patron, *Solon* was pleas'd to be reckon'd a Brother of the *Poetical Tribe*. *Alexander* could not fleep without *Homer* under his Pillow; whofe Works may be juftly ftil'd a-kin to, or at leaft a beautiful Model for *Drammatick Writings*; there runs that Spirit of real Life and Action thro' the Whole. *Socrates* himfelf, in fpite of his confpicuous Wifdom, and vaft Power, was overcome by the more prevailing Wit of a *Comick Poet*: Nor could any thing calm the raging Tyranny of *Phalaris*, but *Stefichorus*'s Mufe.

At

At *Rome* POETRY was not cultivated with that Warmth, or follow'd with that Assiduity as in *Greece*; their Heroes (at least in the Beginning of their Empire) being more eminent for Arms than Arts; but at last, by the Countenance of some Great ones, and the surprizing Beauties of a few of their *Poets*, it began to flourish, and rose to a great Height, but still as far short of the *Grecian* in Splendor, as Merit.

HOWEVER, those excellent *Poets* they could boast, were particularly distinguish'd, and fondly cherish'd by their greatest Philosophers and Princes: The *Scipios* could scarcely live without their *Ennius* and *Terence*: *Cæsar* favour'd, and was himself not the least of *Poets*. *Augustus* and *Mæcenas* pretended to write, as well as patronize; and flew with Raptures from the Grandeur and Cares of Empire, to the beloved Bosoms of *Virgil* and *Horace*. *Seneca* preferr'd his Tragedies to all his other Philosophical Works; nor could the Severity of *Cato*'s *Stoicism* stifle his predominant Passion for POETRY: Nay, *Nero* picqu'd himself more upon the Name of the best Poet, than the Fame of being follow'd as the first Man of the Universe, in all the other Gifts of Fortune: In *Empire* he could rather brook a Rival than in *Parnassus*; so sacrific'd *Lucan* to his Jealousy, for writing *better* Verses.

IF the *Poets* were thus look'd upon by the Ancients with an Eye of Reverence, almost bordering upon divine Worship; we may be certain, that the Persons of their Players, and all Expences incident to their Theatres were not neglected: Their Actors were encourag'd and carefs'd; were often Men of Rank and Figure in Life, Masters of all polite Parts of Learning, and of consequence perfect in the minutest Niceties of their
Profession,

Profeſſion, and skill'd in the juſt Repreſentation of all Characters the World could furniſh the Stage with : Nor did ſome of their principal *Poets* bluſh to perform in their own Plays, tho' perhaps the firſt of the State either in a civil or military Capacity : Indeed I muſt own that their Players, generally ſpeaking, behav'd up to the Virtues and Grandeur of their Stage Characters, in ſome Reſpects even in private Life ; nor were the Names of *Actor* and *Actreſs* then ſynonomous Terms with *Vagabond* and *Strumpet*.

I F our Players complain, that there is no *Tully* to patronize them, we may more juſtly lament, that there is no *Roſcius* for whom a *Cicero* might plead without bluſhing ; nor an *Æſopus* worthy to be admitted into the moſt intimate Friendſhip of the *Wiſe* and the *Great*.

T H E extraordinary Expences of their Theatres, particularly thoſe of the Chorus (which were generally very large,) were always defray'd out of the publick Stock ; not promiſcuouſly, or upon a Level with other common State-Neceſſities, but a particular Fund was laid aſide for that Purpoſe, committed to the Guardianſhip of ſome of the moſt eminent Citizens, not to be touch'd, but upon the Emergency of a Theatrical Deficiency, and held inviolable upon all other Occaſions: *Demoſthenes* was reduc'd to the niceſt Turns of his Rhetorick and Oratory, in daring but to mention to the *Athenians* the medling with that *ſacred Bank,* though Ruin almoſt inevitable ſtar'd them full in the Face ; nor had they any other Means left to ward off an approaching, general Calamity : But thoſe worthy and polite People preferr'd the inculcating Virtue, a genteel Behaviour, and elegant Taſte, to the moſt extended Empire ;

content

content rather to enflave their Bodies than Minds. The chief Magiftrates had entirely the Infpection of the Theatres committed to their Care, and the richeft of the Nobility either bore the Charge of the *Chorus*, in favour of fome particular *Poet*, or that and all other Charges which the Poets and Players could not anfwer, were allow'd out of the publick Treafury: And fo prodigious was the Grandeur and Magnificence of thofe Stages, in *Actors, Muficians, Dancers, Cloaths, Scenes*, and *Machines*; that, by the nicest Computation, a Set of Clouds only for a Comedy, coft the State as much, as a *Coronation* would at this Time in *England*.

We muft likewife obferve, that no publick Edifices were fo much taken Care of, or erected at that amazing Labour and Expence, as the Theatres, Amphitheatres, and other Buildings of that Nature, either amongst the *Grecians* or *Romans*; their Academies, Porticos, Schools, *&c.* were Baubles in comparifon with them, and generally rais'd from fome private Pocket; and indeed they were at moft the Plants, the others the Trees in full Perfection: Nay, the very Temples of thofe fuperftitioufly religious People, fell far fhort of their *Play-Houfes* in the Articles of Beauty, Grandeur and Coft.

The greateft Princes, moft flourifhing Repuplicks, and the wifeft Men, thus interefting themfelves fo arduoufly in the Caufe of POETRY, gave it that Spirit and Vigour we admire in the *Ancients*; and undoubtedly thofe prudent Nations never perceiv'd their Empire leffen'd, their Senfes impair'd, or their Manners corrupted, by the hearty Encouragement given to that Miftrefs of all *Arts*. But, alas! on the other hand, both *Grecians* and *Romans*, with its Fall, faw every Thing

Thing that could be dear to a brave and wife People, trampled under foot; nor could they ever have been conquer'd, had not their P O E T R Y firft languifh'd, and fo ftifled that Life it us'd to infpire. Their Conquerors were *Barbarians*, as void of Humanity, as Sciences, who boafted no Knowledge but Force, and thought Life and Power only given to deftroy the reft of Mankind. —— How oppofite thefe Maxims to the Rules of *Poetry* and Virtue! thofe infeparable Companions.

W E R E I to dwell longer upon this melancholy Subjeɛt, I fhould almoft perfwade my felf to be grave in earneft; therefore I fhall quit it as foon as poffible, and take a peep into our Playhoufes, where every thing one fees, or hears, or imagines, will contribute to our Mirth —— or Indignation.

That our Modern Poets are very bad in the Drammatick Way —— is allowed: *That the Generality of our Players are ten times worfe* —— is not deny'd: *And that the Majority of all Audiences know not whether a Play is good or bad* ——muft be granted. Here then let us fairly ftate the Cafe, and confider to what Caufes this Decay in *Drammatick Poetry*, this Lownefs in Stageaɛtion, and this Depravity of Tafte in the prefent Age is owing.

A s I have the Happinefs to think generally out of the common Road; I fancy, I fhall advance fome Reafons, obvious to very few Criticks, yet when made publick, fhall be granted by all: and without fixing the Fault altogether on Poets, Aɛtors, or Audiences, I fhall make manifeft, in what Points they are all wrong; fo interfperfing fome very new Remarks by way of Cure, I fhall conclude this E s s a y.

T o

To begin then with our Poets. —— I do not here pretend to make any Comparison betwixt our past and present *Dramatick* Writers, or them, and the Antients; neither shall I undertake to praise, or censure any particular PLAYS, by pointing out some hidden Beauties, or neglected Faults: That is a Piece of Criticism, of too refin'd and abstruse a Nature, to be trusted to any one private Judgment: I shall only gently lay my Finger upon those Blots in their Conduct, which are notoriously wrong, tho' hitherto unobserv'd; and which have undoubtedly occasion'd that Inundation of execrable PLAYS, which has overwhelm'd both THEATRES and Press. These I reduce to four Heads: The first is, their mistaken Notions in Choice of Subjects for the Stage: The second, their strange Mismanagement in relation to the Effects of a *Stage-Play*, in giving us TRAGEDIES to make us laugh, and COMEDIES to make us cry: The third, their Ignorance, or total Neglect of the true Sublime: The fourth, their trusting to Narration, rather than Action, the most material Incidents of the *Drama*.

FIRST, then I think our Poets to blame in their Choice of improper Subjects for the Stage; and to their ill Judgment on that Head, is partly owing the bad State of both THEATRES, which are by that Means liable to the severest Censures of above three Parts in four of the People, who are afraid to visit either House: They have, in a Manner, confin'd the *Drama* to prophane *History*, and to the worst Topicks of Prophaness, Rage and Love; so that all our TRAGEDIES are fill'd with the flagrant Crimes and audacious Passions of *Grecian*, *Roman*, or *Turkish* Tyrants; and our COMEDIES very decently deck'd out with our own bold-face Follies and nasty Vices.

F   I

I know they'll anfwer, That if thefe Things are not drawn to the Life, and expos'd, even naked, that it will be impoffible to give an Audience that Abhorrence (which they would have them to imbibe) for thofe deftructive Sins, or ridiculous Affectations which T R A G E D Y and C O M E D Y lafh.

B U T to this I reply, That they paint their Follies fo fair, and fhew their Paffions in fuch glaring Colours, that People are apt rather to grow fond, than afraid of them. The Knowledge of thefe bewitching Allurements banifhes from the *Play-houfe* the greateft part of the Town, who dare not venture, or truft themfelves amidft *Theatrical* Enchantments; and of Confequence, they are debarr'd all that Improvement and Inftruction, which the Stage fhould promote, by recommending Virtue, and putting Vice out of Countenance. 'Tis true, prophane Stories might in fome Meafure anfwer that End, did not their heathenifh Names frighten honeft Chriftian People from coming near them.

T H E Antients (who are faid to have equall'd, if not excell'd us, both in T R A G E D Y and C O M E D Y) thought no part of their Religion either too facred, or folemn for the Stage. They introduc'd their greateft Mifteries with Applaufe; nay, made their *Stage-Plays* the chief part of their Worfhip: So People could pray, and laugh, and cry, and improve at the fame time. *Jupiter* mounted on his Eagle, us'd to throw his Thunder and Lightening about at a ftrange Rate. *Mercury* would fpeak *Prologues* and *Epilogues,* or dance on the high Ropes. *Mars* and *Venus* were often very merry behind the Curtain, while *Bacchus* entertain'd them with Drinking-Catches: *Apollo* flying crofs the Stage in his blazing Machine, would tickle their Ears with his Lyre: *Pallas*
found

found to Arms, and *Diana* fhew her full Moon, while the leffer Deities would fing and caper in Chorus, or fnuff Candles.

Then the Stage fhone out in its full Splendor, and every Man thought it his Duty to promote the Intereft of thofe Poets, or Players, who made it the Study of their Lives to convey fo gently and infenfibly into their Souls, a Love of Virtue, by the politeft and moft pleafing Amufements.

I hope none of my candid Readers will fo far mif-interpret what I have here innocently advanc'd, as to imagine that what I infinuate, is defign'd in the leaft to burlefque even the heathen Religion: No! —— far from my Pen fly fuch impious Thoughts, as idly to reflect upon any thing that boafts the Shadow of Religion.

What I infer from this Obfervation is, That if our Poets would judicioufly choofe from out the Old T——nt or Ap——ha the fineft Hiftorical Parts, and upon fuch fubftantial Foundations, and beautiful Incidents, form all their Theatrical Reprefentations, and introduce them in a proper Manner, upon our Stages; the Gravity of the Subjects, and the Grandeur of fuch Scenes, would invite the Godly thither, and keep the wicked in awe ; and, of Confequence, our Theatres would be crowded with Audiences as religious as polite: Then no body daring to entertain an Objection to the *Play-houfe*. How far this Scheme might contribute to Numbers of People out of Harm's-way, (as Infants are firft fent to School) and make a ftricter Union betwixt Religion and Morality, (according to the Notions the World has of both) I leave the fober Part of Mankind to judge.

I

I am sensible, some People will be very grave, and others as merry, upon meeting with this Proposal: The first will be shock'd at the Impiety of any Project which would bring a Sc——re Story on the Stage, and at once tax with Prophaneness, every Thought, which deviates from the narrow Road of their nonsensical Capacities; the others will ridicule me for advancing as new, what is so openly practis'd abroad in every christian Country; nor are we without frequent Instances of it here at Home, since the first Appearance of a Stage amongst us.

THE Churches in *Italy* and *Spain*, on all Festivals, are turn'd into THEATRES *pro tempore*; and there they exhibit some Sacred Story, by Way of a *Stage-Play*. In *France*, the same Custom prevails: Nay, their best Poets have founded their best PLAYS for the Stage, upon Divine Subjects. In *Germany* and *Holland* you seldom meet with any Theatrical Entertainments, but the Fable is entirely borrow'd from the Scripture. At Home, *Dryden* has given us the *Fall of Man*, and a *Saint Catharine*, which is next Door to the Sign of the *Bible*; and *Milton* his *Sampson Agonistes*; besides, several Authors of an inferior Rank, have built sorry Superstructures on that noble Foundation; and in the Infancy of our *Poetry*, the *Stage-Plays* then presented, were altogether Scriptural.

BUT some squeamish Consciences, as silly as zealous, will object, That we should not in so nice a Point follow the outlandish, heathenish Customs of Papists and Foreigners; and that those PLAYS, but now cited, tho' wrote at Home, yet never were acted —— I partly agree with them there: Thence proceeds my Complaint, I would have them acted, and more attempted in the same Stile, till they got entire Possession

of

of our THEATRES: Then those *Priest-Plays* of the Stage would lay all the *Bug-bears* and *Hob-goblins,* which terrify scrupulous People from coming thither: Then every body might frequent the *Play-Houses* with a Certainty of being improv'd on all Sides, without being look'd upon as Heathens. Then Tradesmen need not hinder their Wives and Prentices; Masters, their Servants; Tutors, their Pupils; nor the religious, their whole sanctify'd Families, from going to an Evening's Exercise.

SHOULD this Project of mine succeed, I make no Doubt of hearing a broad-brimm'd Hat, a starch'd Band and short Cloak, speak an *extempore Prologue* to a PLAY, with as much Form, Grimace and Devotion, as they would say a long Grace to a poach'd Egg.

IT is impossible to enumerate in this small Sketch, the infinite Advantages that must accrue from such a Design, well executed, to the Publick in General, and to the noble Art of *Dramatick Poetry* in particular.

Holland, (a Nation we may look upon amongst the wisest of our Neighbours, and to whom we are deeply indebted on several Scores) will sufficiently instruct us on that Head, if we are not too conceited to follow so prudent a Guide. The Subjects they choose for the Stage, are mostly Scriptural; nor do they ever meddle with any part of it, but with an Intent by some new Turn, or surprizing Thought, to heighten the Story, and improve their People; of which an Example or two may not be reckon'd digressive.

To begin therefore with an *Examen* of one of their most noted Pieces, according to the Rules of the Stage, which is the Sacrifice of I——c. The Subject, I own, seems barren, and promises very little; but the greater the Art of the Poet,

to raife fomething noble and new, from fo poor
a Foundation.

Ab——m goes to *facrifice* I——c, *by fhooting him*
thro' the Head with a Blunderbufs, an Angel pop-
ping from behind a Fuz-Bufh, p——s in the Pan,
On this the Gun miffes Fire; fo I——c efcapes, and
the Angel with a tolerable rough Compliment in the
Low-dutch *Dialect, clofes the Scene.*

HERE the Contrivance is very new, thro'
the whole PLAY, and the Conduct very artful:
The *Cataftrophe* is, (as the *French* term it) to
the laft Degree *fuprenant* and *meweilleux,* and gives
the Audience all that can be imagin'd of an a-
greeable Aftonifhment, which is the chief End
of *Poetry.* This Management fhews what bright
Sparks may be ftruck out of the rough Flint-
ftone of fuch a Subject, by an inventive Genius;
and befides, rectifies a vulgar Error crept in a-
mongft us, That Gun-powder is but a very modern Invention, a lucky Accident of t'other Day;
when by this we are affur'd, that it might have
been us'd by the Patriarchs before the Flood.

IT would be trifling and endlefs to enter into any more Particulars, in fo copious a Manner of Criticifm; let it fuffice to give my Readers an Idea of their prodigious Talents in the
Choice and Improvement of Subjects for the
Stage. In fhort, I have feen the Witch of *En-*
dor, and *Samuel's* Ghoft, by the Help of well-
difpos'd Squibs, f——t Fire at one another, for the
fpace of half an hour, by Way of Salute; which
imprinted the jufteft Notions of Terror on the
Minds of an Audience: Nor could Pity be lefs
predominant, when they confider'd the Uncertainty of this World's Grandeur, in feeing *Ne-*
buchadnezzar fow'd up in a Wolf's Skin, reduc'd
from royal Dainties to a Handful of Grafs.

HOW

How have I seen the *Dutch* amaz'd at the magnificent Decorations of *Bell* and the *Dragon*, introduc'd by way of OPERA, with vaft Succefs! Nor were they lefs pleas'd with the Juftice of Providence, in the feveral wonderful Efcapes of *Tobit* and his *Dog*, thrown in as a merry Interlude.

BEING confin'd within narrow Bounds, I need not touch upon many more Inftances, to fhew what Advantage attends thofe PLAYS, which are taken from *Sacred Hiftory*, rather than *Prophane*. I choofe to ftrengthen my Arguments on this Head from Abroad, knowing it would have the greater Influence at Home, efpecially coming recommended by their Tafte, whofe *Delicateffe* is unexceptionable.

IT may be reckon'd needlefs to point out thofe Parts which would furnifh the properest Theatrical Foundations; but where can an undaunted Bravery of Soul, or the prodigious Effects of Faith, be better exemplify'd, than in *Shadrach*, *Meshach*, and *Abednego*'s being thrown into, and yet preferv'd from the Fiery Furnace? —— as *Daniel* was from the *Lion's Den*.

WHERE do the Triumphs of Virtue, or the juft Rewards of Luft, appear more confpicuous, than in *Sufanna* and the two Elders?—— Where can true Fortitude, or invincible Piety, fhine brighter, than in Heroick *Judith*'s Conqueft over *Holofernes*?—— or Captivating Modefty, than in *Efther*'s over *Ahafuerus*? —— But to defcend thus to fome Circumftances, is to imagine there can be an End of Examples, where the Store is inexhauftible.

I cannot pafs over in Silence, the Force that the Face of Religion has in *Stage-Entertainments*, urg'd from the moft remarkable Inftance the World

World can produce, than which we cannot bring a more powerful Argument to clench the Nail of an Affertion; which is the furprizing Run of Succefs that attended the Farcical, Mufical Dance of *Doctor Faustus,* at both Houfes; which muft be owing to that Religious, Moral, Poetick Juftice, fo finely interwoven thro' the whole Piece; particularly, in the wicked Conjurer's difmal End, by infernal *Fiends* at one Houfe, and a terrible *Dragon* at the other. Thefe lively Ideas of Hell defervedly drew the Town after them. The Criticks may affign what Caufe they pleafe, for what they term an Infatuation; but I infift upon it, I have only touch'd the true one. I am forry the *Beggars Opera* has not either Religion, or Juftice, to countenance its Run, and fcreen it from the Criticks.

The fecond Mifmanagement I charge upon our *Poets,* is their Ignorance in, or Neglect of the true Defign and Nature of a *Stage-Play;* by prefenting us with merry *Tragedies,* or fad *Comedies.* This Difeafe is in a Manner *Epidemick* amongft that Tribe; yet by the ftricteft Enquiry into the original Seeds of P O E T R Y, I cannot fix upon a natural Reafon, whence fo general a Malignity can fpring; of confequence, I muft be pretty much at a Lofs in propofing a Remedy.

I believe it often happens, that an old, or a young *Poet,* takes Pen, Ink and Paper,—— fits down to his Scrutore—— or perhaps a Table ——he finds it neceffary to write a P L A Y——he turns over God knows how many Volumes for a Story—— or he makes one, and then—— he writes a P L A Y: The Difpute is, Muft it be a *Tragedy* or *Comedy?* The Arguments of both Sides are weighty—— It cannot be decided, the Rea-

fons are fo equal—— At laſt he wifely counts his
Buttons—— or truſts to Crofs and Pile —— As
Fortune would have it, *Tragedy* wins the Day :
You fee in the Play-Bill and Title-Page, *T R A-
G E D Y*, in large Red Letters, like a Saint in the
Calendar : Of Confequence, we muſt be Spectators
and Readers of that Performance, in a Deluge of
Tears. Another writes a *Comedy* by the fame
Rules, and wonders, that an Excefs of Mirth does
not crack our Voices, and fplit our Sides : When,
alas! the World does laugh at the Abfurdities of
the firſt, and is griev'd at the Stupidity of the
other.

T H E S E Gentlemen, fure, from their Infancy,
have been only accuſtom'd to Crofs-purpofes ;
and would give Pleaſure to the World by Con-
traries. They never make the Paſſions their Study,
and are utter Strangers to what is true Humour :
Their P O E T R Y has the fame Effect upon an Audience, that the Quack's Medicines had on his
Patients ; he vomited one by a Purge, and pur-
ged another by a Vomit. So with thefe *Poets*, 'tis
laughing and crying ſtill, let *Tragedy* or *Comedy*
be the Caufe.

A N honeſt old Woman (who, like *Moliere's*
Houfe-keeper, judg'd from pure Nature) frank-
ly own'd to her Neighbour, (who carry'd her to
a *Comedy* to make her merry) that they might
call it a *Comedy*, if they would, but, for her Part,
fhe never had been more fleepy or melancholy
at a Sermon.

T H E R E is another Fault to be fpoke to under
this Head, as prepoſterous as the former ; which
is, the blending of Sorrow and Mirth fo cunningly together, that a Man does not know
whether to cry or laugh, without he could play
Heraclitus and *Democritus* at the fame time. Thefe
Cubs

Cubs of POETRY, that have never been lick'd into any true Form, can neither be call'd *Tragedies, Comedies,* nor *Tragi-Comedies*; they are no real Manufacture, but a Sort of Linfy-Woolfy Entertainment; where a Man of Senfe is at a Lofs how to fettle his Looks, unlefs he could new coin his Face, and let one Side wear the Stamp of Grief, and t'other that of Joy: Nay, fo fudden are the Changes from one to the other, that his right Eye muft look grave, and the left fmile at the fame time, left he fhould be furpriz'd into a wrong Behaviour before the Scene is half out.

I muft own, moft of our greateft *Poets* have been particularly to blame in this Point; and have given us PLAYS that are the very *Oglios* of POETRY, no Difh of a Piece with it felf. In the moft grave Affairs of State, you'll have a Dialogue betwixt a Privy-councellor and a Jack-pudding; in the Recital of the moft paffionate Diftrefles of Lovers, a pert Chamber-Maid will tell her Miftrefs a fmutty Story; in the fame Scene you'll have a Husband killing his beloved Wife, and a rampant Widow caterwauling for a Husband; or the Fates of Empires and Republicks tofs'd up with the Humours of *Purgatory* and *Bedlam.* Thus in Matters of the greateft Moment to Mankind, in Virtue, Policy, or Love, the whole will be fo larded with the loweft, moft naufeous Farce, that a fenfible Spectator is readier to puke, than pity the unfortunate *Hero,* or fuffering *Fair.*

THIS Fault (though in it felf fo notorious and defencelefs) has fo far engrofs'd the *Englifh Stage,* that, defpairing of any Redrefs, I cannot mention it with common Patience.

THE third Charge I bring againft our *Poets,* is, their not having a right Idea of, or at leaft

totally

totally neglecting the true *Sublime* in their Writings; nor will they be at the Trouble of turning their Thoughts towards what is new and furprizing. For thefe three thoufand Years, they have been hobling on after one anothers Tails, in the fame dull Pace, and beaten Track; and the fame infipid Tale over and over again, and a hundred times repeated, has furnifh'd the Stage, in all Ages and Languages, with what they call *New Entertainments.*

THE firft *Poets* the World could boaft, were Men of Genius, Spirit, and Invention: They left behind them a few very fine Go-carts, and a parcel of very ftrong Leading-ftrings, for the Ufe of *Infant-Poets*; and Arm'd Chairs, or Crutches, for the *Aged* and *Infirm.* The puny *Moderns* (who prefume upon being call'd their Succeffors) think they are Heroes, if they can creep about with thofe neceffary Machines, and that they do but fcurvily: They are afraid to venture a Step out of them, left they meet with a bloody Nofe, or crack'd Skull; and are fo pleas'd with being paultry Imitators, that they dare not attempt the Honour of being bold Originals.

But then the Ancient Poets *had the wide World of Invention free before them, to range in*; *and every thing they faid, muft be new.* This is readily granted, but not allow'd as an Excufe for our prefent Bards. If much has been faid, how much more is left untouch'd! If Lazinefs, or Stupidity, did not hinder their Search, Fancy is unconfin'd; and, as a Poet is not ty'd down to Truth, there can be no End of agreeable Fiction.

THOSE old Fellows made a terrible Noife and Splutter about a Town call'd *Troy*, its King *Priam*, his Son *Paris*, and a *Grecian* Curtezan, call'd *Helen*: They talk'd fo long of it, and nothing

thing elfe, that they deafened the Ears of the whole World with their Chatt'ring. We, forfooth muft take up the Cudgels, and receive the Fray betwixt *Trojans* and *Grecians*, to the End of Time.

BUT, to render this Affair a little more familiar to my Readers, and explain the Merits of the Caufe, before I appeal to their Judgments,

Let us fuppofe, that the Mafter of the Red-Lion-Inn *in the City of* Brentford, *has an unlucky Boy to his Son, whom we'll call* Paris: *This fame Youth often plays the Truant; and one Day, under Pretence of vifiting an Aunt, who fold Afparagus at* Batterfea, *he croffes the Water, and having ftole fome Money out of the Bar-box, whips to the* Star *and* Garter *at* Mortlack, *in order to fpend it: He there gets acquainted with* Nelly, *the Landlord's Wife; fhe bargains with him to elope from her Hufband, and he carries her home to* Brentford, *telling his Father, he had married a fine Woman, and a great Fortune: The Father believes, and protects them;* Menelaus *at the* Star *and* Garter, *miffes his Wife; Fame informs him where fhe is; he demands her in Form, and is deny'd. Things carry'd thus far, he raifes a Poffe of his Friends, Neighbours and Conftables; furrounds the* Red-Lion, *makes many brave Attacks; and at laft, in the Space of ten Days after, being often repuls'd, he demolifhes the* Red-Lion, *breaks old* Priam's Head, *makes* Paris *beg Pardon on his Knees, and brings back* Nelly's *crack'd Pipkin to* Mortlack *in Triumph: The Man has his Mare again, and all is well.*

IN fine, from a Story not one bit better or truer than this, have all our *Epick* and *Dramatick Poems* been borrow'd for thefe three thoufand Years; and from this Body of a Tree have fprouted I know not how many Branches to amufe us. One General was ten Years a wandering Home, another

another was kill'd by his Wife, as foon as he came Home; a third was forc'd into a ftrange Country by contrary Winds, and built a City there; a fourth had a terrible Difpute with *Neptune* and *Eolus,* fo was drown'd by the Way; and a fifth got fafe to *Italy* (as they fay) and laid a Foundation for another *Romance.*

But, in order to give our young *Poets* a jufter Idea of what I mean; to enliven their Underftandings, and refcue them from the pitiful Slavery of always treading in the direct Foot-fteps of the Ancients, I fhall give but one Inftance of the Ingenuity, Fire and Strength of Expreffion, of a poor *French Stroler.*

The Prince of a Tribe of *Dramacick Wanderers,* once fix'd the Seat of his Empire in the largeft Barn of one of the *Hans-Towns*: His vaft Equipage of tatter'd Scenes, various Inftruments, turnifh'd Tinfel, and empty Band-boxes, delighted the Populace, and gave Wonder to the Magiftrates. After a Week's neceffary Preparation, he promis'd the City a moft entertaining and magnificent P L A Y, upon the Story of St. *Peter's* following our S A V I O U R into *Galilee.* The Play-Bills gave the Town Hopes of fine M A C H I N E R Y, gay S C E N E S, and exquifite M U S I C K, furprizing D A N C I N G, and all thofe additional Ornaments of the Stage, which are requir'd to coax a *High-Dutch Audience* into fwallowing Wit.

The long-expected Night comes, the Houfe quickly fills; Crowds that could not enter, were fo unfortunate as to be oblig'd to carry back their Money. Prodigious was the Expectation of the happy Mortals within; as great the Vexation of the Wretches excluded. At laft, the wifh'd for Minute comes, the Curtain flies up, and he who perfonated our S A V I O U R, appears with good St.

G   *Peter*

Peter at his Heels; whom, with an Air of Maje-
fty, he commands to follow him into *Galilee*;
then quits the Stage--- and St. *Peter* follows. From
behind the Scenes, they immediately convey their
Perfons, with the Treafure of their Wit. So grand
an Opening of a P L A Y promifing wonderful things
to come, the Audience, with unfpeakable Impa-
tience, waited their Return to proceed with the
Bufinefs of the Stage—— but all in vain —— Moment fucceeds to Moment; no Tidings, no Appearance of our S A V I O U R, or St. *Peter*, to finifh
the P L A Y. The Audience, enquiring into the Reafons of their Delay, were inform'd, that indeed
they had taken Poft - Horfes, and were by that
Time got out of the Territories of the faid Town,
in their Way to *Galilee*.

N o w thofe Novices in polite Literature, who
are ignorant of the true Art of *Dramatick Poetry*, will imagine, that this Audience was bit, as
we emphatically exprefs it; but I boldly maintain, that no Audience ever enjoy'd a Stage-Entertainment in a higher Degree of Perfection.
To give a fine Surprize, and raife our Paffions,
then gently let them fink, is the greateft Height
the *Drama* can arrive to; which certainly was
their Cafe exactly: And if what was new, or out
of the Way could pleafe, they, fure, had Reafon
to be charm'd! And, in Vindication of that excellent Mafter of his Art, as Poet and Player, I
prefume to fay, That the few Words he repeated, had more of the true *Sublime* in them, according to *Longinus*, than any one P L A Y now in
being. *That Simplicity of Expreffion, without a Poverty of Stile! That Grandeur of Elocution!* ——
yet void of Bombaft. How delicate the Sentiments!
—— *yet free from the leaft Affectation.* This happy
Conjunction of fo many Beauties, has fix'd upon

it

it the Mark of the true *Sublime,* according to the
great Critick juſt mention'd; and, as ſuch, I recommend it to all our young *Poets,* hoping that,
for the future, they'll take Care to introduce, in
all their Writings, that noble Simplicity, which is
the Quinteſſence of Nature and Art, in P o e t r y
or P r o s e.

Fourthly, I accuſe our *Dramatiſts* of a grand
Miſtake, which they are frequently guilty of, particularly in *Tragedy.* This is too far truſting the
moſt eſſential Parts of their P l a y s, upon which
the Main of the Plot turns, rather to tireſome
Narration, than the Force of Action; in direct
Oppoſition to a poſitive Maxim of *Horace,* that
conſummate Critick, and exquiſite Poet; who
ſays —— *Some Things are acted, others only told;
but what we hear, moves leſs than what we ſee:
Spectators only have their Eyes to truſt; but Auditors muſt truſt their Ears and you.*

B y this Conduct they deprive the Stage of one
of its greateſt Beauties; and, indeed, what we
look upon as the moſt material Difference betwixt the *Epick* and *Dramatick Poetry.*

O u r Actors too muſt prove better Orators
than we can boaſt at preſent, if they pretend to
move an Audience as much, by telling them,
ſuch and ſuch an Affair happen'd —— ſo and ſo
—— at that and t'other Time —— As the Action
it ſelf will affect their Underſtandings, when faith-
fully repreſented before their Eyes, they'll expect we ſhould ſuppoſe it all to be brought a-
bout in the *Green-Room;* but it might as well be
tranſacted at *Grand Cairo,* or *Greenland.*

I f a *Poet* would have me to mourn his *Diſtreſs'd Widow,* let her appear upon the Stage, ſuitable to her Character, like the Picture of *Charity,*
with an Infant at each Breaſt, one on her Back,

and a Couple led: Then what Heart of *Adamant* could refrain from Tears, to see them weep?

I F from the Rage of a *Jealous Husband*, I am to guess at what he inwardly feels, let me first view him, brandishing his Wife's Heart on the Point of his Sword, red with the Blood of every Man that but spoke to her.

I F the justest Idea of an absolute Tyrant is to be imprinted on the Minds of the Spectators, shew us the Monster surrounded with Guards, Arms, Legs, Racks, Gibbets, and Axes; then we are sure, whenever he speaks, each Word pronounces Death and Terror.

I must confess, that as to the Articles of Stabbing, Poysoning, and Tortures, our *Poets* have play'd their Parts, and laid about them very handsomely; and several *Tragedies* have ow'd their Success to a Ruffian in an old Red Coat, a Carbuncle Face, and Black Perriwig; who is sure always to come off with Applause, especially in the Slaughter-Scene.

BUT I am principally concern'd, that some small Love-Affairs, are not transacted in so clear a Manner of Negotiation, and to the entire Satisfaction of an Audience, as I could wish: Indeed, in some PLAYS, the Affair of a Rape has been push'd a tolerable Length; nor has any thing but the critical Minute been hid from our longing Eyes; yet had they gone a little farther, then we might have seen a just Resentment of the Villainy in every Spectator's Eyes, each Hand prepar'd to assassinate the Ravisher.

I am sensible that this Defect in our PLAYS, is partly owing to the innate Modesty of our *Poets*, and partly to the excessively nice Stomachs and well-bred Rules of our own, and the *French* Criticks; for one of the most noted of them observes, ferves, that an excellent *Tragedy* of *Corneille*'s was damn'd to all Intents and Purpofes, only for a Rape's being mention'd in it. The fhocking Idea fo difgufted thofe fqueamifh Knight-Errants, thofe very civil Heroes, that their fine-fpun Notions of Love and Honour, could not digeft the naughty Word.

But why fhould we plan out a Method of Behaviour to our felves in this Point, from their puny Appetites and weak Defires? We *Englifh* fcorn fuch trifling Kick-fhaws; what is fubftantial, alone charms us; and, when we feed, it muft be Knuckle-deep in a Sirloin. Let not then the Forms of their Romantick Love and Honour, regulate our Tafte. We are convinc'd, that the more naturally things are reprefented on the Stage, the more fhocking, or agreeable they prove, according to the Heinoufnefs, or Innocence of the Fact. How can we fhew a juft Abhorrence of that Crime we fleep over, when 'tis told? Let the Reprefentation be faithful, and every Paffion is rous'd; the Sight blows up the Coals of Indignation, and Rivets a Deteftation in our Souls! Thus the wife *Spartans* made their Slaves get drunk, that their Children might imbibe the trueft Idea of, and fix'd Averfion for that beaftly Vice.

But I only prefume to fpeak my humble Opinion, in an Affair of fo great Confequence: I fubmit my Thoughts on this Head, and all others, to a general Council of the Learned; not to any *Pope-Critick* who pretends to be infallible.

Having declar'd my principal Objections to the Conduct of the Mafters of our POETRY, and, I think, in every Particular made good my Charge; I fhall next attack, in Form, their Journeymen, in their Quarters; *viz.* the Managers and Actors of our *Play-Houfes*, or, *vice versá*, the

G 3   Actors

Aʼtors and Managers, they being allow'd, by some unaccountable Blunder in the Politicks of that vast Empire, to be both; and permitted to sit as Judges, when they are at most, but a Party concern'd.

So many petty Kings in one Kingdom occasion a great Confusion and Distractions in the State: Each Monarch studies only to enrich himself, nor is the publick Welfare or Pleasure taken Notice of, but where their private separate Interests require it. To this *Aristocracy* then are owing several of the following Misfortunes, which have occasion'd the Decay of the *Dramatick Art,* as will be manifest to every unbiass'd Reader, without pointing to Particulars.

My Complaints against the Managers of our *Play-Houses,* are near as numerous as against the *Poets :* For, to their Mismanagement I impute the Scandal the Stage and their Profession lies under, by their mistaken Choice of *Poets, Plays* and *Players,* and their almost total Neglect of those Decorations which are essentially necessary to the Beauty and Life of the Stage.

If our *Poets* are to blame in their Choice of Subjects for the *Theatre,* the Managers are as much out in their Judgment of the P L A Y S, when brought to their fiery Trial. They don't consider a P L A Y as to its Merit; the Reputation it would bring to their Art, or the Pleasure, or Instruction it would give the Town; but what Expences must we be at, to fit it for the Stage? What Time must we lose, to study the Parts? and what Money will it bring in, to answer our Pains and Expences?

We may proceed with those *Stock-Plays* we are perfect in, or revive those which have lain dor-

mant

mant half an Age: They'll be new to the Town, and fave us the Trouble of getting by Rote, more Parts than we can remember; and anticipate the Charge of Cloaths, Scenes, and the *Poet's* third Night.

Thus argue *Lazinefs, Ignorance* and *Avarice:* This is the Care they take of encouraging Poetry, and obliging the Town. Their Behaviour is recent in every Memory, when both Companies were united under their Banner: The Spectators, Poets and Actors of thofe Days, can but in Death forget it. We feldom then had an Opera to entertain us, and our Musick was in a tolerable bad Way: Play we had none, but what, and when they pleas'd to give us one: So even our Men of Senfe, and Ladies of Fafhion, were forc'd to run for Amufement to the *Puppet-Show* and *Bear-Garden.* Either the underling Actors were dignify'd with the principal Characters; or, if the *Heads* condefcended to favour the Town, they but trifled, yawn'd and flept three Hours away. They grudg'd the fmalleft Expence to invite, or amufe Company; they were fenfible they had no other Houfe to go to; a new Scene, or fuit of Cloaths, a new Dance, or Piece of Musick, were as rare as a Comet; and when they blaz'd forth, the Prices were rais'd, and the Town pay'd the Piper. Thus they enrich'd themfelves, ftarv'd their Players, and fool'd our Nobility and Gentry.

Since the Eftablifhment of the two *Theatres,* our Ufage has been kinder, and their Behaviour modefter; and 'tis abfolutely proper, that two Houfes fhould always fubfift; not that Wit thrives better than before, they affecting only to encourage the Heel, and not the Head: But the

the Dread of a powerful Rival may keep both in Awe, though neither is to be trusted.

I f a Poet appears at their critical Tribunal, he is judg'd in the general Way of the World. *What is his Name, his Character and Fortune?* —— *Is he a Whig or Tory?* —— *What great Men countenance him?* —— *Is he known, or supported at* Will's? —— *Does he frequent* Button's? —— *What says the* Lion's *Face to him there?* —— *or the rest of the witty Wooden Heads?* —— *What thinks* Co--ly *of the Affair?* —— *Will the Gentleman allow his* P L A Y *to be alter'd, and resign the Profits of his third Night, for the Name of a Poet?*

T h i s they call sitting as Judges upon the Body of a P l a y, in order to see Poetick Justice impartially distributed, for the Credit, Pleasure and Improvement of the Nation. Thus Gentlemen are to be treated, who (however they succeed) design their Labours to delight and instruct Mankind by those Upstarts in Manners, as well as Fortune, and who are as great Strangers to Sense, as to Gentility; who have as little Knowledge in judging of such an Affair, as they have Right to manage a *Theatre*; nor can any thing but the grossest and most general Infatuation, account for either.

I f one of their own Fraternity is deliver'd of a Bastard; however ridiculous, vile, or mishapen the Changling is, it must be publickly christen'd, finely dress'd, and put to Nurse at the publick Charge: But had Men of Wit and Reputation, above all Bribery, and every Way unprejudic'd, canvass'd the P l a y s, with a Power to receive or refuse what has gone thro' their Hands, many valuable Entertainments would be rescued from Obscurity, and a vast Quantity of execrable Trash be buried in Oblivion. But it is needless to dwell any longer on so disagreeable a Subject; since, in order to make their own Drofs pafs at Home, the Gold they have refus'd, is allow'd Sterling in another Kingdom.

WERE the Managers of our *Theatres* as follicitous about the true Ufe of the Stage to the World, and the Dignity of their Profeffion, as they are about filling their Pockets, in order to enable them to W—re, and D—nk, and G—me, as if they had as much Right to thofe Vices, as the firft Men of Quality in the Kingdom; they would then give all due Encouragement to the Poets, to ftick clofe to facred Subjects; and by once making fuch a *Dramatick* Law, they might, with a well-bred Confidence, refufe all PLAYS built on prophane Foundation.

THEN our Stage would rife in Grandeur and Reputation, equal to the Plans they follow'd; and perhaps, might be permitted, by our Superiours, to entertain us prudently, and gravely, even on *Sundays* and *Holidays:* And inftead of our *Play-Houfes* being filenc'd on *Wednefdays* and *Fridays* in *Lent*, and other *Fafts* and *Feftivals*, they might be open'd to our Edification, as well as Amufement.

ALL civiliz'd Nations in *Europe* allow PLAYS and OPERAS on *Sunday Nights*, but the *Dutch* and we, or fome other infignificant, petty States, below our Notice; yet our confcientious Neighbours juft mention'd, approve of private and publick Gaming in Affemblies, Coffee-houfes, &c. on thofe Evenings, when Divine Service is over. Now the numerous Mifchiefs arifing from that Liberty to all civil Societies, are fo fcandaloufly notorious, that the moft innocent Game cannot be brought upon the Parallel with the moft faulty Stage-Entertainment we ever knew.

MORE-

MOREOVER, we fhould confider, that above two Parts in three of any Audience, can find out no manner of Way fo agreeably inftructive, and virtuoufly amufing, as a PLAY, to kill Time; and Time will be as uneafy to them on a *Sunday Evening* as any other.

BESIDES, all our Tradefmen, and others of an inferior Rank, (who are oblig'd to labour hard fix Days of the Week, and are by their Callings depriv'd of fuch Diverfions) may have then an Opportunity of improving, in a moral and polite Way, as well as their Betters: For, let our Divines preach up what Doctrines they pleafe, *Sundays* and *Holidays* being, as the *Presbyterian* Parfon call'd them, *Idle days*; People of that Rank will then unbend their Minds from the Cares of the World, and hunt out Amufements of fome Sort or other: Therefore let us give them thofe which may prove pleafing, harmlefs and inftructive.

THERE are but few of our meaneft Mechanicks now, that will condefcend to fpend thofe Evenings only over a Pfalm, a Slice of cold Beef and Carrot; fo grunt, lovingly, Arm in Arm to Bed: The Tafte, even of the Dregs of the People, is at prefent more refin'd; and we that toil for the publick Good, ought to give it fuitable Encouragement: For, as Mr. *Dennis* wifely obferves, in his *Remarks* upon Mr. *Collier's Thundering Effay* againft the Stage—— " Nor will the " People of this Age be fatisfy'd, to be always en-"tertain'd with Prayers and Sermons, but require " other Diverfions."

IT is evident, indeed, that if the higher Powers fhould take this Propofal of mine into Confideration, and fhelter it under the Wings of Authority, our Taverns and Bawdy-houfes would
be

be confiderable Sufferers in the Manufactures of Wine and Flefh, which the vaft Trade of that Day calls for, it being their weekly Market : But whither Wh——ing and Dr——nefs, or feeing a PLAY, is moft offenfive to Religion or Morality, I leave the pious and virtuous Part of Mankind to judge. I think it appears very plain, that Nature requires a gentle raifing of the Spirits, after the Fatigue of that Day ; and the generality of People are agreed to have it one way or t'other.

WE all are fenfible, that this Affair of innocent Recreations, was not only allow'd, but encourag'd, in the Days of a moft religious King, and zealous Metropolitan. They knew that the Genius of the Nation demanded this Relief on fuch Occafions : For that reafon, the *Book of Sports* after Divine Service was publifh'd by Royal Authority, to prevent their running into greater Exceffes.

BUT, if the pure Simplicity of undebauch'd Nature can have any Weight with us, I need only appeal to the unaffected Innocence and rural Cuftoms of the *Welfh*, who never fail fpending in this laudable Manner, their *Sunday Evenings*. The honeft Parfon, after Preaching to, and Catechifing his Parifh, with a Cup of Ale gives them a Tune on the Fiddle, while they lovingly dance after their Paftor. The Phyfician of the Soul acting in this, like the Phyfician of the Body, cloathing the black Pill of Religion with the golden Garment of Mirth.

THE next Error in Management of the Mafters of our *Play-houfes* is vifible, in a wrong Difpofition, or Choice of proper Actors for the Stage.

HERE are a Company of Players enter'd as the King's Servants, who (as *Hamlet* has it) are

fit

fit either for *Tragedy*, *Comedy*, *Hiſtory*, *Paſtoral*, *Paſtorical-Comical -Hiſtorical - Paſtoral* , *Tragical-Hi-ſtorical*. This Sett of Gentlemen and Ladies are to go thro' all P L A Y s, and all Characters, in as many different Shapes, as the World and T H E A T R E can vary them.

T H E ſame Man muſt one Day keep juſtly up to the Grandeur of a Monarch; the next, per-ſonate as exactly the miſerable Beggar : Now a Tyrant defying the gods, and breathing Deſtru-ction to Mankind; anon a whining Lover, expir-ing for a Frown. In one P L A Y he muſt put on the ridiculous Fop, in another a ſlovenly Juſtice of Peace, or Courtier, or Cit, or Stateſman, or Captain of the Militia; juſt as his Lot is that Evening.

T H E Women too muſt paſs thro' the ſame Variety of Characters. The romping Country Hoyden to Night, muſt ſhine out the fine Lady of the P L A Y to Morrow: One Day as ſtarch'd as a formal City Matron; the next, as flippant as a Court Cocquet in *Tragedy :* A proud ambitious Queen dwindles in *Comedy*, to a Pert , Jilting Chamber-maid; and ſhe who yeſterday was the gentleſt, beſt natur'd Creature alive, this Even-ing muſt have Jealouſy flaming in her Eyes, and Revenge brooding in her Heart.

I think, the Faults we find in our beſt and oldeſt Actors, and the little Hopes we have of any tolerable ſpringing up, are owing to this odd Jumble of Characters in the ſame Perſon, and obliging a Man to change his Air, Voice, Face and Motions, as often and eaſily as he might a Vizor-Maſque. In that Particular, the Antients had the Advantage of us, that Diſguiſe to a Man's Countenance, by an Alteration of Speech, very much favouring the Deceit.

B u t

But in acting to Perfection, as well as in Writing, a Genius is requir'd; and it is impossible for one Person truly to form himself to so many different Parts: Therefore, where Nature has furnish'd any Man with that happy Talent, he should stick to that Character he's most adapted to; for in throwing himself out of his natural Bias, he'll run wide of all the rest he aims at. Where an Actor is born with a Notion of any Part in Life, of which we may form a proper Stage-Character, and studies by Art (which must have its Part in the Affair) to model himself entirely to it; there he'll be perfect, and may represent some others tolerably; but they must appear forc'd and affected: But one Robe can sit easy on him, and that which sits not easy, cannot please. I believe, this general Rule will admit of as few Exceptions as any that we know.

Some wonderful Adepts in Criticism, and Sticklers for the present Management of our Theatres, will very civilly and cunningly demand, *What's to be done in this Case? The Masters of a Play-house, cannot pretend to keep a different Actor for every different Part.* I grant it, not for every different Part, but for every general Character, at least, they may: Nay, I insist upon it, to do the Town and the Stage Justice on that Head, several ought to be kept to represent the same general Character. One Man may be very capable of representing a King, or Hero, as describ'd in such a Play, that may be highly unfit to enter into those Parts, as their Pictures are drawn in another. An Actor may shine in the Parts of *Don Sebastian*, or *Mark Anthony*, and be hiss'd in those of *Maximin*, or *Bajazet*. Thus widely too may differ the Humours of old Men in *Comedy*, and an admirable *Foresight* fit

H   out

out a fcurvy *Don Cholerick Snap Shorto de Tefty*.
Nature delights in Variety, and is not content
to divide the World into Heroes, Cowards, wife
Men, Fools, Divines, or Atheifts, but makes
every Individual differ in fome Particularity from
all the reft of that Species, and every Ideot upon Earth has fome Folly cleaving to him, a Secret to the reft of the Herd.

As a negligent blind-fold Choice of Actors
for the Stage, is the Source from whence fpring
thefe Evils fo juftly complain'd of, I can think
of no Redrefs, but cautioning the Managers of
our *Play-houfes*, to choofe for the future, prudently and circumfpectly; which can only be brought
about, by a careful Vifitation of the moft publick,
or generally frequented Places of this M E T R O-
P O L I S; where they may readily fpy out People
born to reprefent, in a natural and eafy Way,
every Character that Life can fhew, or the Stage
demand: Thofe who may be entirely of a-piece
with the Parts they are to appear in; and whofe
Stations in the World may not fcorn moderate
Propofals.

As the Accidents in Life of the confpicuous
Part of the World, furnifh the Stage with Characters, by a natural Reprefentation of, and ex-
pofing their moft ridiculous Follies, or dange-
rous Paffions: So, in the loweft Scenes of Life,
we may, by a curious View, difcover an Imitation or Refemblance of the Behaviour of their
Betters; from whom we may borrow Perfons,
cut out by Nature, to appear juftly in all Branches
of the Theatrical Bufinefs.

T H E *Dutch* (whom I am oblig'd to name fo
often, with Regret to my Countrymen, in the
Articles of Politenefs and Penetration) allow a
confiderable Penfion to fome Men, eminent for
their

their great Sagacity, who are conſtant Survey-
ors of all publick Meetings, and Crowds. They
carefully inſpect the very Refuſe of low Life, in
order to cull out proper Perſons to ſupply all
Dramatical Characters.   This Project has ſuc-
ceeded to Admiration; for their Diſcernment is
ſuch, that they read immediately in every Countenance, or judge nicely from ſome Particularity of Behaviour, what every Man is moſt capable of, by exerting his Top-talent.

They'll fix upon a Stateſman, from a Tailor's
threading his Needle, and diſcover an invincible Hero, in the Shoulders of a brawny Dray-
man.   A Cobler's eaſy Whiſtle will diſtinguiſh
the fine Gentleman; as the Management of his
Awl will point out a General.   A ſurly Skipper
never fails in furniſhing a charming Tyrant; as
the Hen-peck'd Husband makes the moſt ſub-
miſſive Lover.   If they are in diſtreſs for an able
Lawyer, the Fiſh-market ſupplies them; and they
borrow all their Beaus from the Baker's Flower-
tub: Nay, I have known them very happily
gueſs at a Judge in the Care of a Kennel-ſweep-
er, and catch at a Critick, in the Dexterity of a
Hang-man.

T H E I R little Theatrical World is in the ſame
Manner ſupply'd with female Characters; and
the Queen, the fine Lady, the Prude, the Cocquet, the Jilt, the Termagant, are occaſionly
pick'd out from amongſt broken Tradeſmen's
Wives, gay Sempſtreſſes, demure Widows, Boors
Daughters, City Goſſips, and bawling Oiſter-wo-
men.

T H E Y all return next Morning to their ſeveral Trades, and unlike our Actors and Actreſſes,
lay aſide their borrow'd Dignities with the *Play-
houſe* dreſs.   The Publick are entertain'd at an

eafy Rate; nor are they forc'd into an idle, ufe-lefs Life; for they work by Day to maintain their Families, and by Night to divert their Neighbours.

I T will not be improper to obferve here, that in feveral Towns in *Holland*, the Revenues of the T H E A T R E are wholly appropriated to the Maintenance of fome Hofpitals; as the Stews at *Rome*, keep the Head of the Church in Pocket-money. This Oeconomy tallies exactly with my Project, advanc'd in the preceeding E S S A Y, relating to the *Opera-houfe*.

B U T, to Inftance a few Domeftick Examples. Can any reafonable Man fuppofe, that the late Worfhipful Sir *Ja----s B---ker*, Knight, was defign'd by Heaven to be only a Cypher in Life; the Scorn of Wife-men, the But of Ridicule to Fools, or a Banter upon all the Dignities of the Great. To what End then ferv'd his Air of Wif-dom? his Philofophical Countenance, and So-lemnity of Addrefs? —— No! —— he was born to be an Actor. As Fortune favour'd him with no Station adequate to his Merit, he fhould have been feiz'd by the Stage, and at leaft have appear'd, in Imagination, to himfelf, and the World, what he ought to have been in Reality. In his being excluded the T H E A T R E S, the Town was depriv'd of a fedate Privy-Counfellor, a folemn Ambaffadour, and an awful Doge of *Venice*.

N o body can imagine that ——*P——ne*, Efq; was fent into Life, only to pace twenty times a Day round the Mall; regardlefs of the Crowds of Beaus and Belles, to write, in tranfitory Chalk thofe valuable Scraps of Politicks which engage the admiring Eyes of all Paffengers. How con-fummate a Statefman! How profound a Politi-cian here is loft! One, who may have Cunning
enough

enough to fet Fools together by the Ears, and Prudence to fcreen himfelf from the Scrutinies of the wifeft : But his Merits being neglected by the World ; yet what a Figure might he make in the Bufinefs of the Stage, it's Miniature ?

A R E we to believe that C —— t *H*——*r*'s terrible Countenance was chizzell'd out by Nature, only to prefide at a *Mafquerade,* frighten Wh---res of Rank into decent Behaviour, or grace a Board of O——a D——rs ? Impoffible ! That juft Copy of *Gorgon,* was only made to fit the Shoulders of a Firft-rate Tyrant. How is the Stage cheated of a *Maximin* ; Perfecution in every Feature ! —— The very Figure of *Dionyfius !* Nay, *Phalaris* himfelf ! For who can look at him, without expecting the brazen Bull to follow ? But thus contrary to the Defigns of Nature, Mortals often are put to a wrong Ufe : For want of a capable Actor, no fuch Part is attempted ; we are difappointed in our Pleafures, and he, in the End of his Creation.

L E T us next infpect Taverns, Coffee-houfes, and Gaming tables. How many *Tragick* Heroes are there to be met with ! Fellows ! —— who are only proper to exprefs thofe Paffions to the Life, which are never vented but in Words, and evaporate into Air : Thofe Drums of the Creation, fent into the World to make a Noife, and be beat upon. Your *Mohuns, Harts, Bettertons,* and *Booths,* are but Apes of them ; for they are the Men, who, like *Maximin,* can brave all the Gods, rage like *Hotfpur,* and rave like *Othello.* On the Stage, thofe Bellows of Converfation might ftretch their Lungs for the publick Good, which are now the Bane of all Civil Society, and a Nufance to all Ears within reach of their Throats.

L E T

LET us venture farther, and visit the Churches, Drawing-rooms, and Front-boxes. How many shall we find there that out-pitch, a Bar's length, any Character a Poetical Fancy ever form'd?

'TIS true, the Stage is look'd upon as a magnifying Glass, and allow'd to shew Vices, and Follies, full blown. Every Thing ought to be represented there, larger than the Life, the readier to distaste the Beholders; and that the smallest Error being made plain on the Surface, no part of wrong Behaviour should escape their Eyes unregarded:

YET, on the Stage of Life, we every Day meet with those that are as ridiculously affected as *Lord Foppington*, as stupidly vicious as *Lord Brute*; as fawning as *Lord Plausible*; as impertinent as *Novel*; as impotently fond as *Limberham*; as treacherous as *Maskwell*; as superstitious as *Foresight*; as subtil as *Volpone*; as humoursome as *Morose*; as silly as *Sir Martin*; as hypocritical as *Tartuff*, and as jealous as *Fondle-Wife*.

WERE it proper to find Fault with the other Sex, any Man that was resolv'd to spy Blemishes in them, and examin'd their Behaviour in the Middle of an OPERA, or a Sermon, or pry'd into their Conduct in an Assembly, or Closet; might find the most glaring Female Characters that ever Poet drew, very tenderly touch'd; and all the *Olivias, Latitias, Belindas, Lucretias, Isabellas, Marias* COMEDY has given us, are but Foils to the more brillant Follies the Town every Day throws in our Way.

NOW, as by all Political Constitutions, every body ought, in their several Stations, to be in some respect conducive to the publick Good, I would have an Embargo laid upon the Persons of all those Gentlemen and Ladies, who have so

natural

natural a Turn to thofe fmall Foibles, and their
Bodies feiz'd for the Ufe of the Stage; that as
they boldly appear in open Defiance of the Reformation intended, they may fhine out there to
fome purpofe, and hinder others from falling into the fame Errors.

I look upon this innate Propenfity to what is
ridiculous, as a Diftemper, and. pity it as a Species of civiliz'd Madnefs: Therefore, let their
Births and Fortunes be ever fo great, I would
allow them the Liberty of difplaying their Parts
in the moft publick Manner; that at once they
may divert and improve their fellow-Subjects,
and humour their own Frenzy: Perhaps, we may
eafier conquer the Difeafe, by giving Way to,
than oppofing it.

From what I have here urg'd on this Head,
I think the Neceffity of furnifhing the Stage with
Actors, after this Manner, muft at firft fight appear plain to every Frequenter of a *Play-houfe*,
nor can there be any other Method of advancing a juft Supply, in Propriety, Number, and
Expedition: But, as the Obftinate and Self-con-
ceited, are not eafily convinc'd of the Truth;
if there are any fuch, let them but confider
W——ks as a Heroe, *B——th* as a fine Gentleman, *M —— ls* as a Lover, *C——er* an old General, *D--y N---is* a Tyrant, *O——ld* a Prude,
P——er a Cocquet, and *B——ker* an Emprefs;
which Difpofition of Characters we commonly
meet with: Then let them fay, we have no reafon of Complaint. 'Tis true, there are but a
few good Actors for numberlefs Parts; but, as I
have propos'd a Remedy, no body will pity their
Indifpofition, if they refufe a Cure.

If I might touch upon Things, P --- C ---or
E ---- this Affair may admit of feveral new
Hints

Hints for the Service of the Publick; nor would
it prove the worst Rule in the Choice of our - -
- - and our - - - - - and the - - - - - and them - - -
- - - and those - - - - - - - and that - - - - - . by these
prudent and political Maxims, the Nation just recommended, succesfully regulate their S - - - -
and their S - - - - -; but I am of Opinion, this
Point will be more fully and pertinently spoke
to in the E s s a y upon M a s q u e r a d e s.

I come now to the third Article of high Crimes
and Misdemeanors charg'd upon our Theatrical
Managers; which is made manifest in their strange
Negligence of, and prodigious Oeconomy in the
Decorations of the Stage; which are so visibly
essential both to *Tragedy* and *Comedy*, and con-
sist of S c e n e r y, M a c h i n e r y, H a b i t s,
A t t e n d a n c e, M u s i c k and D a n c i n g.

I t is morally impossible for any P o e t, or
Master of a *Play-House*, to be too expensive in
the Beauty or Grandeur of their S c e n e s and
M a c h i n e s: The more just and surprizing they
appear, the sooner will the Spectator be led insensibly into imagining every thing real, and, of
consequence, prove the easier perswaded of the
Instruction intended: Besides, they are absolutely necessary in all Parts of a P l a y, where the
Plot requires the Intervention of some supernatural Power, in order to conquer Difficulties,
and solve Misteries: For, what is a God, or a
Devil, or a Conjurer, —— without Moving
Clouds, Blazing Chariots, Flying Dragons, and
Enchanted Castles? —— Airy Sprites, Terrestri-
al Hob-goblins, and Infernal Demons, must, at
a Word, descend, rise, and vanish. These things,
justly introduc'd, strike an Awe upon the Audience; and, while they are amaz'd and delighted,
they are instructed. This gives the S t a g e a
Character

Character with the World, and P O E T S and A C-
T O R S are esteem'd Demi-gods. Thus, when
People are prepossess'd in Favour of their Power,
they dare not but embrace their Doctrines.

A B B O T *Hedelin* observes, *That the Ornaments*
of the Stage, so sensibly delight us, by a Kind of
witty Magick, as to raise from the Dead Heroes of
past Ages. They present, as it were to our Eyes, a
new Heaven and Earth; while we are so agreeably
deceiv'd, as to imagine every thing present: Even
People of Understanding take them for Enchantments,
and are pleas'd with the Dexterity of the Artists,
and the neat Execution of so many Contrivances.
For this End the Ancients bestow'd the richest Deco-
rations upon their T H E A T R E S : *The Heavens would*
open for their gods to descend, and converse with
Men; the Air would be fill'd with Thunder, Ligh-
tning and Storms; the Sea would shew Tempests,
Ship-wrecks, and Sea-fights; the Earth would pro-
duce Gardens, Forests, Desarts, Palaces and Tem-
ples; out of its Bosom would rise Furies, Demons,
and all the Prodigies of their fabulous Hell; and the
P O E T S *never fail'd to fill their* P L A Y S *with such*
Incidents as requir'd those magnificent Decorations.

T H E Habits of the Actors likewise have a
prodigious Influence on the Minds of an Audience. We see daily, in the great World, a vast
Deference shewn to the Figure of a Suit of Cloaths;
and how regularly Degrees of Respect rise, from
the Gold and Silver Button and Button-hole, to
Lace and Embroidery. How nicely are the Di-
stances betwixt Cloth, Velvet, and Brocade, observ'd? Much more in the T H E A T R E should
this Distinction prevail, where our Senses are to
be touch'd, pleas'd, and taken by Surprize; and
where every Spectator, indeed, is to receive an
Impression of the Character of the Person from his
Dress;

Dreſs; and the firſt Ideas are generally moſt laſting.

TRAGEDY borrows vaſt Advantages from the additional Ornaments of Feathers and high Heels; and it is impoſſible, but that two Foot and a Half of Plume and Buskin muſt go a great Length, in giving an Audience a juſt Notion of a Hero. That great Appearance gives an Air of Grandeur to every thing he ſays, or does. The beſt *Grecian* POETS, who brought TRAGEDY to its Perfection, firſt gave Birth to this Invention: They found it of Service, and all other Nations continued it. In *Rome*, commenc'd once a famous Diſpute betwixt two eminent *Tragedians*, which beſt repreſented *Agamemnon*; he that ſtep'd loftily, and on tip-toes, or, he who appear'd penſive, as if concern'd for the Safety of his People; but the tall Man carry'd it. Theſe uſeful Allies to the *Drama*, take more with the Generality of People, than the brighteſt Thoughts, or juſteſt Expreſſions; and, I defy any of our beſt tragick Bards, ſo readily to give an Audience a true Idea of a Queen, by the nobleſt Sentiments, or fineſt Language, as the Wardrobe-Keeper can, by half a Dozen lac'd Pages, and as many Yards of embroider'd Tail; and, indeed, there ſhould be ſomething particularly adapted to the Look and Dreſs of every ACTOR, which ſhould, at firſt View, ſpeak his Character, before he opens his Mouth; and, as the Frown ſhews the King, the Stride, the Hero, the thoughtful Air, the Stateſman, and the ſilly Smile, the Fop; ſo do the Robe, the Truncheon, the Bundle of Papers, and Clock'd Stockings.

THE Appearance of a Retinue ſuitable to every diſtinct Character of the *Drama*, (which ſhould
make

make a Figure on the Stage) is another Point of very great Confequence, and ought to be principally regarded. What is a Tyrant without his Guards? or a Princefs, without her Maids of Honour? A General, without a Troop of Officers? Or, a firft Minifter, without a Levee of Spies and Dependants? A Lawyer, without a Flock of Clients? Or, a Beau, without a Train of Lacquies?

A juft Number of Attendants gives an Air of Dignity to, and diftinguifhes the proper Superiority of each Character; befides, when the Stage is crowded, the Greatnefs of the Shew cafts a Mift, as it were, over the Eyes of the Spectators, and makes the thinneft Plot appear full of Bufinefs. Keep the Stage fill'd thus, you'll inftill Life and Spirit into the dulleft P L A Y; the Paffions will never flag, nor the Action cool.

I have known a *Tragedy* fucceed, by the irrefiftible Force of a Squadron of *Turkifh Turbans* and *Scimiters*; and, another owe the whole of its Merit to the graceful Proceffion of a *Mufti*, and a Tribe of Priefts. A P O E T who fights cunning, will judicioufly throw into every Act a Triumph, a Wedding, a Funeral, a Chriftening, a Feaft, or fome fuch Spectacle, which muft be manag'd by a Multitude. Thus, by a well-difpos'd Succeffion of Crowds in every Scene, he lies, as it were, fave under Cover from all Criticifm.

A N D, indeed, I am inclinable to believe, that this was the chief Defign of the Ancients, in eftablifhing and encouraging, at fo prodigious an Expence, their C H O R U S: For by this Means, the Stage could never be empty; which prov'd of infinite Service to their P O E T S, and contributed vaftly to the Satisfaction of the People.

T H E

THE *French* Critick juft mention'd, (whofe Authority, in Stage-Affairs, is undoubted) fays, *That the moft magnificent Part of the Reprefentations of the Ancients confifted, in their feldom fuffering an Actor to come upon the Stage alone;* and remarks, *That if a Prince, Princefs, or any other Perfon of eminent Quality appear'd, they were follow'd by a large Retinue, fometimes Soldiers, fometimes Courtiers; but always thofe who were proper Attendants to the Ground-work of that Scene. A rich Citizen would not enter without many Servants; and even a publick Courtezan fcorn'd to make her Appearance, but furrounded with Maids; and, in fhort, every Body was well accompany'd, without fome particular Reafon requir'd their being alone:* For, they did not underftand that *Hibernicifm,* fo judicioufly us'd by our modern POETS, of an Actor's making a *Soliloquy* in the middle of a Crowd.

As to MUSICK and DANCING, I cannot object a Deficiency in thofe Articles to our Stage Directors: They cannot well be more expenfive in thofe Entertainments, without it were poffible to bring about the compleat Re-eftablifhment of the old CHORUS: Therefore, if I blame them on that Head, it is, becaufe they are rather extravagant than fparing, efpecially in the latter; which deprives us of Decorations more effential to the *Drama.* But of this we fhall talk amply in the next ESSAY.

I am at laft arriv'd at the finifhing Stroke of this ESSAY, which was to confider, To what Caufes is owing the vitious Tafte of the Town, and how far the Decay of *Dramatick Poetry* is owing to Spectators, or Readers of it. But this Affair is of that Confequence to the Relifh and Encouragement of every thing polite; its Faults

are

are so notorious, and Amendments so necessary, that I shall reserve the further Consideration of it, till I come to the ESSAY upon AUDIENCES in general; where I have so many Orders of People to speak to in a different Way; so many mistaken Judgments to set right; so many Kinds of Criticks to call Names; and so much more to that Purpose, and all, that I must beg of my Readers to suspend their Curiosity, in Relation to themselves, till the Fifth ESSAY, when I intend to play the Devil with them all.

ESSAY

ESSAY III.
OF DANCING,
RELIGIOUS and DRAMATICAL.

An Historical Account of the MIMES *and* PANTOMIMES *of the Ancients; with a short Parallel betwixt them and our modern* ARLEQUINS *and* SCARAMOUCHES; *and a learned Criticism on our present* GROTESQUE DANCES. *To whch are added, Some Reflections upon* DANCING, *of a publick and private Nature; with a Side-step towards* TUMBLERS, POSTURE-MASTERS, *and* ROPE-DANCERS.

S no Man can deny the vast Veneration the Antients, on all Occasions, profess'd for DANCING, I need not be too copious on that Head, or lay too weighty a Stress of Arguments, where there is but a small Foundation for Dispute. To be prolix, in tracing it to the remotest Ages of Antiquity, would be amusing the World with trifling

trifling Flourifhes, and cutting Capers to very little Purpofe; my principal Aim being to point out its Beauties, and make manifeft fome Steps in it of the utmoft Importance to the Publick, not yet difcover'd.

But, in order to profecute this laudable Defign regularly, and give compleat Satisfaction to all my Readers, learned and illiterate, by improving one, and fhewing the others my Reading, I muft beg Leave to throw in fome fmall Hints, neceffary to clear up its Original, and manifeft the Purity of the Spring from whence fo beautiful a Stream does flow.

Both facred and profane Hiftory talk much in Favour of DANCING. All Ages have fhewn their Efteem for it, from the Beginning of Time to this Day: And, to a DANCE and a SONG, in Honour of *Bacchus,* we owe the Rife of all *Stage-Entertainments*; and, of confequence, all that Inftruction and Delight the World has from time to time receiv'd, either from TRAGEDY, COMEDY, or OPERA.

NAY, fhould we view DANCING in a private, as well as publick Light, it would appear to us as healthful in one, as agreeable in the other. But having confin'd my felf within the Circle of the Town-Diverfions, I fhall not, at prefent, touch any farther upon that Subject, than in obferving, That I look upon a DANCING-MASTER as a very ufeful Member in a Commonwealth: Nor can I well avoid making a fmall Excurfion, towards the End of this ESSAY, in recommending fome new Movements abfolutely effential to the moft material Points of private, as well as publick Life.

But, to proceed methodically.—I juft hinted before, that the God *Bacchus,* having firft brought

the

the Art of planting of Grapes into *Greece* (for which I heartily thank him) *Icarius* (to whom he imparted the Secret) finding a Goat too free with his Grapes, facrific'd the Beaft to the Honour of that Deity; at the fame time giving an Entertainment of MUSICK and DANCING. This Solemnity pleas'd, and grew into an annual Cuftom, every Year adding fomething new to the firft Plan; and the POETS intermedling with the Affair, firft added an ACTOR; another *Two*; the next *Three*; till by degrees, and new-modelling, it was fo far improv'd, that at laft it ended in a regular TRAGEDY; and that which was only defign'd as a Sacrifice, became a finifh'd STAGE-PLAY.

THUS the THEATRES rofe by, and borrow'd DANCING from the Temples; and what was at firft a forry Hymn, by way of Chorus, in a blind ridiculous Religion, gave Birth to the nobleft Amufement, and moft inftructive Entertainment, that the politeft Nations of the World could ever boaft.

BUT we are not to fuppofe that DANCING was confin'd to this Part of their Worfhip alone: No, the World grew fo fond of Religious Agility, that the Feftivals of each particular Deity fhow'd away with a different DANCE. *Ceres, Venus, Priapus,* and the whole Rag-man-roll of Gods and Goddeffes, invented various Geftures and Motions appropriated to their feveral Rites. *Bacchus,* indeed, had his Mifteries, in a more efpecial Manner, celebrated by DANCING; as may be gather'd from the wild Rants and frolickfome Capers the *Bacchanal Priefts* made ufe of, during their mad Performances and Enthufiaftick Solemnities.

BUT,

BUT, whilſt we are poking into Antiquity (were it proper to carry this Affair higher, than either mentioning it as a Part of a publick religious Ceremony, or a private elegant Entertainment) we might inſtance, from ſeveral of the moſt antient POETS, Places, where the Gods themſelves are introduc'd dancing. In *Pindar*, *Apollo* is called, by Way of Excellence, The DANCER.

IN *Homer*, he plays upon his Harp, and dances at the ſame time: Nay, *Jupiter* himſelf, in the Fragment of an old *Greek* Poem (the Author of which is uncertain) is uſher'd in as the Father of gods and Men, in a Minuet-Step.

WE learn, from the Right Reverend Biſhop *Potter*'s *Antiquities* of Greece, *That from the moſt antient Times,* MUSICK *and* DANCING *were the principal Diverſions at all Entertainments, and that, in every Step of private Life,* DANCING *was particularly eſteem'd an Accompliſhment becoming all Perſons of Honour and Wiſdom* Epaminondas (who always was look'd upon as the Chief of the *Grecian* Heroes) is celebrated for being a fine DANCER, and playing very genteely on the Flute.

'TIS true, the ſame profound Author gives us to underſtand, *That the* Romans *look'd upon theſe Amuſements as trivial, and not worthy to be mention'd; though in* Greece, *they were thought very commendable.* In anſwer to this ill-grounded Aſſertion, I muſt obſerve, That his Authorities are only cited from a very few old, moroſe Orators and Hiſtorians, who, of conſequence, muſt blame what they are unfit for, or did not comprehend. To their narrow-ſoul'd Opinions, we object the Practice of all the politeſt *Romans*, who beheld DANCING with a ſuitable Regard and favourable Eye, both in their Religious Worſhip, and Civil Amuſements. The moſt eſteem-

I 3   ed

ed Tribe of their Priefts were call'd *Salii*, from *Saliendo*, Dancing : Nay, they were founded by *Numa* himfelf, the *Roman Licurgus* ; and to their Care was entrufted the famous Target which drop'd from Heaven ; upon the fafe keeping of which, the Fate of their Empire depended. At their yearly Proceffion (which was one of the moft fplendid Sights of *Old Rome*) they travers'd all the Streets with nimble Motions, prodigious Agility, and handfome Turns of the Body ; as we are inform'd by feveral wife Authors.

As to their well - judg'd Amufements in private Life, even *Brutus*, *Catiline*, *Julius Cæfar*, *Mark Anthony*, &c. fome of their moft diftinguifh'd great ones, were preferr'd to their Fellow-Citizens, more for their DANCING, than any noted Martial Exploit.

BUT how can we reckon the Art of DAN-CING to be defpis'd, either by the Religious, Military, or polite Men of *Rome?* when the firft made ufe of it, more or lefs, in all the Mifteries of their Religion ; which is already made fufficiently plain : The fecond, by its Affiftance, qualify'd themfelves for all Feats of War, as is evident by the *Saltatio Pyrrhica*, and *Troja Ludus* ; which were only military DANCING-BOUTS : And, for the third, I may venture to affirm, That no Nation ever look'd upon a Man as polite, that could not dance.

THE Inftitution and Progrefs of the *Troja-Ludus* is known to every School-Boy ; and the Defcription of it under their little Leader *Afcanius*, at the Games for *Anchifes*'s Death, fo very full and beautiful, in the inimitable Lines of *Virgil*, that as every body has him in *Latin* or *Englifh*, I need fay nothing more of it here ; only that it was always perform'd on Horfeback, as the *Pyrrhica Salta-*

tio

tio was a-Foot: The Original of which is not quite fo clear. The Accounts given us of it by Hiftorians, Criticks, and Commentators, all widely differing from, and contradicting one another. Some afcribe its Foundation to *Minerva*'s leading up a Warlike-like D A N C E, after the Conqueft of the Giants by the Gods: Others hold its Rife to be from the D A N C E S of the *Corybantes*, who took Care of young *Jupiter*; and, in their mad Fits, danc'd about, clafhing their Spears againft their Shields, to drown the Infants Cries, that *Salum* might not find him out, and eat him. Thefe, indeed, have an Eye to the Affair it felf; but account not in the leaft for its Name; therefore the moft probable Conjecture is, That it had its Name and Steps from *Pyrrhus*, Son to *Achilles*, who inftituted thefe warlike Motions to the Honour of his Father, at his Funeral Games: And what adds to its Probability is, the exact Defcription we find of the *Pyrrhick* D A N C E in *Homer*, perfectly delineated upon the Shield of *Achilles*, in the Account he gives us of the Armour made for him by *Vulcan*. From whence we may reafonably fuppofe, he borrow'd the Defign.

BUT what are all thefe trifling D A N C E S to thofe celebrated ones of *Old Greece!* where, at all the folemn Games, fuch as the *Olympick, Nemaan, Elaan, Pythian,* &c. thofe Prizes of Honour were gain'd by the Strength, Agility, or Swiftnefs of the Body: Where the Victors were efteem'd fuperior to the Conquerors of the World, and their immortal Fame founded upon the lafting Bafis of a well-regulated D A N C E.

HOWEVER plaufible and juft this Account of the firft publick Appearance of D A N C I N G, may feem to every thinking, or unthinking Reader,

I will

I will boldly maintain, that (after canvaffing all the Poets, Criticks, Hiftorians, *&c.* either of this, or former Ages, on that Head) I take this noble Art to be of a much older Date than any of them have allow'd it. I could give undeniable Authorities for this, from facred Hiftory; as, *Miriam* the Prophetefs, and her Damfels, going out with *Timbrels* and with *Dances*. The Daughters of *Shiloh* went every Year to dance, only for their Diverfion. *David* himfelf danc'd before the Ark; and *Herodias* danc'd *John* the *Baptift*'s Head off, *&c*. But to wave all Inftances of this. Nature, left we difoblige any Body by a feeming Offence, I fhall only cite what Conjectures or Proofs I think are for my Purpofe, from profane Hiftory, and fupport my Arguments by honeft Heathen Quotations.

CERTAINLY, DANCING is much antienter than any Author, *Grecian* or *Roman*, makes out. If we judge by any Light they give us into that Affair, 'tis already prov'd, That it was firft us'd in Religious Worfhip, at leaft publickly. Now as *Rome* had its Religion, Morals, Laws, and every Thing polite or ufeful, from *Old Greece*; on the other Hand, *Greece* was as much indebted, for all thefe valuable Bleffings, to *Old Egypt*: At leaft, for the principal Part, however the whole may be difputed.

NOR will this appear a bare Conjecture, but a well-grounded Affertion, when we reflect, that all former Ages and different Parts of the known World, made DANCING a principal Ingredient in a Religious Hodge-Podge: And as *Egypt* is the oldeft Nation we can well give an Account of, undoubtedly from thence the firft *Grecian* Sages brought their Divine, Civil and polite Learning; as on the other hand, the *Romans* borrow'd
all

all from them. And as it is notorious, that thefe three pious, wife, genteel Nations danc'd over the largeſt Share of their Prayers, fo it is eaſy to account for the firſt Inſtitution and Progreſs of RELIGIOUS DANCING.

BUT to bring this Point nearer home than the firſt Eſtabliſhment of Religious Dances in *Greece*; even down to the Beginning of the *Mimes* and *Pantomimes*, which was long after. I ſay, thefe dumb Reprefentations of proper Fables by Motions, Geſtures, Attitudes, *&c.* muſt be entirely taken from the old *Egyptians*; as any curious Antiquary may readily difcover, in the near Refemblance betwixt thefe Twin-Brothers, *viz.* The *Hieroglyphicks* of one, and *Dances* of the other; or indeed, (to fpeak more properly) what is every Step in thefe *Dances*, but a fignificant *Hieroglyphical* Expreſſion?

SINCE DANCING then, either *Theatrical*, (as it is commonly introduc'd on the *Stage* without any particular Meaning) or *Dramatical* (when we have a Story properly *danc'd*, fo as to form a perfect Entertainment to be underſtood) is what I am now principally to fpeak to. I think it will not be impertinent here to take a more particular View of their firſt Rife in *Greece*, either before the *Chorus* was found out, or as they were introduc'd as Parts of the *Chorus*, after the Invention of that Supplement to a *Stage-Entertainment*; when we may confider DANCING in the Infancy of its Merit, fo trace it down to thoſe Days when the *Mimes* and *Pantomimes* came fo much into Vogue, that they were admir'd by the greateſt Princes, Poets, and Philofophers, both *Grecian* and *Roman:* When we may look upon DANCING in general to ſtand tip-toe on the very Pinnacle of Perfection.

FOR

FOR several Ages the Profession of DANCING remain'd in a quiet, unpolish'd State, contriving a friendly Alliance betwixt the *Altar* and the *Stage,* and proving a very humble Servant to both, till some old *Greek* (whose Brains lay in his Heels) thought there might be something more made of DANCING, than just pleasing the Eye ; wisely judging, That if *Dancers* could arrive at speaking to the Mind without Words, Mankind might be instructed without the Trouble of Speech. But who first chalk'd out the Steps for a dumb *Tragedy* or *Comedy,* I could never yet discover ; only I imagine, he must be very expert in the *Egyptian* Hieroglyphicks. Having once got, firm Footing in *Greece,* it long flourish'd there before it was transplanted to *Rome,* where that Art likewise throve wonderfully for several Centuries.

BEFORE I proceed any farther, some of my Readers may be inquisitive to find out a Distinction betwixt the *Mimes* and *Pantomimes,* as they may happen to be mention'd separately, or together. As I do not suppose those curious Persons to be any Conjurers in Criticism ; the most plain and satisfactory Account I can give them, in so material a Point, is to set full before them the Difference betwixt his Grace of *Y*——*k,* and his Grace of *C*——*ry* ; one being *Pr* ——*te* of *E*——*nd,* the other of *all E*——*nd.*

THE most rational then, and succinct Method I can pursue, in explaining the Rise and Progress of the *Mimes* and *Pantomimes,* take as follows. The old *Grecian* COMEDY being restrain'd of its Licentiousness, in abusing nominally Persons of the highest Stations and brightest Characters, the Stage was oblig'd to have recourse to feign'd Stories, which were confin'd to the meanest Events in low Life, after the Manner of our

Modern

Modern COMEDIES: But long before this they had loft their *Chorus* of MUSICK and DANCING; either becaufe they could not, in thofe Reprefentations, preferve a *Chorus* with any Decency; or, that the Magiftrates refus'd being at the Trouble or Expence of a *Chorus* for COMEDY; which Reafon indeed feems beft grounded.

THUS the old COMEDY and its *Chorus* being laid afide, the new COMEDY was receiv'd, with what we call Interludes of SINGING and DANCING, in a Way of *Mimickry* and *Buffoonery*, in Place of the *Chorus*; as being more of a-piece with *Comick-Poetry*, and more anfwerable to its Nature.

FROM thefe Plants then I fancy, (for there is no more in it) the *Mimes* and *Pantomimes* in *Greece* fprung up; from whence they were ufher'd into *Rome* with vaft Applaufe.

IT is certain, they were of very old ftanding in *Greece*, being mention'd by *Ariftotle*; nay, by *Efchylus* himfelf. They were held fo much in Efteem, that they were introduc'd at all publick Shews, and private Feafts; and were every where receiv'd with Encomiums fuitable to their diftinguifh'd Merit. *Plutarch* calls them *Dumb Poems*; as, *vice versâ*, he does POETRY, a *Speaking-dance*. So juft was their Expreffion of every Paffion, that the leaft Motion of Head, Arm, or Foot, had fo far its due Weight with the Audience, that nothing (which could be made intelligible by Words) was left imperfect, or the Senfe loft in their Action. *Ariftotle* (who was the jufteft and moft learn'd Critick in POETRY, as well as one of the Firft-rate Philofophers) fo much admir'd their Mimick Art, that he call'd one of them a divine Dancer, for having fo well danc'd a whole *Tragedy* of *Efchylus's*, call'd, *The feven before*

fore Thebes: Which alone is sufficient to stifle the ridiculous Notions of some pretended Dablers in Antiquity who would insinuate, That the two first of this Tribe that were famous, were *Pylades* and *Bathyllus,* who came from *Greece* to *Rome* in the Time of *Augustus*; when it is rather more than probable, that this Art (which had been so long cultivated amongst the *Grecians,* with the greatest Care and Success) was with their Empire rather in its Decline, before its first Appearance in *Italy.*

N o t but *Pylades* and *Bathyllus* were both eminent, in their Way, to a vast Degree; one being as noted for imitating the *Tragick,* as the other the *Comick* Passions. *Seneca* mentions them with great Respect, and from the Consideration of their different Excellencies, lays it down as an infallible Maxim, That no Man should undertake to profess any Science, but what he is design'd by Nature to excel in: Which I think fully corroborates my Project mention'd in the precedent E s s a y, where I advanc'd some Rules for better supplying the Stage with proper Actors; and will, I hope, bear as great Weight in a following E s s a y, when I shall produce some Hints very New (yet undeniably useful and solid) for trying and qualifying all People for those Employments Nature has fitted them for.

T h e r e is another Argument which strengthens the imagin'd Antiquity of the *Pantomimes,* which arises from my past Reflections upon the *Pyrrhick* and *Trojan* D a n c e s, which were partly of this Kind: And, as they were introduc'd in the earliest Accounts we have of those two celebrated Nations, 'tis reasonable to believe, that the *Mimes* had an Eye to their Performances, both in their Original and Progress.

S o m e

SOME People may here object (and not without Cause) to the wanton Gestures, and lascivious Behaviour of the *Mimes* in general; which were Incendiaries to vitious Love, Provocatives to all Beastliness, and Shocks to modest Eyes. Part of this Charge I allow, and will not defend it; what was blameable in them, I give up; but must desire my Reader's Patience in observing two Things. This Accusation, in the first Place, touches not the *Grecian Pantomimes*: This Art was allow'd no such Excess amongst the *Greeks*; tho' it was held there in the highest Esteem. Those polite and prudent People encourag'd no Diversions, but what could stand the Test of Virtue as well as Pleasure; and tho' some of their Amusements might only aim at an agreeable Ingenuity, yet they were never suffer'd to look a-squint at Vice. In the second Place, we learn from this, that the *Mimick Art* soon degenerated with the *Romans*: The *Grecian* Masters being gone, and no skilful Successors to support their Stage, People were oblig'd to take up with the Refuse of their Society; who, in order to carry on their Trade, (by the Inclinations of the Generality of their Spectators, and the Countenance of some lustful Emperours) grew so impure in their Actions, and nauseous in their Obscenities, that even corrupted *Rome* it self was asham'd to be pleas'd with a Diversion so notoriously scandalous, and fairly laid them aside.

BUT, before I intirely leave this Subject, I cannot avoid taking Notice of some absurd Accounts handed down to us by very grave, learned Authors in Relation to the *Mimes*; particularlarly Mr. *Kennet* in his *Roman Antiquities*: Who says, that *Scaliger* defines *Mimickry* to be a POEM imitating any sort of Actions, so as to make

them

them appear ridiculous. This Definition, I am sure, is highly imperfect, ridiculous, and wide of the Mark: For, every School-boy knows, that in the true Art of the *Mimes*, there never was any Speech made use of; as is already sufficiently prov'd from the Authors, both *Grecian* and *Roman*, above cited. Indeed, there were a Set of Farce Writers and Actors, who, by Way of Interlude, either betwixt the Acts, or at the End of a Play, rehears'd several odd Pieces of P o-E T R Y; but how they came by the Name of *Mimes*, I cannot comprehend: For, I take *Mimickry* to be a just Explanation of all Actions of Life, by Motions alone without Words. This Definition may not be according to Mood and Figure; but 'tis just and true: For, in that consisted the Merit of the *Pantomimes*.

Mr. *Kennet* himself owns, that the Original of what he calls the *Mimi*, was owing to a Set of Actors, who after the *Chorus* went off the Stage, diverted the Audience with apish Postures, and antick Dances: This indeed was a Part of *Mimickry*, but the poorest: For *Laberius* and *Tublius*, (whom he stiles the two famous *Pantomimi*) with their imperfect odd *Drama*, were Farce Writers, and Farce Actors, noted indeed in their Way; and the first of them (tho' of the *Equestrian Order*) was oblig'd by *Cæsar* to act in one of his Farces: But, neither that Part of his *Prologue* cited, or what *Horace* mentions of him in the tenth *Satire* of his first Book, insinuate in the least his being one of the *Mimi*: it being undeniable, that the two first that visited *Rome* in that Character, were *Pylades* and *Batlyllus*, before spoken of, and fully.

B u t what a Right Reverend Author means by a total Neglect of the *Mimi*, tho' so very particular

cular in the other Antiquities of *Greece*; I cannot
account for: This I am fure of, that he treats of
many Cuftoms at large, of lefs moment in general to Mankind, and in particular to the learned World: nor is there one of their mifcellany
Cuftoms there treated of, but is a Trifle in comparifon to a thorough Knowledge of the *Panto-
mime* Art.

HAVING been very plain and particular on
this Head, as far as it relates to the *Antients*; it
will not be improper now to confider how far
the *Moderns* have imitated them in this Art; fo
make a fort of Connexion betwixt thofe Times
and the prefent Age, in the Cafe before us.

I believe, that from fome faint Notions of
thefe dumb *Orators*, imprinted on the Minds of
the late *Greeks*, or fome remaining Tracks left of
their former Foot-fteps, the Cuftom arofe of
having *Mutes* in the *Grand Signior's Seraglio*, and
which is fo ftrictly obferv'd in all the Palaces of
the Tyrants of the *Eaft*: For, they being no Blab-
bers, Secrets of the greateft Moment are alway
entrufted with them. They are the moft cffici-
ous and handy, as well as filent Servants; and
as they do not difturb one with their impertinent
Voices, fo they cannot tell Tales out of School;
which Perfections would highly recommend them
to the generality of our fine Ladies: And on the
other Side, I fancy moft *Britifh* Husbands would
not be difpleas'd, if the mute Article was by
fome Means or other introduc'd in Matrimonial
Life.

WHAT very much confirms my Belief in this
Point of the *Mutes* being related to the *Mimes*,
is, that to this Day they often act little Pieces
in the *Mimick* Way to divert the *Grand Signior*;

which

which is indeed the only Theatrical *Entertainment* the *Turks* have any Notion of.

As the *Sultan* has furnish'd the Privacies of his Court from the Remains of the old *Mimes*; so has the *Italians* supply'd their *Comick* Stages with Actors from their Relicks in *Rome*: For from their Ashes (*Phœnix-like*) have sprung up our Modern *Arlequins*, *Scaramouches* and *Punchinello's*, which must be apparent to all who are conversant with the History of one Set, and the Performances of the other.

I must own, that the best *Italian* COMEDY is a tolerable Imitation of the old *Pantomimes*, only a little *Gothicis'd*; most of the other *Antique* Arts have in a great measure retriev'd their pristine Glory: *Painting*, *Sculpture*, and *Architecture*, have for these three last Centuries flourish'd prodigiously: And, as I have already observ'd, I am inclinable to think, that the present State of our MUSICK by far exceeds any thing of that Kind, ever known to *Greece* or *Rome*: Only POETRY, and this its dumb younger Sister, fly a low pitch, in comparison with the high Flights of their Ancestors.

IF any Nation can be brought to a juster Understanding or Performance of the old *Mimickry*, than we have in Modern Times met with; it must undoubtedly be attempted after the Manner of the *Italian* COMEDY: That is, by preserving what is just and beautiful in the *Antick* Action, but rejecting their ridiculous Innovations in bad, low Dialogues; and worse vocal MUSICK.

THIS Affair is of greater Moment to Mankind than may appear at first View, and should be manag'd with Sense and Discretion; not by a Set of ignorant, strolling Scoundrels ((such as

for

for some Years past have infected both Sides of the *Hay-Market* with their nonsensical *Jargon*, and *Jack-pudding* Action ;) but by a chosen Society of learned *Antiquaries* and penetrating *Virtuosi* ; who may gather from old *Urns*, *Vales*, *Statues*, *Bustos*, *Bass-Releives*, *Intaglias*, *Cameas*, and *Monumental Inscriptions* ; an intire Set of *Vizor-masks*, *Features*, *Grimaces*, *Steps*, *Motions*, *Attitudes*, significant *Postures*, and learn'd *Directions*, in order to instruct a young *Group* of *Mimicks*, in all that was peculiar to, or us'd by the antient *Pantomimes*. Then these Gentlemen, by the necessary Assistance of some *Tumblers*, *Posture-masters*, and *Rope-dancers*, might produce a Set of *Actors* to amaze the World; who might by the strongest and finest Turns of *Argument*, enforce all Precepts of *Religion*, and *Morality*, by their dumb *Eloquence*, and silent *Rhetorick*.

As for those poor Wretches, known here by the Title of the *Italian-Comedians* ; I shall not at present meddle any farther with their absurd Performances, till I come to mention, them as pretending to the Form of a Theatre.

THE true *Italian* COMEDY, is neither perfect *Farce* nor old *Mimickry* ; for, tho' they often make use of very proper and emphatical Motions, and really manage Arms, Legs, and Heads to very good purpose; yet their wretched Stuff of *Farce* quite destroys the Merit of their Action, and is an Obstacle to their Improvement; so in aiming at both, are in effect neither : The nearest Resemblance they bear to any part of the *Antique Stage*, is that Set of *Farce-Performers*, call'd by Mr. *Kennet*, the *Mimi*.

I acknowledge I have often met Abroad with very clever Fellows upon the *Italian Stage*, in every respect design'd by Nature to make excel-

K 3   lent

lent *Mimicks*; could they have been content to make the use of all Members but their Tongues: For, according to an establish'd Rule of the old *Pantomimes*, they may open their Mouths, but muſt never ſpeak.

THE nearest then of all Modern Inventions to the Primitive *Mimick Art*, are ſome *Grotesque* DANCES, which have been lately very happily introduc'd upon the *Engliſh* Stage, with Applauſe almoſt equal to their Merit; they being a Glory to our Nation, an Ornament to our THEA-TRES, and the Teſt of Politeneſs in our preſent *Gou.* They have, indeed, in the compaſs of a few Years arriv'd to that Perfection; and in ſome Reſpects ſo far kept up to the Severity of the Rules, and Juſtneſs of the Meaſures of the *Antique Mimes*, that they may boldly demand a Continuance of the Succeſs they have met with (eſpecially thoſe perform'd at *Lincoln's-Inn Fields*,) could they be prevail'd upon to ſtick to their DANCING, and baniſh their *Songſters*: But it is impoſſible to make them ſenſible, that their Vocal MUSICK is as inconſiſtent with the Main of their *Entertainments*, as the *Comick Poetry* of the *Italians* with a juſt Imitation of the old *Mimes*. Thus by an ill-judg'd Jumble, and wrong blending of two Arts in one Piece, both the true *Italian* COMEDY, and our *Grotesque Dramatical* DANCES, have miſs'd their Point; they form Alliances which will ruin them, and by joining execrable POETRY and vile MUSICK to beautiful Scenes of juſt *Grotesque* DANCING, the Perfection of one is loſt in the Stupidity of the other; and inſtead of a ſingle, compleat *Entertainment*, they will be both reduc'd to the low State of *Buffoonery*, tho' they aim at ſoaring to the moſt exalted Pitch of true *Mimickry*: And, indeed,

Indeed, our Theatrical DANCING, in thus mixing *Scenery*, *Machinery*, and *Musick*, Vocal and Instrumental, with their Steps, comes nearer to the Nature of an old *Grecian Chorus*, than that of their Reprefentations, or Interludes by *Pantomimes*; which will appear evident to all Capacities in the next ESSAY, where I fhall examine all Particulars relating to a *Chorus*.

As for thofe humorous DANCES exhibited at *Drury-lane*; I have not yet difcover'd, whether they are defign'd as a *Burlefque* upon the other Houfe, or themfelves: But, as their *Mimes* are arriv'd at the *Ne-plus-ultra* of Badnefs in that Way; if they cannot improve, I think 'tis high time they fhould leave off, fince they cannot do worfe. I muft obferve one Thing, tho' in their Favour; which is, that their Defigns anfwer more to the Spirit of the old *Mimes*, they keeping up intirely to the Life and Beauty of Action, however lame in the Execution: not clogging their *Entertainments* with thofe monftrous Loads of harmonious Rubbifh, we are tired with at the other Houfe. One would fwear, that both THEATRES were afraid of doing too well, or giving Pleafure too exquifite to their Audiences; therefore are fure to throw in fome Allay; one is not content to act well, unlefs they are allow'd to dance ill at the fame time; the other charms us with their DANCES, therefore are at fome Pains and Expence to fquawl and fcrape us out of our Senfes.

BUT, in order to make a juft Application of all that has been faid on this Head, and not to find out Difeafes without propofing Remedies, let us at once come to the moft material Point, and confider what is to be encourag'd, and what amended in this Noble Art; and how far fuch

an

an Amufement may be render'd of the utmoft Confequence to the Republick of Letters.

In our prefent vifible Decay of all Senfe, efpecially *Poetick*; and of all Poetry, particularly *Dramatick*; the Art of Dancing fhould again wholly ingrofs the Stage, as it did formerly in its Infancy: For, fince we can no longer boaft the Shadow of thofe Beauties, for whofe Sakes we banifh'd it thence; why fhould any one now object to its Reftoration? If we confider this Art of *Mimickry* thoroughly, either in its former flourifhing State, or in the Addition of fome late Improvements; I believe, every impartial Judge will allow, that it may be prodigioufly advanc'd in this Age, not only to its priftine Height, but, perhaps, (if taken in a right Light) more to the Advantage of Mankind in general, than has been yet known from any publick Amufement. And, fince Nonfenfe has fo long ufurp'd the Provinces of Tongue and Pen, we may chance to improve, by dumb Wit: And, fince Head-pieces are at a Lofs in giving us proper Documents, we may look for Inftruction from Arms and Legs.

I am fenfible, that fome Book-learn'd Criticks, or formal, ignorant Humourifts, will immediately reproach me with the vaft Progrefs thefe Stage Dances have already made amongft us; and that any farther Encouragement given them, would prove the utter Ruin of that fmall, expiring Spirit of Poetry left. To this I readily anfwer, That *Dramatick* Poetry is at prefent at fo low an Ebb of Merit, that 'tis neither worth minding, nor retrieving; nor can its Place be better fupply'd, than by that inftructive Art, which was the Admiration even of the greateft Poets, when the Stage was in its full-blown Flower of Perfection.

BUT

BUT, what would thofe very wife Gentle-men fay, fhould I fcrew my Argument a Note higher, and maintain, that Poetry it felf may be brought to a greater Pitch of Inftruction and Delight by thefe DANCES, than by the Works of any Poet now living; and in one Night's *Entertainment*, we may skim the Cream of all the different Kinds of that Noble Art. But, in or-der to fortify my Affertions by fome Examples; let us only fuppofe one of my old Friend *Bays*'s Grand DANCES.

ENTER firft, a ftrapping two-handed Fellow, with a bright Shield, a broad Sword, and a fui-table Plume of Feathers; moving exactly to a Trumpet-tune; frowning and laying about him as if the Devil was in him. Won't he give us a juft Idea of the Fire and Grandeur of *Heroick Poe-try* in general? Then, if he falls in Love with all the Women; kills all the Men he meets, and at laft ftabs or poifons himfelf; this will have a particular Regard to that part of it, call'd *Dra-matick*, as twelve or twenty-four very high Ca-pers, and Military Flourifhes, with a juft Paufe at the End of each, will to the *Epick*.

If a Giant and Dwarf hop about Hand in Hand; the long Stride of one, and fhort Step of the other; figure out to the meaneft Capacity the Beauties of *Pindarique Poems*: Should the tall Fel-low fometimes ftare, foam and gallop full drive, as if poffefs'd with a Fury; anon, all of a fud-den ftand ftock ftill, as if quite out of Breath; while the little Shaver is playing fome genteel Tricks; toying, finging, fmiling, by Starts; they thus point out to us the unequal Enthufiafm of the great *Ode*, and Pleafantry of the fmall *One*, with the Variety of the *Lyrick*.

AN

AN Upholder's Retinue moving gravely round a Coffin, attended by fome Bedlamite Lovers, curfing, crying, bleffing, laughing, fighing, as if their Hearts would break; the different Poftures of this mad, whimfical, melancholy *Group*, will juftly comprehend all Sorts of *Elegiack* Complaints.

AN open, fincere Countenance, generally drefs'd in Frowns, with a Looking-glafs in one Hand, and the Balance of Juftice in the other; explains to us the neceffary Truths of bold *Satire*: as a Vizard Mask, Dark Lanthorn, and frequent Whifpers, do its Counter-part, a private *Lampoon*.

A Set of Hay-makers, a fprightly Jig, rural Love, with a River-God or two, and as many Wood *Nymphs*; denote the natural Simplicity, and Innocence of *Paftoral*.

A *Pigmy*, with a diminutive, but very keen Dagger, cutting and pricking every body as high as he can reach, gives us at once the Sting in the Tail of an *Epigram*.

THE *Heroic-comick*, may be diftinguifh'd by a purple Robe and Sceptre, with a *Satyr*'s Hoofs and Horns; as its Half-brother *Burlefque* (who's generally more Knave than Fool) may by a *Jack-pudding*'s Coat over a Philofopher's Garment.

THUS the *Anacreontick* may be defcrib'd by a Train of jolly Lads, and blooming Laffes, led by *Bacchus* and *Venus*, playing, drinking, loving, moving in the eafieft Manner, to the fofteft MUSICK: As the Modern Imitation of them, the *Philippick*, and the Improvement upon the *Philippick*, call'd the *Lilliputian*, may, by fome Infants, that juft can go and fpeak, fhining in their innocent PLAYS, catching Butter-flies,

blowing

blowing Bubbles, tossing Balls: *Witty Master! Pretty Miss!*

THEN if a Dancer would in a more particular Manner chalk out some private Subjects; it may be easily brought about in the following Method:

BY a pale Complexion, dirty Shirt, uncomb'd Wig, and distracted Step, the Love-sick Songster is known; as a tolerable deal of Lace and Fringe, clock'd Stockings, and a Minuet Step, are certain Signs of genteel Poetry; the Wit of the *Beau-monde*; or, as *Waller* has it, *soft Words, with nothing in them, &c.* A blind Man with an *Antique* Robe, and Modern Brocade Waste-coat; a Sceptre in his Hand, and Buskins on his Legs; who loves the roughest Roads, treads loftily, but seldom stumbles, is an exact Emblem of *Blank Verse*: As a Morris-dancer, adorn'd with Garlands of Flowers, fetter'd with silken Cords, and deck'd all round with Bells, does *Rhime*: And so a fruitful Genius, may proceed *ad Infinitum.*

NOW could our Eye at one View take in all these, jumbled together in a Grand Dance, at the same time we should enjoy the Quintessence of all Kinds of POETRY, as significantly explain'd to us as the Nature of an Eclipse was by the *Hays* in the *Rehearsal.* The Success of which Dance, and Justness of the Representation, shew to what Perfection such Entertainments may be brought in natural, and all other Sorts of Philosophy.

I am perswaded, that DANCING is the only Method of making all Parts of the Mathematicks to be easily comprehended by the dullest Capacities; nor can I think of any Means so proper of rendering familiar to a young Lad's Understanding any Problem of *Euclid,* as dancing it

2   over

over to him. Sir *I - - - c N - - - - n* often own'd to me, he was entirely of my Opinion. Mr. *R - - - ly*, Dr. *Ha - - - ly*, and the reft of our principal Mathematicians, will come readily into it, if they once confider the various Natures of Motions abfolute, and relative, regular and irregular, of Bodies mix'd and fimple, elaftick and volatile, with all the reft of the neceffary Jargon, in the proper Terms of Art: And would thofe Gentlemen be at a little Pains with fome of the bad Clock-work Machines belonging to both *Play-Houfes*, I am confident no Lecture or tedious Harangue, fpun out by a trifling Superfluity of Words, could give fo much Satisfaction to an Audience, or fo true Notions of the Elements of Things, as a *Mathematical Dance*.

I need not proceed to fet off every other particular Art in this Light; any Man that is Mafter of a ready Head and Heel, will quickly reduce, from Speculation to Practice, all Branches of any other Science, in the fame Manner I propofe. As thefe Grotefque Dances have met with a favourable Reception from all true Judges of Wit and Politenefs, even where there was but little of the *Utile* mix'd with the *Dulci :* What might we not expect from Entertainments upon the fore-mention'd Plans, efpecially at the *New Houfe*, under the Direction, and conducted by *J - - - - - - n R——h*, Efq; who is Mafter of an unparallel'd Genius to excel in that Way: And I will venture to proclaim him the the greateft Poet, Philofopher, and Mathematician now in Being, if he pleafes to exert his nimble Talents according to the Schemes I have here laid down for throwing thefe Arts into proper Motion and Figure.

I fear it might be highly refented by feveral of my kind Readers, if, in an E S S A Y upon

Theatrical

Theatrical Dancing, no honourable Mention fhould be made of *Tumblers*, *Pofture - Mafters*, and *Rope-Dancers*; therefore I fhall not wholly negleƈt, nor dwell too long upon that Subjeƈt: The two firſt we look upon as humble Creepers in D A N- C I N G, as the laſt are generally High - flyers: They all have their Merits in their different Sta- tions. *Tumbling* and *Poſtures* require as great Agility and Dexterity, and their various Tricks may appear as pleaſing to the Eye, as the brave Attempts of *Rope-Dancing*: But this laſt is more furprizing and hazardous, giving the Speƈtator a fort of painful Pleaſure; and, indeed, a naturally fteady Head, and bold Heart, are more requifite in this myſterious Science, than that mean Cun- ning, fupple Limbs, feemingly diflocated Joints, flexible Hams, and artificial bending any Way; which is all the two firſt can boaſt of.

'T I S true, thefe low Movers have infinitely of late, got the Advantage over the High - flyers; yet the laſt, with the Generality of People, are ſtill in great Efteem, and live in Hopes of one Day or another having Liberty again to divert both Court, Town and Country. And though for fome Years paſt the laudable Art of R O P E- D A N C I N G has been held in great Contempt in the refin'd Neighbourhood of St. *James*'s; yet, I can't fay, but of late they have got Ground remarkably, by the fine Performances of Signior *Violante* and his Lady; who have given vaſt Con- tent to all Ranks of People, and flatter the High- flyers with a Profpeƈt of being once more in Requeſt. A Time may come, when their Anta- goniſts fhall be oblig'd to refign the Power they gain'd by *Poſtures*, *Grimace* and *Agility*: And if they care not to dance on, they may fwing in a Rope, and quaver their Toes in the Air, though

L   now

now they're confin'd to *Terra Firma*: I fay, this is not improbable, efpecially fince Signior *Violante* has taken Poffeffion of the higheft Part of the Steeple of the K——g's own Parifh-Church, in order to fhew his Skill to Multitudes of admiring Spectators. 'Tis true, the chief *Pofture-Mafter* of that Parifh had a Stop put to his fhewing any more there; but we expect Orders from a higher Power to permit him to perform.

BEFORE I take my Leave of *Stage-Dancing*, it will not be thought impertinent, if I remind my Readers here of what I advanc'd in my firft ESSAY, about the Recitative of an OPERA being danc'd: I believe they'll all enter more readily into that Project, now that the Nature and Beauty of DANCING is more fully explain'd.

THE Ufe that may be made of thefe *Theatrical Grotefque Dances* is, I hope, by this Time fo obvious to every thinking *Briton*, and the Advantages accruing from them fo demonftrable, that I fhall not any longer infift upon their extraordinary Merit, but apply fome new Steps in DANCING to private Life, which may be of the utmoft Confequence to the *Publick Good*.

I defire that our prefent worthy Set of *Dancing-Mafters* would not be difpleas'd, if I propofe erecting feveral publick Schools in this *Metropolis*, and other great Towns of this Ifland; in order to inftruct all our Youth in fpeaking *Dances*, or a *Dancing Speech*. They are themfelves yet ignorant of that myfterious Part of DANCING; but as they could qualify themfelves for fuch a laudable Work, they fhould preferably to others be encourag'd; in the mean time we fhould have skillful Mafters brought from *Turkey*, *Perfia*, &c. protected by the Government, and paid at the Publick Expence.   THE

THE Benefits arifing from this Art to the Majority of a trading Nation, may be eafily made manifeft from the ready and quiet Difpatch of Bufinefs in this and all great Cities; for a Nod, a Shrug, a wry Face; the Motion of a Leg or Arm, right or left; nay, the Difpofition of a different Finger (according to the old Cuftom of fpeaking with our Fingers) will, without the Appearance of any Hurry, or the fhocking Noife of ftunning Voices, facilitate, to Admiration, the moft expeditious Manner of Commerce amongft the bufy Part of Mankind: Not fo much as a Humm will be heard in the *Royal Exchange,* but the whole Crowd will appear as ferene as a *Quaker's Meeting,* when the Spirit works not on the Flefh. Then we might fee an *European* calmly dancing a Bargain with an *Afiatick*; a *Briftol* Merchant drawing a Bill on *Scanderoon* with one fmart Caper; a *Jew* bowing himfelf into the Favour of a *Chriftian*; and one of the Pure ones, without the Expence even of *Yea* or *Nay,* outwit a *Chancery* Sollicitor with a clean Hop. In fuch a Medley of foreign Tongues, as muft neceffarily attend the Trade of fuch a Town as *London,* where you meet all Nations of the known World in a Compafs of an Acre of Ground, what can we expect but *Babel* it felf, in the tranfacting of Bufinefs. Now this Hint of mine, rightly improv'd, would enable every one to manage his Affairs, without being skill'd in the Mother-Tongue of him he deals with: And I am certain, that it is next to a Demonftration (if I may be allow'd the *Paradox*) that the only Method of attaining an univerfal Language, is to be *Dumb.* A Tofs of the Head, a Wink of an Eye, or Shrug of the Shoulders, will diftinguifh whether you deal in *South-Sea, India,* or *Bank-*

Stock;

Stock; an Arm or Leg will tell whether you are a Buyer or Seller. And as to Numbers, every Child knows, we may reckon to Millions by our Fingers in the readiest Manner of Accompts; and to the greatest Exactness in Arithmetick. Besides, every different Movement at once proclaims the Man's Country you would deal with. If you see a Gentleman move slowly along in a grave Sarabrand Step, as if he was afraid to dislocate his Bones, or fall a-pieces, you, at once, know him to be a *Spaniard*. If you see another cut fifty Capers in the making one Bow, always gay, always in Motion, and never out of Countenance, you're certain he's a *Frenchman:* This last tho' must be allow'd the Liberty of his Tongue, in some few particular Monosyllables, or he's undone for ever. The *English* (those *Tragi-Comedians* of the World) with one merry Leg, and one sad, are known to all Nations upon Earth by a grave Jig peculiar to themselves. The *Germans* are as noted for their long Stride, Turky-Cock Strut, and dancing in the Ox-Stile; as the *Low-Dutch* are for their aukward Imitation of the *French, a-la-Clumsie.* Thus, without observing even the Countenances of People (which might be of great Advantage in this Affair) or any Part or Kind of Speech, every Man's Birth and Business is made manifest by his Country-Steps.

SOMETHING, in the Nature of these DANCES, was begun and carry'd on in the Way. of Trade, about the Year *Seventeen Hundred and Twenty*; but the Masters of those Times and *Dancing-Schools* (tho' otherwise vast Proficients in their Calling) made their Scholars dance so long, and cut Capers so high, that all *Europe* grew quite sick of their Method in Business.

I can-

I cannot help obferving here, that as the firft Inftitution of DANCING was religious, fo there is no Part of publick or private Life, to which it would prove more ferviceable or becoming, in the way of dumb Oratory, than to the P—— pit : It appears already, by the modeft and well-judg'd Endeavours of a young Gentleman (who is as juft an Actor, as a profound Scholar) to be a Science in all Refpects highly proper in and worthy of that Place and Function.

No Words, without proper Motions, can have any tolerable Effect, as to inculcating found Doctrine with a fuitable Vehemence: And if any Pr——ft labours under the Infirmity of a bad Elocution, a ftammering Utterance, or any kind of Impediment in Speech, every Member of his Body may affift in edifying his Congregation; and his Ser——n be fluently and elegantly deliver'd by Signs and Tokens, and Movements, and all that, what fignifies it, whether he fpeaks or no, fo he is underftood to the Purpofe. Nor would it be amifs, were all our Pu——ts made of a commodious Largenefs, and then our Par ns might have Space fufficient to fhew us, that we muft be content with a Sort of a rough, hobling *Courant*, to get to H——n; or, that if we don't take fpecial Care, we may flide in a fine eafy Minuet-Step (before we are aware) to the D---l: In fhort, one might * * * * * * and fo * * * * * and thus * * * * * and * * * * * ** and then * * * * * * but more of this * * * * * another Time * * * * * as my Project thrives in its Infancy.

It may be naturally expected, by the Majority of my Readers, that, in a general Difcourfe upon DANCING, the *French* Nation fhould make a greater Figure, efpecially as I have

L 3   thought

thought fit to touch upon other Countries, both antique and modern in this ESSAY. But being oblig'd, by feveral material and unavoidable Hints, to ftretch this Subject to its utmoft Extent, and no principal Part that they excel in being neglected, I thought it proper to tofs their Merit, on that Head, by the Lump into the Scale : Befides, were I to enter into a formal Detail of the Beauties of DANCING, and a *Frenchman* at the fame time, new Matter would, every Moment, flow in fo copioufiy, that I fhould never know when to make an End.

I hope, (tho' I have promis'd not to meddle but with the *Publick Entertainments*) that what I have advanc'd in relation to fome Parts of private Life, will not be look'd upon as altogether abfurd ; but that I fhall be pardon'd for fuch feafonable Digreffions, without the Trouble of digreffing any farther, in order to excufe my felf : So conclude very pertinently with that wife Affertion of *Epicurus*, "That the whole Frame, Con- "trivance, and Structure of this Globe, is but an "orderly Movement, by Atoms juftly difpos'd for "that End. Oppofite to which, was that confus'd "Jumble of jarring Atoms during the Reign of "*Chaos*; before this World was tun'd by the Mu- "SICK of the Spheres, into a regular DANCE.

E S S A Y IV.

OF CHORUSSES,

Antique and Modern; in great Esteem with the ANTIENTS, *neglected by the present Age. Of their Use and Beauty in all* STAGE-ENTERTAINMENTS. *To which are added, Some Reflections upon the* English CHORUS *of* CAT-CALLS.

N ESSAY, explaining the Nature, Use and Beauty of a Grand CHO-RUS, as practis'd by the Antients, may be thought very impertinent at this Time of Day, being entirely banish'd the *Play-House,* and only the Name preserv'd in the *Opera.* This shall not deter me from introducing it amongst our publick Diversions, though laid
aside,

aside, either with an Intent to shew the World what Notion Antiquity had of it, or by describing it exactly, leave a just Plan, in case any generous, poetical Patriot, should attempt re-establishing it in our THEATRES.

THE Antients look'd upon the CHORUS, *As a Troop of Actors, representing a Number of those Persons, who were, or probably might be, present at the Time of the Representation of a particular Fable: They interfer'd with the Business of the Stage, either by Side-Speeches, or in Dialogue with the Characters of the* DRAMA, *or sung and danc'd, to mark the Intervals of the Acts.*

BUT if we consider a CHORUS historically, we must take it in three different Views: *First,* As it was the Whole of a *Stage-Entertainment*; *Next,* As it was brought in as an Interlude only, or Appendix to TRAGEDY and COMEDY; *Lastly,* As it was totally lost in *Greece* and *Rome,* and but the Shadow of it left remaining with the Moderns. But however they have neglected or despis'd the reviving what was so essential to the very Life and Being of a STAGE; yet I have that Deference for the Judgment of the Antients, who thought it even necessary, that I have set apart this whole ESSAY, to give my Countrymen (who do not dip into Antiquity to search for such Things) an Idea of its Beauty and Grandeur.

I observ'd, in my last ESSAY upon DANCING, that the Original of all *Theatrical Entertainments* was entirely owing to a merry Sacrifice, instituted to the Honour of the jolly God *Bacchus:* It consisted equally of SINGING and DANCING in a rude unpolish'd Way; and was the Whole of what we have since call'd, a CHORUS, as far as such a Performance was made up of MUSICK, Vocal or Instrumental, and DANCE.

The

The POETS, taking the Hint, thought this Affair capable of Improvement, so threw in one Actor after another so fast, that in about fourscore Years the *Drama* was fram'd into regular TRAGEDY and COMEDY; and, from this wild Beginning, sprang the politest STAGES of *Greece*. Thus we see, at first, the Whole was but a CHORUS: Tho' the POETS had made this Alteration in this rough *Entertainment*; they had too great a Deference for the old Plan, not to retain some Part of it, at least in Memory of their common Parent: So preserv'd entirely the MUSICK and DANCING of the OLD CHORUS, but exhibited after a juster and more beautiful Manner; and embellish'd it with all the Magnificence of *Scenes*, *Cloaths* and *Machines*, that Thought could invent, or Art supply: Nay, to push the Matter still farther, they oblig'd the CHORUS to enter into the Business it felt of every PLAY: Thus it became not an additional only, but an essential Part of all *Stage-Representations*; and the Use of it look'd upon at least as necessary, as the Ornament.

IN this Station the CHORUS remain'd undisturb'd, from the Establishment, to the Ruin of the *Grecian Stage*: The Office of the CHORUS was to *Sing* and *Dance* in Notes and Measures, either of a Piece with the PLAY then represented in general, or some particular occasional Part; they frequently convers'd with the Characters on the *Stage*; especially the chief of them, call'd the *Coryphæus*, maintain'd the Dialogue, when there was but one Person of the *Drama* present; the Antients not allowing of *Soliloquies*, or but rarely; and it was very common for them to fill up any little requisite Vacancy by some Conversation amongst themselves *a propos* to the Affair in hand.   THUS

Thus the Chorus being generally upon the Stage, and except, in some few Examples, continuing there during the whole Representation, they were always ready to ask or answer Questions, and moralize betwixt the *Scenes*; and by this means never suffer'd the Plot to cool, or the Business of the *Stage* to fall: Then their Singing and Dancing betwixt the *Acts*; not only explain'd to the Audience the just Interspaces, but their Songs and Dances being allied to the Subject of the Play, kept the *Fable* entire; at the same time they gave the Spectators the most exquisite Delight; and added an Air of Magnificence and Surprize to the *Stage* and *Audience*.

The Chorus being fix'd upon this solid Basis, was found so beneficial and diverting, that it could not be lost but in the total Destruction of the Theatre. Comedy, indeed, was obliged to part with its Chorus in a short Time after its Institution; but Tragedy preserv'd it to the very last. This Conduct, in relation to the different Kinds of *Dramatick Poetry*, was unavoidable; and the Reasons for proceeding in this Manner have been given in a former Essay.

The *Romans* first alter'd the Office and Behaviour of the Chorus, and, with that Empire, it by degrees dwindled, till it sunk to nothing. Their Successors, the Moderns, found it fallen to the Earth, they kept it down, and seem not inclinable to be at any Expence or Trouble to raise from Obscurity, and almost Oblivion, the noblest Ornament of the *Stage*.

I must take Notice tho', before I go on any farther, that from all my Observations upon the *Dramatick Poetry* of the *Romans*, and Reflections upon all their Writers of any Kind, I have no

Grounds

Grounds to believe, that with them the CHORUS ever appear'd in that Luſtre, or Credit, as at *Athens*; but was in all Reſpects carry'd on in a meaner Method of Coſt and Deſign: The *Grecian* CHORUS as much exceeding it, as their *Dramatick Poets* did thoſe of *Rome*.

IT is not a difficult Task to account for the Ruin of the CHORUS amongſt the *Antients*. The *Grecians* loſt it with their Stage, and the *Romans* with their Empire: All fine Arts being look'd upon as Foes to Barbarity, in civilizing, not de-populating the World. We cannot ſuppoſe, that the *Goths*, *Huns*, *Vandals* and *Lombards* had them much in Eſteem: But it will not prove ſo eaſy to give a good and ſenſible Reaſon, why, with the Reſtoration of all fine Arts, and polite Amuſe-ments, the *Chorus* too ſhould not recover its pri-ſtine Glory.

IN *Comedy* a CHORUS has been found uſe-leſs, even by the *Grecians* themſelves; therefore juſtly laid aſide: And, I ſo far deſpair of ever ſeeing it brought upon the Stage in *Tragedy*, or a Poſſibility of ſucceeding in it, tho' attempted (there lie ſo many unſurmountable Rubs in the Way, as the Stage is manag'd with us) that I would be content, it ſhould reſign all Pretenſi-ons to an Intereſt in the *Play-houſe*; was it but judiciouſly introduc'd in our OPERAS. I am ſenſible, that three Parts in four of the genteel Audiences, which crowd all Performances at the H—y-m——t, will immediately ſquall out, Pray when had we an OPERA without a CHORUS? To theſe I poſitively anſwer, That we never had an OPERA with one: The Name may be ſpelt the ſame way, but the Preſent is as unlike the Paſt, as a modern *Italian* differs from an old *Greek*. What we palm upon the World now,

cannot

cannot boaft of being the Ghoft of an *Antique*
C H O R U S.

B U T to bring this Difpute nearer a Conclu-
fion, by fetting it in a jufter Point of View; let
us inquire more particularly into the Nature of
an old C H O R U S; the Ufe the *Antients* made
of it, and their prudent Management of it; in
the vaft Variety of C H O R U S E S adapted to every
Subject; which Confiderations join'd to our Remarks upon the Behaviour of the Moderns in
that Way, may lay down fome Rules, and advance fome Reafons for its Revival here.

I N order to compafs this End, I fhall briefly
recapitulate fome Points already fpoke to; fo
throw the Whole into a more regular and eafy
Method of being underftood.

T H E Duty of the Ancient C H O R U S, confifted of two Parts: In the firft, they fpoke with
the other Characters in the Bufinefs of the Play,
and then appear'd as Actors concern'd in the
Intrigues of the *Drama* then reprefented. In the
fecond, they mark'd the Intervals of the *Acts* by
M U S I C K, Vocal and Inftrumental, and D A N C E;
or perhaps fung in the *Acts* fome Things relating to the Subject then brought upon the Stage.

T H E Characters of the Perfons which made
up the C H O R U S of different P L A Y S, were as
various as the Fables could be, on which they
were founded; or, as the teeming Imaginations,
and whimfical Fancies of Poets could make them.
Tho' the *Antients* abfolutely tied themfelves down
to this Rule; that the C H O R U S was fuppos'd to
be a Company of thofe Perfons, who might moft
probably be prefent on that individual Place,
where the Scene of the P L A Y, then in Reprefentation, lay.

T H U S

THUS in the *Hecuba* of *Euripides*, the CHO-
RUS confifted of *Trojan* Women, Captives, as
fhe her felf then was; and in his *Cyclops* of *Sa-
tires*, no others daring to ftay near the Den of
Polyphemus.

IN the *Antigone* of *Sophocles*, the CHORUS
was made up of old Men, fent for to Council
by *Creon*: And in his *Ajax*, of Seamen, who
came to offer their Service to their Prince, on
hearing of his Diftraction.

IN the *Prometheus* of *Efchylus*, the Nymphs of
the Ocean furnifh'd a CHORUS; he being chain'd
to a Rock in the Sea, and no other living Creature near him: And, in the *Seven before Thebes*,
the young Women of the Town.

THUS we may obferve, how ftrictly they confin'd themfelves to what was proper on this
Head; but ftill the Latitude in the Characters of
the CHORUS, was as large as in Subjects; and
in *Comedy* generally very entertaining: Of which
I fhall inftance but a few Examples; fince the
Province of *Comedy* quickly was oblig'd to refign
its Pretenfions to a CHORUS.

Ariftophanes, particularly of all the *Comick* Poets, was the moft ingenious in the Whim and
Contrivance of his CHORUS; tho' ftill with a
nice Regard to Propriety. In one Play he
gives us a CHORUS of Clouds, in order to ridicule the *Sophifms* of *Socrates*: In another, one
of Birds; to which fome *Athenians* prattle about
building feveral Caftles in the Air. In a third, he
introduces a Neft of Wafps, to hinder an humorous old Fellow from going abroad; which they
perform'd, by ftinging him home to fome Tune:
Nay, he once entertain'd his Audience with a
mufical CHORUS of Frogs, while *Bacchus* is
paffing *Styx* to vifit *Pluto*. This fome People

M   may

may look upon, as carrying the Jeſt too far; and what was very unbecoming the Dignity and Gravity of any *Stage-plays*: But, ſtill we may obſerve in all theſe Fancies, tho' of a very odd Turn, that they have an Eye to what is proper to the Subject in Hand.

From theſe few Citations, we may learn the Nature of an *Antique* C H O R U S, both in *Tragedy* and *Comedy*; and they'll ſerve to ſhew us what Liberties their Poets took in that Part of their Plays; from whence we may gather, that even thoſe deſign'd meerly for Mirth, were not againſt the Rules of their Art.

For Example, Let us but ſuppoſe the Scene of an O P E R A, laid in *H--l--nd*, or Hell; What can be more proper than a C H O R U S of Frogs; yet the Probability is preſerv'd; for that is the Harmony to be expected in thoſe Regions.

The Conſequences I would naturally draw from the Authority of theſe Quotations, will be contain'd in a ſmall Compaſs: For I allow any unprejudic'd Perſon to determine, what wonderful Effects a well-judg'd C H O R U S might produce in an *Italian* O P E R A; where the Variety of Subjects I have propos'd in my firſt E S S A Y, would allow that vaſt Latitude in the Choice of proper Perſons to form a C H O R U S, as would equal, if not ſurpaſs, the *Grecian* Stage, in Humour and Grandeur.

This will be more apparent, if we conſider, that in forming our O P E R A S upon the Plans of *Engliſh* Fables, either in the heroick or familiar Stile, we take in the utmoſt Extent of the *Antique* C H O R U S, either as it related to *Tragedy* or *Comedy*; and, according to the Nature of each particular Story, make uſe of the Grandeur and Severity of one, or the Novelty and Pleaſantry

of

of the other; while both may be attended with Variety and Magnificence in a different Taste.

THIS CHORUS should consist of MUSICK, Vocal and Instrumental, differing from what makes up the Body of each Act; but yet expressive of the Subject then on the Stage: Next of DANCING, and Sounds proper to accompany those Motions: Then no Cost should be spar'd in the proper Decoration of Scenery, Machinery and Habits, that the Spectators may be pleas'd and amaz'd. Thus the CHORUS need not break in upon the main Thread of the Design, by appearing in any Part of an ACT; but be rather conducive to the carrying it on, by being introduc'd as an Interlude, to fill up the Vacancies betwixt the *Acts*; which are now pass'd over in dull Chit-chat, or in our duller Gaping and Staring at one another; so never suffer the Business of the Stage to drop; amuse the Audience with an agreeable Variety, and preserve the Entertainment, from the Beginning to End, all of a-piece; and the Whole might be finish'd by a Grand CHORUS, or a *Tout-ensemble* of Voices, Instruments, Dancers, &c.

NOW, if we reflect upon the Novelty and Variety of the *Antients* in their CHORUSSES, even when they had the greatest Regard to the strictest Rules of Poetry; what Liberties might we not allow to OPERAS, which are not confin'd to the Probable, but can call Gods, and Devils, and Machines upon the Stage (as fast as a Juggler does his Balls) where they may prophecy, or dance; solve Difficulties, or sing a Song; assist a Hero, or kiss a Shepherdess; thus unravel the most intricate Plots in a trice, by a very natural Catastrophe, and as easily as *Alexander* unty'd the *Gordian-Knot*.

BY

By this Management, the OPERA will be established upon a lasting Foundation, without injuring the *Play-houses*, or their Manufactures. *Tragedy* shall be allow'd to make the most of its Terror and Pity; and *Comedy* of its Wit and Mirth: whilst the OPERAS shall subsist and flourish, by the absolute Power of the *Marvellous*, the *Etonnant*, and all that.

WAS our Musical THEATRE but once grac'd with such a CHORUS as is here specify'd, what Groves of Musical Warblers! what Troops of dancing Deities would ravish us! What rising Mountains, sinking Valleys, enamel'd Meads, and winding Streams, would appear in perspective, with enchanted Palaces and Gardens to surprize us! A new Creation should arise at the Prompter's Whistle, and Nature's Self be lost in what seem'd but natural: Then would Tapestry Figures and Joint-stools cut Capers to improve our Understanding; Jet-caus and Cascades pour out Instruction; and flying Dragons, and walking Statues, demonstrate the great Truths of R——n, by amazing us.

ALL such Spectacles and Decorations were allow'd to be a Part of the *Antique* CHORUS; and by all Judges of the *Opera-stage*, are look'd upon as essential to it: So in this happy Conjunction, here propos'd, every Being, natural or supernatural, is order'd to obey its Commands. I am perswaded, that any Man, who has just Notions of what is surprizing, wonderful, metaphysical, and all that, will readily comprehend, what Pleasure and Profit must result from this Design.

WE dare not be positive, that the *Greeks* or *Romans* were so polite, as to have any Taste for an entire Musical Entertainment, consisting of

Recita-

Recitative and Airs, like our OPERAS: But, this we may be affur'd of, had thofe prudent, genteel Nations, once harbour'd an Idea of fuch a Stage Diverfion; they would not have forgot its moft effential Part, a proper CHORUS.

A fuperior Genius ought to prefide in the Conduct of thefe Affairs, left we be miftaken in the End propos'd, and have our Performances turn'd into Ridicule, when we expect they fhould be admir'd. This was the very Cafe in an OPERA once exhibited at the H----y---m---t; a CHORUS of wild Sparrows was let fly behind the Scenes, but they were never heard (the Undertakers being out in their Choice of a Singing-bird) nor feen, but in their Effects, upon the Ladies Heads. Now, had the Wife-acres planted fome tuneful Flageolets behind the Scenes, and let feveral artificial Nightingales appear hopping to and fro in the Grove; Art there, by imitating, would have out-done Nature. This Example may fuffice to give the Managers of thefe Entertainments a Caution, not to be deceiv'd into things unnatural, by trufting to Nature too far.

OF all the Moderns, the *French* alone have enter'd a little into the Defign of an antique CHORUS: They are but Copiers, 'tis true, and if the Refemblance be faint, and the Colouring and Features want the Spirit and Life of the Original; yet they are as like, as a *Frenchman* of this Age can be to a Citizen of *Sparta*. Their MUSICK I have not touch'd upon in any regular Method of Criticifm; but I cannot help thinking their CHORUSSES the moft harmonious, moft beautiful, and moft magnificent Part of their OPERAS; every Act there ends with a Grand CHORUS adapted to the Bufinefs of that Scene, which concludes each particular Act: Sometimes

M 3   you

you have a Stage fill'd with quavering Nymphs and capering Shepherds, animated by the sweet Notes of *Flut-douxes* and rural *Bag-pipes*; anon a Troop of Blood-thirsty Warriors, with clashing Arms and sounding Trumpets, give you the Fury of a *Battle* in Air and Motion: And now the idle Gods and Goddesses chant and foot it away with celestial Steps and Graces; the very Musick of the Spheres ravishing the mortal Ears of the Audience; who kindly join the Stage, till the whole House appears a Heathen Paradise.

They have likewise made some small Attempts towards introducing an antique Chorus into their *Tragedies*, *Comedies*, and *Ballets*; but with Success answerable to such wretched Stuff: Though Abbot *Hedelin* laid them down the justest and most beautiful Rules for their Instruction: Though Cardinal *Richlieu* encourag'd such an Enterprize; and tho' afterwards *Racine*, *Moliere*, and *Baptist Lully* were principally concern'd in the Management of the Whole, they could not perfect so great a Work; whether for Want of a suitable Genius, or a Fund sufficient to defray so vast an Expence, I will not determine.

In Fine, a Chorus rightly introduc'd in an Opera, must give the World the *NE PLUS ULTRA* of Musick; and, I think it manifest, that by the wilful and careless Omission of it on the present *Italian Stage*, we lose the Perfection of *Harmony*; and never allow our Composers an Opportunity of exerting their highest Talents, and displaying the Greatness of a Genius, by shewing what the Force of Musick can produce.

We may have an Idea of this from some Parts of our Church-Musick; which though generally very bad, yet demonstrates, that those

full

full Parts of Musick, either in Church or Theatre, shew the Quinteslence of Art in the Composer, and must give equal Delight to an Audience.

That pitiful Farce of Sounds, that less than the Shadow of what it represents, which passes upon us at the Conclusion of our Operas for a Grand Chorus, is a *Burlesque* upon the Name, Design and Grandeur of the Thing; one may have as much, and as good for a Half-penny from a friendly Alliance of *Ballad-Singers* at *Pye-Corner*, or *Fleet - Bridge*. That which should be the Life, the Soul of the collective Body of Musick, Dancing, and Machinery, poorly drops into a few scurvy Scrapes, and Bows, and Curtseys from our Singers, and their Tinsel Attendant Snuff-Candles and Oyster-Girls; and the All of *Harmony* dwindles into a few sorry canting Notes, fit only to accompany a *Wapping Crowdero*: And this is to be esteem'd the finishing Stroke, to close one of the noblest Entertainments, that Art, in Conjunction with Nature, can produce, to charm Mankind.

I freely acknowledge, that the *English* Dramatick Operas of the last Age, by far exceeded our *Italian* in that Point; for every Act concluded with a Piece of Musick, Dancing and Scenery, consonant to the Affairs then in Agitation; conducted, in some Respects, after the Manner of the Antients; or rather, in the Stile of the *French*, whose Fashions then prevailed in every thing polite. And as our Theatrical Managers were sensible, that we had a very mechanical Genius; they contriv'd so their little ornamental Incidents, as to humour that *Gou*; when *Elbow - Chairs* danc'd, *Flower-pots* sung, *Ghosts* walk'd, and *Devils* flew to divert us.

There

THERE is one thing more I muſt obſerve, to the Shame of the Maſters of our THEATRES in general; which is, that the only juſt Remains of a true CHORUS appear in the artful Management of our *Puppet-Shews*; and, indeed, the entire Performance of theſe ſmall, itinerant, wooden Actors, is a kind of Grand CHORUS in Miniature; eſpecially their Prompter anſwers exactly to the Character and Buſineſs of the *Coryphæus* with the Antients; whoſe Office it is, to explain to the Audience, the moſt intricate Parts of what they ſee and hear, or to tell what is to come; to make wiſe Reflexions on what is paſt, or what may be; to enter into moral Dialogues pertinent to the Subject with his little Play - Fellows; nay, he generally talks as much to the Purpoſe as any of them; his Behaviour (with the Humours of *Punch*, and the MUSICK, DANCING and MACHINES, which are beautifully and prudently ſcatter'd up and down thro' the Whole) exactly diſcharges the Duty of an antique CHORUS.

To apply more particularly to our ſelves (by way of drawing towards a Concluſion) the Sum of what has been urg'd on this Head; let us but conſider a CHORUS either in a critical, a political, or an ornamental Capacity, and judge how far it effects our Intereſt in all.

As far as Criticiſm is concern'd in this Affair, I think we are ſafe, as to the Judgment, Uſe and Beauty of a CHORUS: The whole Tenour of this ESSAY, and ſeveral undeniable Arguments diſpers'd here and there in the others, with the general Conſent of all the Antients, and the Approbation of the moſt Learned amongſt the Moderns, have determin'd in our Favour, and confirmed the Neceſſity of it in every Particular.

But

But as the Manner of reasoning on this Head will not have its due Weight with the Generality of People, 'tis needless to insist any farther on that; but to speak to their Understanding, Interest and Pleasure, in the two other Points.

In sound Policy, I am certain, every *True Briton* ought to give the greatest Encouragement imaginable to a Grand CHORUS; the unavoidable and vast Expences which necessarily attend the Grandeur of such an Undertaking, must of course, bring along with them infinite Advantages to a trading People, in the Disposal of all Manufactures, Foreign and Domestick: Besides, the full Employment it will give to Hundreds of our Poor; who otherwise must steal or starve. Nor will it be amiss, if I here remind my Readers of my Project of establishing a *Musical Academy* in one of our Largest HOSPITALS; for were a CHORUS, proper to their Stage, once settled, no *Beggar* need walk *London* Streets; so great would be the Demand, for Crowds of Attendants to fill the spacious STAGE; and, on this Foundation alone, more *Aged, Infirm,* and *reduc'd Persons* (besides *Orphans,* and all real Objects of Charity) might be supported, than in all the Hospitals belonging to this City and its Liberties.

However, other Diversions may be design'd only to affect the Ear or Eye; those of the Stage speak to the Mind, in order to improve us; but such is the Depravity of human Nature, that if we are not pleas'd, we will not be instructed; therefore all the additional Ornaments to *Stage - Entertainments* are highly necessary to entice us in, else we should never sit out a tedious Lecture of Morality. This the Antients prudently considered, and artfully threw in those agreeable, amazing
zing

zing Spectacles, and Decorations of all Kinds, which were Parts of their CHORUS; thus luring them cunningly into a Reformation of Manners.

THEY were sensible, that the Majority of all Audiences would never appear in a THEATRE, were they not more charm'd with the Beauty of the SCENES, the Surprize of the MACHINE-RY, the Magnificence of the HABITS, and Variety of MUSICK and DANCING, than with the fine Language, the noble Sentiments, the Precepts, and divine Lessons contain'd in a TRAGEDY or COMEDY: Therefore the Poets, the Inventors, and the Magistrates, the Encouragers of the CHORUS, spar'd no Labour nor Expence to draw Numbers of People of all Ranks to their PLAYS, spite of themselves: For knowing that the Generality of Mankind are, naturally speaking, in a State of Infancy the greatest Part of their Lives; they were oblig'd to perswade them to swallow the black Potion of *Instruction*, by promising the Sugar-Plumb of *Delight*.

I have now, as briefly as possible, trac'd every Foot-step of a CHORUS, in its Rise, Progress and Declension with the Antients, and shewn how far the Moderns are mistaken in their Notions of that Part of a *Stage-Entertainment*, explain'd its infinite Use and Beauty, and propos'd the most reasonable Method of attaining to it with the most moderate Expence: But there still remains to be spoken to, a CHORUS altogether of *British* Growth, a genuine Plant of this Isle: I mean a CONSORT of CAT-CALLS; which so often makes a vast *Eclat* in our THEATRES.

I confess, this Affair does not properly belong to the STAGE, the usual Station of a CHORUS in all former Ages; nor does the Performance of it in the leaſt depend upon the Characters of any *Drama* repreſented, or any Perſon belonging to it, as an additional *Actor, Singer* or *Dancer*; but wholly regards the Behaviour of the Audience, when they have a Fancy to turn Performers inſtead of Spectators: Yet, as it alway makes its Appearance by way of a full C H O R U S, I thought it could no where be introduc'd with that Juſtice, as in this E S S A Y ; therefore chooſe to tack this Domeſtick Invention to its Tail.

I fear, that in my hiſtorical Enquiries after the Origine of this polite Inſtrument, I ſhall have no Foundation to build upon, but Conjecture; ſo my Readers muſt be ſatisfied with Gueſs-Work. However, I ſhall omit nothing in the Way of Reading, or Intelligence from other Hands, that can give me any Light into its Antiquity or Merit.

By its Etymology, it ſhould be of *Britiſh* Extraction; for I have turn'd over a Thouſand Volumes of *French* Criticks, and *Low-Dutch* Commentators; yet met with no ſingle Hint that touch'd upon its Invention or Uſe; ſo loſt my Time and Labour.

I was mightily puzzel'd to find out ſomething in Antiquity, upon which I could ground the moſt trifling Surmiſe relating to its Birth; but my Search made me no wiſer: Nor was there any thing anſwer'd in the leaſt to my Purpoſe; excepting the C H O R U S *of Frogs* in a Comedy of *Ariſtophanes*, before-mention'd; from whence I imagine, ſome of our modern Criticks (whoſe only Merit lies in a blind Admiration of the Antients) ſtole the Conceit, and fix'd this Inſtrument upon a Level with that M U S I C K: And as the Buſineſs of the O L D C H O R U S was to ask Queſtions of, or make Reſponſes to, any Perſon of the *Drama, ma,* during the Reprefentation; or jointly, by SINGING and DANCING, to make the Intervals of the Acts: So I have perceiv'd, that the Performers on CAT-CALLS, are employ'd fingly in the Time of Action, or in a Body betwixt the Acts; the Obfervation of which Rule looks with an Eye towards the CHORUS of the Antients, in the Inftitution of theirs.

UPON mature Confideration, the Criticks, for feveral weighty Reafons, muft have been the Inventors of this Inftrument; either as a Signal to gather their Forces together, when difpers'd about the Houfe; or when to fall on, and when to make an orderly Retreat; it has exactly the fame Compafs of Notes with a Hunting-horn; and is us'd for much the fame Purpofe, either to throw a Pack on, or call them from their Prey: And fome Mafters, who have carefully ftudy'd Compofition on the CAT-CALL, will immediately tell you the Fate of every PLAY or OPERA, where its Sounds are heard: They diftinguifh with the greateft Eafe, whether the poor Hare of a *Poet* or *Compofer,* is only to be merrily run down, by way of pure Diverfion; or kill'd outright, for the Benefit of the critical Kennel.

N. B. *I am now practifing very hard, to qualify me for a Judge in this Performance.*

I am enclinable to think, that the *Criticks* rather hope to intimidate the Poets by this Noife; as the ftrongeft Lungs have often the beft of an Argument, by filencing an Opponent: 'Tis certain a CAT-CALL frequently has this Effect upon the Poets to a wonderful Degree, though generally very bold Rogues; which may proceed from fome fecret Antipathy in Nature, not yet accounted for by Philofophers; as the Crowing of a Cock frightens a Lion: Perhaps POETRY

infpires

infpires her Difciples with an Averfion to a *Cat*;
the folemn Demurenefs of one not being agreeable to the Wit and Life of the other: So the
Criticks fight cunning, like the Gentleman who,
in a Duel, drove his Antagonift out of the Field,
by popping a Kitten in his Face, whenever he
came near him; knowing he could not ftand the
Sight of that Creature.

IF thofe profound Naturalifts, the Gentlemen
of the R——l S——y, can fmell out any thing in
the wonderful Antipathies of contrary Qualities,
which will in the leaft countenance this Affertion of mine, we may be very pofitive, that the
Criticks, in their Searches into Myfteries, had before difcover'd the *Arcanum*, and borrow'd the
Hint of a CAT-CALL, from the nightly Sere-
nades of thofe Love-fick Creatures upon the
Tops of Houfes: And, if we were nicely to
make our Remarks upon the Life and Converfation of feveral young Noblemen and Gentlemen, who are particularly fond of that Inftrument, we fhould difcover, that they are much
given to Catterwauling.

A very ingenious, but whimfical *Virtuofo* of
my Acquaintance, ftrenuoufly avows, and infifts
upon it, That the CAT-CALL is one of the moft
antient Inftruments we read of. Some People
may urge, That what he advances is at beft but
a witty Suppofition; but I'm of Opinion, that
he has both an hiftorical and poetical Foundation to ground his Argument on; and, if it is
not abfolutely Matter of Fact, I'm convinc'd,
that it is a very pretty and juft Prefumption. His
Manner of making it appear runs thus--- He fays,
" The CAT-CALL was the Inftrument play'd
" on by *Pan*, in his Contention with *Apollo*, for
" the Prize in the Art of MUSICK. *Ovid* very

N " properly

" properly calls it the fhrill Pipe. *Midas* being
" conftituted Umpire in this Caufe, very wifely
" gave the Palm to *Pan*'s harfh Notes; but be-
" ing juftly honour'd with Affes Ears, for his
" rafh and ignorant Judgment, he ever after
" made ufe of that Pipe to filence all Harmony;
" then left it as a Legacy to his lawful Succef-
" fors of the Family of the *Long-Ears* (*alias Cri-*
" *ticks*) who, upon all Occafions, make ufe of
" it to demolifh P O E T R Y and M U S I C K; of
" both which Arts, *Apollo* is Patron."

I can't tell whether the *Criticks* will allow this
to be found Doctrine; but they'll find many Te-
nets worfe fupported in *Thomas Aquinas*.

I fhall quote out of *Gefner*, in his Hiftory of
four-footed Beafts, one Paffage, which bears fome
fmall Refemblance to the Affair in Hand. He
gives a very remarkable Account of two Creatures in *Ethiopia*, who are at continual Enmity;
the firft participates of the Natures of our Hares
and Foxes, being as timerous as one, and witty
as the other, without its Malice, by reafon of a
particular good Nature inherent to this Creature, and a Difpofition to feveral little entertaining Gambols: It is a Favourite with, and protected by all the Beafts, but that which is its
profefs'd Foe; which, by the Defcription, I take
to be a Sort of wild Cat, or Cat-a-mountain; a
Species of fmall Tygers. This lives in a continued Purfuit of the other; and wherever it meets
them, they are devour'd as lawful Prey, unlefs
refcued by fome of the other Beafts. If this
makes nothing to my Purpofe, in relation to
the Cat-call; yet it exactly defcribes the Nature
and Behaviour of *Poets* and *Criticks*.

T H I S is all I could gather to fatisfy my Readers,
as to the Invention of this Mufical Machine. As
to

to its proper Ufe and Application, 'tis too well known, to be enlarg'd on here; but I intend to publifh in a little Time, by Subfcription, a very large Folio, with all the Rules neceffary to make a compleat Performer on this Inftrument; with Directions how, when, where, and why any Gentleman fhould play on it fingle, or in Concert; with a juft Scale of Notes, and Variety of Airs in all the Keys, and adapted to all Occafions, for the Ufe of thofe who do not compofe *Extempore.*

HAVING in this ESSAY impartially ftated the Effence, Ufe, and Lofs of a CHORUS, I leave every Man to make what Reflections, and draw what Inferences he thinks moft pertinent to the Subject. I only beg Leave to conclude with my humble Opinion, that a CHORUS is allowable in a *Comedy,* proper in a *Tragedy,* and neceffary in an OPERA.

ESSAY

E S S A Y V.

OF AUDIENCES;

The several Orders of SPECTA-
TORS *that form an* ENGLISH
AUDIENCE. *Their Behaviour
in the* THEATRES *consider'd.
Their Manner of judging, in Pub-
lick and Private, set in a true
Light: With a particular Ac-
count of the whole Race of* CRI-
TICKS.

N this ESSAY, I propose speaking to that Part of the second, in
which the Decay of our *Dramatick Poetry* was imputed to the bad
Taste, and little Encouragement
of the Town for that Art. This
Point, and several others as ma-
terial, I reduce to one general Head, *An Audience;* which may be justly look'd upon as the

Primum

Primum Mobile of all Diverſions; by whoſe Ge-
neroſity they are ſupported, and by whoſe Smiles,
or Frowns, they flouriſh or languiſh.

My Panegyricks ſhall be very modeſt, and my
Cenſures very gentle, as to the Beauties or Blemiſhes in the Behaviour of this formidable and
numerous Body: I ſhall ſet the Glaſs of Truth full
before them, by which their Errors will readily
reflect upon themſelves, and from whence they
may draw ſome natural Inferences, the eaſier to
reform them: And, in order to beſpeak the Favour of my courteous Readers (who, I ſuppoſe,
will generally prove the Majority of an AUDI-
ENCE at *Opera*, or *Play-Houſe*) I declare, with
the Air of a free-born *Britiſh* Subject, that as it
is Truth I chooſe for my Guide, to lead me ſtea-
dily through this Labyrinth of Errors, I am uncon-
cern'd whether they treat me as a too ſevere Sa-
tyriſt, a ſcandalous Lampooner, or Inſipid Tri-
fler, being alike inſenſible to the Threats or Fa-
vours of the *Many*, ſo they do me Juſtice, and
pay for my Book before they read it.

Tho' the fundamental Matters of an OPERA
or PLAY, as to the Buſineſs of the Stage, are
very different, and as ſuch have been ſeparately
conſider'd, yet I ſhall not make uſe of that Method in relation to their SPECTATORS; the
Behaviour of an Audience at either, being much
upon the ſame Footing, and equally notorious;
ſo I ſhall jumble them together, thro' every Article of this ESSAY, in order to ſave my Reader ſome Time, and my ſelf ſome Paper.

But though I throw the two AUDIENCES
into the ſame Point of View, as to the Regulation, of my approving or cenſuring their Conduct, yet I muſt beg my Readers to take one
eſſential Difference along with them, and cloſely

obſerve

obferve it whenever they are mention'd. The
Inhabitants of the Boxes at the *Play-Houfe*, make
up Pit and Box at the *Opera*. The Pit at the *Play-
Houfe* is the firft Gallery in the *Opera*. The firft
Gallery and middle Part of the upper Gallery in
the *Play-Houfe*, have no Reprefentatives in the
Opera; there are but few of that Country who
care to part with a Crown for a Song. As for
the Gentry at each End of the Upper Gallery in
the *Play-Houfe*, they enjoy that entire Region to
themfelves at the *Opera*, with Space to range,
and Liberty to make as much Noife as they pleafe ;
which grieves me not a little, nor fhall I part
with them unreprimanded: I wifh my Pen, at
every Stroke, was a Cat-of-nine-tails for their
Sakes, and our own, that their Manners might
be mended, and our Diverfions not interrupted;
but I fhall talk with them by and by, when I
have finifh'd with their Mafters.

FIRST, then, I fhall ftrive to bring the feveral
Degrees that compofe a regular AUDIENCE,
to bear upon the Parallel with the four principal Orders of Architecture. Under the *Dorick*
and *Ionick*, I comprehend the Pit and firft Galleries, I looking upon them as the moft plain,
folid and fubftantial Bafis of an AUDIENCE,
intermix'd with fome People polite, and of good
Fafhion, who refemble the *Ionick :* Then the *Dorick*, allowing of fome Affes or Goats Heads in
the Cornifh, by way of Ornament, that refers to
the critical Part of that Order; the Boxes being
fome Steps higher, and altogether form'd in a
genteeler and more elegant Tafte than the former, I fix them as my *Corinthian*, that Order
being very beautiful, and defign'd much for Shew:
Then the Upper Galleries anfwer exactly to the
Compofite , and that Order differing from the
Corinthian

Corinthian chiefly in the Capitol, I judge it thus: That Part which is the modefteft, I borrow from the *Ionick* in the Pit; the other is entirely *Corinthian*, either as they belong to that Order in the Boxes, or as their Capitols are generally caft in that Brafs.

THE Pit then in the *Play-Houfes*, and firft Gallery in the *Opera*, are fupported either by fome of our moft fubftantial, plain, fober Tradefmen, their Wives and Children, in the *Dorick* Stile; or by Officers of the Army, Members of Parliament, and Gentlemen of good Character and plentiful Fortunes, in the *Ionick*; with a few Criticks, who are divided betwixt the two.

I have not much to fay to the Quality from *Cheapfide*, *Ludgate - Hill*, *Covent - Garden*, or the *Strand*, as to their erring in Point of Judgment; but a great deal as to their Behaviour in the THEATRES. They are generally fo very impatient to gain the Centre of the Pit, or the firft Row of the Gallery, that they hurry from Dinner with Spoufe under one Arm, and the Remnants of an unfinifh'd Meal, in a colour'd Handkerchief, under the other. As the Plot of the *Play* begins to thicken, their Appetites grow fharp, having not been fufficiently ftuffed at Noon; then their greateft Concern is, how they may be fatisfied with Decency and Oeconomy, that no curious Neighbour may difcover their Treafure, and long for a Morfel. Thus reftrain'd by the orderly Management of their portable Larder, it is impoffible for them to have any Regard to the Bufinefs of the STAGE; but by that Time the Poet begins to unravel his Defign by an *Artful Cataftrophe*, which ftrikes an attentive Silence upon the fenfible Part of the AUDIENCE, their natural Cloak-Bags are fill'd for a Journey; they
ftretch,

ftretch, and cry —— *Lord !* —— *when will thæfe*
tirefome People have done ? —— *I wiſh we had a*
Dance, and were a-bed.

I have had the ill Fortune to ſit three Hours
in ſuch an elegant Neighbourhood often, and
have ſeen the manly Concern due to the Weak-
neſs of human Nature in *Mark Anthony*'s Fall,
neglected for the Leg of a cold Pullet, or a *Na-*
ples Biſket; and *Monimia*'s Diſtreſs (which ſhould
draw Tears from every generous, or virtuous Eye)
drowned in a Glaſs of Sack; as if the Diverſion
or Inſtruction of a P L A Y was only to be taken
in at the Mouth, while the Eyes, Ears or Soul,
were entirely foreign to the Affair in hand; or
as if the *Play-Houſe* was rather a Twelve-penny
Ordinary, than the nobleſt Entertainment which
Nature, in conjunction with Art, can produce.

T H E young Plants of this Tribe (who hire
their Swords at ſome neighbouring Cutler's, in
order to appear as Gentlemen there) are too apt
to imitate the exterior Signs of a ſmart, rakiſh
Gentility; and affect Airs wholly appropriated to
the other End of the Town: They take Ill Manners to be Senſe; Rudeneſs, an eaſy Politeneſs;
and that nothing is ſo faſhionable as to be noiſy :
But I caution them for the future, to leave off
talking Bawdy to the Orange-Women, romping
over People's Backs from Seat to Seat, and ſhewing the Keenneſs or Pleaſantry of their Wit,
by making the Women that ſit next them *bluſh.*

T H E female Part of this Band are generally
of the Family of the Notables, and think it highly incumbent on them, whenever they go abroad,
to ſhew themſelves as ſtirring as in their own
Kitchen, and as loud as in their own Bed, left
they ſhould forfeit the Character of a clever Houſe-
wife. They are ſo very courteous, they get immediately

mediately acquainted with you, without Ceremony offer you a Pippin half roasted with the Warmth of a large Hip, and at once communicate to you the Secrets of the whole Family. In Civility you are oblig'd to listen to *Susan's Intrigue with their 'Prentice* Tom ; *how* Ralph, *their eldest Son, was a hopeful Boy as ever the Sun shone on, only he had the Rickets ; and how poor* Molly *look'd wonderous pale, and eat every earthly thing.* This Alarum ceases not but with the P L A Y ; you must bear it, and lose the innocent Griefs of poor *Desdemona,* in the tedious Tale of *Dame such - a - one's tenth Child's breeding its Teeth ;* and be deprived of the agreeably anxious Expectation depending upon the Discovery of *Othello's* Handkerchief, for the dirty History of an unfortunate *Double-Clout.* I can use no other Reprimand to their Sex, but to entreat them, for the future, to gossip it at Home, or a Neighbour's House, and not disturb all who sit near them, at any publick Diversion, by the Recital of their private Affairs. By coming to a P L A Y, they lose their Money, and turn common Nusances : If they do it in order to see and be seen, that laudable Curiosity should be confin'd to their going to Church.

T H E second Division of these two Orders, consists of Gentlemen of sober Behaviour, good Nature, and plentiful Fortunes ; mix'd with others in handsome Posts, Civil and Military. To these Gentlemen I can scarcely make an Objection, either in Point of Judgment, or Behaviour. Were they alone to sit as Umpires on any Performance, design'd as a publick Amusement, the Author might hope for Applause, proceeding from good Sense, and Criticism from good Nature ; their Fortunes, Education and Generosity, set them above judging with Envy, Ignorance, or ill Manners :

ners: If there is a Shadow of a Fault, it is in their cenfuring too favourably fome Things they know are not perfectly right.

As to their Behaviour in the *Play-houfe*, it is altogether made up of Decency and good Humour; they are fo unwilling to offend, that they never fhew their Difpleafure by the leaft Noife; unlefs fome of the younger Sort, who are but juft out of Leading-ftrings, get into Wit's Corner, or make an Elopement into the Side-Boxes: They having a natural Tendency to a Rattle, fometimes are fond of Playing upon that Inftrument, which fhould never be feen but in the Hands of a Pedant, or Fool.

THE poor Criticks, who are partly compos'd of thefe two Orders, muft fatisfy their Ignorance and Spleen; they fpunge upon their Bellies for half a Crown; and we muft allow them, in Return, to fhew their ill Nature to the Authors of new Plays, and Actors of old; they come prepar'd to find Fault, and muft be indulg'd, or they could not fleep. This Favour I muft beg of them, that when they are out of Humour at any *Entertainment* (which always happens, when they are not the Authors) that their Cenfure may be as quiet as their Applaufe, which is always exprefs'd in Silence; and not to hinder thofe who would be diverted, becaufe they are refolv'd to be difpleas'd. It is not neceffary to take any farther Notice of them, till I come to the Rife, Progrefs, and prefent State of *Criticifm*.

By a gentle Afcent, I foon arrive at the Station of the *Corinthian* Order, which includes the Pit and Boxes at the OPERA, and Front and Side-boxes at the *Play-houfes*, with fome inconfiderable Stragglers behind the Scenes, and the

Flying-

Flying-fquadron, who fcorn to be fettled any where.

We look upon the Natives of this Region, as fo many fmall Divinities; the Ladies, from the Luftre of their Jewels, and the Power of their Eyes; the Men, from the Fame of their Places, Titles and Fortunes. Honour therefore calls upon them, to behave and judge in that polite, fedate Manner, that every Look, or Word of theirs, may be an infallible Rule for other Parts of the AUDIENCE to walk by: But the Regularity of their Conduct is fo little anfwerable to this Maxim, that if their Behaviour is not altogether fo loudly offenfive, as what we fuffer from thofe of a meaner Rank, yet they are, to the Full, as regardlefs of the Bufinefs of the Stage.

DURING the Time of the Reprefentation, the Ladies are fo employ'd in finding out all their Acquaintance, Male and Female, left a Bow, or Curtfy fhould efcape them; criticifing on Fafhions in Drefs, whifpering crofs the Benches, with fignificant Nods, and Hints of Civil Scandal of this, and that, and t'other Body;—— they fcarcely know whether they are at OPERA or PLAY.

WHILE the Belles are ogling the Beaus, and the Beaus admiring themfelves, the Affairs of real Moment (which fhould have feduc'd them there) are entirely neglected.

THE Gentlemen are fo taken up with their own Intrigues, or watching thofe of their Neighbours, that they never mind them on the Stage. A fmall Sketch of fmutty Converfation is preferable with them to any Scene in the *Plain-Dealer*, tho' but with an Orange Wench: Nor is there one of them, but would rather boaft a Smile
from

from the reigning Toaft, than liften to the mourn-
ing *Belvidera.*

THE Ladies tattle too much to one another
to heed *Comedy*, it is too much of a-piece with
their daily Life; then they are fo bufy in fecur-
ing an Old Lover, or gaining a New, that all
their Attention is feiz'd, before it can reach the
Stage. Domeftick Griefs from unlucky Cards
and Dice, give fuch real Pangs to other Hearts,
that poor *Jaffeir* mounts the Scaffold unregarded; for what are *Cleopatra*'s Misfortunes to an
ill Run at *Quadrille*, or *Baffet!* tho' all the World
was loft for Love.

IF by fome unavoidable Incidents in the Fable of PLAY or OPERA, a *Stage-Entertainment*
is lengthened with a few Additional Speeches or
Airs, a quarter of an Hour beyond the ufual
Time — they ftretch, —— they yawn,—— they
die! Lard! —— we can be fatisfied at an eafier
Rate; thefe horrid Poets and Actors think one
never has enough for ones Money! —— When
will the Curtain drop! —— And what pray may
occafion this ftrange Uneafinefs! —— An affembly at my Lady *Hazard*'s —— a Drawing-room-
Night—a new Gown to be fhewn there; —— or
an Appointment at Mrs. * * * *or at Madam * *
* * * or at my Lady * * * * * *. And it is
certain, that could they with Decency decamp,
as foon as the Ceremonies of being feen, point-
ed at, and bow'd to, were finifhed, they would,
without Hefitation, quit the Houfe before the End
of the fhorteft firft Act.

UPON fumming up the Evidence, in the Cafe
of the Conduct of the Boxes in this Particular,
and from my own private Remarks, I vow, I
think they are altogether as heedlefs of a PLAY,

or

or OPERA, as a Sermon;——which is a burning Shame!

I have taken more Notice of the Behaviour of the fair Sex in this Place, than the Men; becaufe I fhall fpeak to the latter in other Terms, when Judges and Criticks come in Form before me.

I cannot pafs over in Silence, a Species of Animals belonging to this Order, whom I look upon as the *Hermaphrodites* of the Theatre; being neither Auditors nor Actors perfectly, and imperfectly both; I mean thofe Gentlemen who pafs their Evenings behind the Scenes, and who are fo bufy in neglecting the *Entertainment,* that they obftruct the View of the AUDIENCE in the juft Difcernment of the Reprefentation; and are a prodigious Hindrance to the Actors, in the Exactnefs of the Performance; the Beauty of which often depends upon a fmall Nicety.

I confefs my felf at a Lofs, when I would account for the Reafons, which induce Gentlemen thus to lofe their Money and Time; unlefs they think that their Complexions or Cloaths may appear to the beft Advantage, by the Glare of a Stage Light; and that the Spectators cannot obferve a bad Face, aukward Body, or crooked Leg, while their Eyes are dazzled with the Luftre of Powder, Brocade and Embroidery: Whatever are their Motives, I wifh they would confine themfelves to the Green Room, or the Actreffes Shifts, and not occafion fo many Confufions, by obftructing proper Enters and Exits; when Tupees and Feathers make up part of a *Turkifh* Emperour's Train; and a fring'd Waftcoat or clock'd Stockings, are taken for the Drefs of a *Grecian* or *Roman* Heroe.

THIS is not to be underftood, as any Reflection upon that Part of an AUDIENCE, who

O   are

are cramm'd behind the Scenes of a Benefit-Night: The Stage being for that Time for the Use of the House, and no body coming with a Design to be amus'd, there can be no Offence.

As I labour in climbing the steep Hill of *Parnassus*, I must call in at the first Gallery in the *Play-house*, to which nothing in the *Opera-house* answers: They are partly of the *Dorick* Order, or rather one more simple and heavy; so we'll imagine them the *Tuscan* in a wrong Scituation.

As to Judgment, they seldom err, where pure Nature is the Test; if they are mistaken in Point of Art, it is thro' Ignorance; they judge according to their Knowledge, and are Strangers to Partiality or Prejudice; unless some malicious Wits take Shelter amongst them, in order to hiss *Incog* in some obscure Corner; or that some Party-stroke hits pat with, or opposes their political Principles. They generally come with an Intent to see the PLAY, and of consequence laugh heartily, and cry plentifully, as tickel'd by *Comedy*, or affected by *Tragedy*; if they are displeas'd, they shew more Modesty and good Nature than most other Parts of the House.

THEIR Errors in Behaviour are much of the same Kind with those of their *Dorick* Relations in the Pit; and if they cannot arrive at that Height of Luxury, to swallow Sweetmeats and *Canary*; their Pockets are lin'd with bad Fruit; and by the time their Wives and Daughters have devour'd mellow Apples, and suck'd green Oranges; the Ladies begin to be grip'd, and are oblig'd to move off, for Air and Ease.

I must caution them in the two following Particulars: If they find it necessary to whet their Judgment, or set the Teeth of their Understanding on Edge, by dealing in such Trash; that

they

they would not be fo liberal of their Fragments
of Peel and Core to the Stage and Pit: Or that
their lovely Females would not fo often miftake
the various colour'd Inhabitants of the Boxes for
Beds of Tulips, and water them fo plentifully,
perhaps in a wrong Seafon; but reftrain from
every Thing liquid, that warm Showers may not
defcend.

I have at laft, with much Difficulty, foar'd to
the higheft Region in the Sphere of Wit and Politenefs; and muft, according to promife, talk a
little to the Gentlemen of the Regiment of the
Rain-bow, who reign here in their Altitudes; thus,
like other Architects, conclude with the Roof of
the Houfe.

THEY are introduc'd here as that Part of the
Compofite Capital, which is borrow'd from the
Corinthian, and take up the whole Upper-Gallery
at the OPERA, and the two Ends at the *Play-
Houfe*. The whole Town (or at leaft the Lovers
of POETRY and MUSICK) are indebted to them
many fevere Reprimands, for their frequent Dif-
orders at both Places; I wifh heartily, that my
Power could carry my Refentment farther, that
they might be thoroughly fenfible of my being
in Earneft; but being deny'd that Authority, I
muft be content to have a Lafh at them in my
Way.

As Liberty and Property are the boafted Priviledges, nay, the very Life and Soul of an *Eng-
lifhman*; fo the moft valuable Bleffings may be
abus'd, and often apply'd to a very wrong Purpofe: Nor is this in any Particular more notorious, than as made manifeft in the Cafe now before us.

OUR Servants (becaufe not Slaves) are fuffer'd to difturb at Will our politeft Amufements:

O 2   At

At an immenſe Sum we ſupport theſe *Entertainments,* and they are allow'd *gratis* to put the Negative upon our hearing them : The Bread they eat, the Cloaths they wear are ours; yet, with one in their Belly, and the other on their Back, their Rudeneſs dare ſtand betwixt Us and our Pleaſures; and the meaneſt Footman unpuniſh'd, fly in the Face of the whole Court.

'Tis well I write this, where the Truth from fatal Experience cannot be call'd in Queſtion; for no ſuch Liberties or Inſolencies would be tolerated in any Part of the Globe, but *Great Britain.*

THEY can bring no Plea for this Priviledge, but Preſcription, or being at Hand, if wanted. As to the firſt, it is never too late to alter a bad Cuſtom, eſpecially when it does not anſwer the End propos'd. As to the ſecond, proper Methods may be found out to keep them within Call, than their being mounted up three-pair of Stairs; could they remain quiet, or improve there, the Impoſition might be wink'd at; but as their Delight is to be noiſy, let ſome large Place be fitted up near each THEATRE, where in the Bear-garden Stile, they may amuſe one another.

I own, moſt of thoſe Errors in Judgment charg'd upon that Part of the AUDIENCE, which unfortunately takes up its Station below Stairs, may be occaſion'd by the Diſtractions rais'd by thoſe noiſy Fellows: For, who can judge ſedately of POETRY or MUSICK in *Bedlam* or a *Brothel?* Or, what is worſe, in THEATRES, with Galleries ſet aſide for Livery Servants to Bully and Swear in?

THIS Part of my ESSAY, is not deſign'd for their Peruſal, but their Maſters; who might
with

with Eafe redrefs thofe Grievances, if once heartily and unanimoufly join'd: Tho' no fingle Perfon could well negotiate an Affair of fuch Confequence, with fo large, and fo unruly a Body; yet, take them feparately, every Man is Mafter of his own Family, and has Law, Juftice, and the Government on his Side.

If there be any Neceffity refulting from fome particular Merit, that fuch Fellows fhould be indulg'd in Liberties unbecoming their Station; the good-natur'd Condefcenfion would be more properly fhewn in Private; where their impertinent Follies can incommode no body, but thofe who think themfelves oblig'd to bear them. If this gentle Ufage gains not upon their brutal Tempers; there are Means to tame the wildeft Beafts: If their Mafters rich Liveries but ferve to warm them into ill Manners, and blow them up with Pride; ftrip them, and put them, on for three Months, a *Bridewell* Jacket, only lac'd with plain Black and Blew, but laid on pretty thick, and in a little time you'll find a ftrange Alteration.

I do not pretend to prefcribe here any Rules for a *Domeftick* Regulation; every Man is the propereft Judge of what is right or wrong in his own Family. But, were I to propofe a Reformation of fo publick an Evil as we now complain of, it fhould be in the Terms of a great Critick, who prefented to Cardinal *Richlieu* a Plan for eftablifhing the Grandeur, Ufe and Decency of the *French* THEATRE —— *and the King fhall forbid all Pages or Footmen to enter the* THEATRES *upon pain of Death.*

THE canvaffing thus the various Miftakes in Behaviour, which infect the feveral Degrees of an AUDIENCE; makes me reflect, with Indignation,

tion, upon the wide Difference betwixt the *Antients* and us on that Head. No Prince there was too great, no Philosopher too wife, nor no Mechanick too ignorant, to be pleas'd and inftructed by the Stage; they confider'd what they had in View, in coming there, and behav'd up to that Confideration; the moft rigid Stoick would confefs an Emotion of Pleafure from what was beautiful; and the loweft of the People demean with the Gravity of an old Senator. Their Silence and Attention were fo remarkable, that a *Grecian* or *Roman* A U D I E N C E appear'd rather an Affembly of Nobles, met in Confultation about the weightieft Affairs, than a promifcuous Multitude of all Ranks, come there to amufe themfelves; no rude Clamour fhock'd the liftning Ear; all was quiet, except the decent Expreffion of thofe Paffions the *Drama* was defign'd to move; and they were to the Purpofe, but never loud. The Contraft betwixt that Age and ours, is fo ftrong, it needs no Illuftration to add to the Colouring.

I cannot avoid taking Notice here of the Ignorance, and mifapply'd Zeal of fome late Divines, who have fo ftrenuoufly labour'd for a Reformation, or rather Demolition, of the Stage. They have all along unhappily chofe the wrong Side of the Queftion; and when they arraign'd our Poets of encouraging Impiety, Immorality, Abufe of the Clergy, Difrefpect to our Superiors, *&c.* they fhould rather have tofs'd their Wit and Learning into t'other Scale, and catechiz'd their Flock, who follow'd P L A Y S fo eagerly, yet fo blindly, that every Trifle took them off from attending diligently to that fage Inftruction, thofe moral Precepts, that Love to Virtue, and Hatred to Vice, which every Man

must

muſt find in moſt *Entertainments* of the THE-
ATRE.

HAVING lightly touch'd every Particular in
the Behaviour of an AUDIENCE, which oc-
curr'd to me; the Affair of CRITICISM in general
comes next before me. I run ſo haſtily thro'
the different Ranks that fill a crowded Houſe,
and the Majority of them are ſo fully employ'd
otherways than in heeding the *Entertainment,*
that neither they, nor I were at leiſure to criticiſe, till we got out of Doors. The Chocolate
and Coffee-houſes, the Drawing-rooms, the Aſ-
ſemblies, the Toilets and the Tea-tables are the
Judgment-Seats, where POETRY and MUSICK
are try'd; nor is it improper to rank them under the Title of an AUDIENCE, ſince we are
to ſuppoſe, they who ſit as Judges there, have
been preſent at every Repreſentation; and thoroughly examin'd every Particular upon the Spot,
before they make their Opinions publick.

I comprehend then, under two general Heads,
all Spectators of *Stage Entertainments*; who pretending to cenſure or commend any Piece, may
be call'd *Judges* or *Criticks*. The firſt Order
takes in the whole World; for every body upon
Earth will judge, and if they are not allow'd the
Liberty, they will take it. Their Opinions are
as various as their Faces, or Humours; as uncertain as the Wind, and as ill founded as common Fame; they ſpeak without thinking, and
think without reaſoning. The ſecond is, that
ſelected Part of the Whole, who look upon
themſelves, as the only People capable of
that Province; they boaſt themſelves to be the
genuine Off-ſpring of *Ariſtotle,* or the greateſt
Men of Antiquity: They talk of nothing but
poetick Laws, which muſt not be infring'd, **and**
Rules

Rules of Art, to guide blind Nature, and keep within juſt Bounds the Extravagancies of a great Genius. They erect a formal Tribunal, or Court of Inquiſition, before whoſe Bar all Writers muſt appear; Nature and Art preſide; the Criticks are the Accuſers; and the antient Freeholders of *Parnaſſus* the lawful Jury.

THUS far all goes well. Now let us by their Practice form a juſt Idea of their Right and Skill in judging and criticiſing.

THE Method of judging, now moſt in Vogue, is hearing Sounds by other Ears, reliſhing Wit by other Underſtandings, and taking the Beauty of any thing in Perſpective from other Eyes than our own; tho' we have no Reaſon to think they enjoy any Senſe to greater Perfection than our ſelves. Tho' I would have the World in general to appear very diſcreet in the Matter of Judgment; yet I cannot approve of this ſlaviſh Complaiſance, to reſign the nobleſt Faculty of the Mind, to a mean Dependance upon a few faſhionable Head-pieces, who may chance to be the moſt ignorant of Men.

IF you offer to cenſure or applaud any thing in Contradiction to the Sentiments of ſuch and ſuch Perſons, —— you are immediately ſtopp'd ſhort —— *How Sir!* —— *do you conſider what you advance?* —— *My Lord* Drivler, *and Sir* Timothy Trifle *are entirely of another Opinion.* —— That may be, Sir; —— but I judge for my ſelf, as if they were not in being: —— *How ſhall we then fix upon what is excellent in* POETRY *or* MUSICK, *but from the general Voice of the* Beau-Monde? *and what thoſe Gentlemen determine, no other muſt contradict:* —— I am ſorry for it, Sir; I will not implicitly give into a general Character of any Performance; —— but if any
                                                              Man

Man gives a Reason : —— *Reason's a Fool ; there's no true Judgment in superior Sense ; Superiority of Numbers alone is infallible : Would you have me whipp'd round the Town for a cross-grain'd Puppy, because I think I'm in a right Scent, when the full Cry of the Pack is against me ?*

THUS a few eminent Ninnies may lead by the Nose the Judgment of half the Town ; and when once they have fix'd the Stamp of Merit upon any dull Work, every fashionable Body must come into it, or bravely dare to stem the Current of popular Opinion. I met once with a small Conversation-Piece at a Tea-Table, the rough Draught of which I'll present my Readers, it being drawn exactly in this neat Manner of judging, and will give a just Taste of the Whole.

Lady PLYANT, *and Beau* MODISH.

B. Mod. *I suppose, your Ladiship honour'd the new* OPERA *with your Presence.*

L. Ply. *Certainly, Mr. Modish, I never miss the first Night.*

B. Mod. *Was your Ladiship mightily pleas'd ?*

L. Ply.. *I cannot say —— but so so —— tolerable enough —— what I minded of the thing : But I shall not declare my self, till its Character is established by the Town.*

B. Mod. *Was it approv'd of by that* Audience ?

L. Ply. *Some strange Creatures seem'd in Raptures ; the Claps came from the Gallery ; but few Admirers below Stairs, and those, mighty ill dress'd.*

B. Mod. *Then it must be damn'd Stuff ! —— there's nothing sure, in Life, so impertinent, as Criticks of either Sex in* Long-Lane *or* Monmouth Street *Suits : They pretend to judge of Fashions in*
POETRY

POETRY *or* MUSICK, *and cannot put on their own Cloaths;* —— *Prepofterous!*

L. Ply. *Moft abfurd and ridiculous!*

B. Mod. *Dem-me, if I have not heard an aukward Thing in Pattins, and a draggle-tail'd Callicoe, cry, Fogh! at the prettieft and fofteft Air in the World; and a rough-hewn tramontane Fellow call the genteeleft fmootheft Verfe imaginable, infipid Nonfenfe, who never wore a Pair of clean Gloves in his Life, fhav'd but once a Month, and fcarce knew a Barber's Shop from a Chocolate-Houfe, or a Coach from a Wheel-barrow.*

L. Ply. *Intolerable! for my Part, I would no more applaud what is cenfur'd by the well-bred, well-drefs'd World, than walk to Court in a Ruff and Fardingale, repeating fome Lines of* Chaucer.

B. Mod. *I'm entirely of your Ladifhip's Mind; a Singularity of Judgment is mighty foolifh!* —— *one looks as filly as a Dog on the Stage, the whole Houfe hoots, and the poor Creature knows not which Way to run: I always give my Opinion fecure; I fortify it in Matters of that Moment with Ravelins of Embroidery, Counterfcarps of Brocade, and Baftions of Whale-bone; I call to my Alliance a large Stock of perfum'd Powder from my own Sex, and unerring Darts from the Eyes of the Fair; then, undaunted, I dare approve or damn.*

L. Ply. *You judge perfectly right, Mr.* Modifh; *you have mighty juft Notions of Things: I think there's a new* PLAY *to Night.*

B. Mod. *So the Bills fay* —— *I fhall go to view the Company, and I expect to fee Lady* Fanny Faddle *there; but I dare fwear the* PLAY *is fomething ftrangely horrid; for I have not heard it once mention'd by the Wits at* Button's, *or the Quality at* Will's. *As for the Author's Character or Family, they are as great Strangers to my Knowledge,*

ledge, as I defire his Poetry *may be to my Ears or Underftanding.*

So much I thought neceffary to plan out in the fafhionable Way of judging; though I could enlarge mightily upon this Head, and tell how * * * * * and where * * * * * the greateft * * * * and wifeft * * * * * do and fay * * * * * a thoufand * * * * * better or worfe * * * * and thus * * * * Fame.

ANOTHER very flagrant Practice us'd in the Art of Judging, is praifing or condemning thofe OPERAS and PLAYS we have been at; but never heard a Note of, nor know one Word of: As if being within the Walls of a THEATRE gave immediately the Faculty of Judgment; as the *Tripos* did the *Pythian* Prieftefs the Spirit of Prophecy.

SOME honeft Gentlemen prefs by Three o'Clock into the firft Row of the Gallery of the *Opera*, or back Seat of the Pit in the *Play-Houfe*; pleafed with their Succefs, and tir'd with expecting the Entertainment, they fall faft afleep before the Overture, or firft MUSICK, and fairly take out their Time and Money in Snoring, till rous'd by the CHORUS or DANCE at the End of the PLAY; they ftart up—— gape—— and cry *Damn'd Mufick!* —— a moft execrable PLAY!

OTHERS (to be fure People of Fafhion, and great Lovers of POETRY and MUSICK) lie the whole time perdue in a Corner with a fine Girl —— Snugg's the Word; and for any thing they know of what's tranfacted on the Stage, the *Theatre* might have been a *Conventicle*, and the *Entertainment* a plain *Tub-Sermon*, furbelow'd with fome fober Sighs and Groans.

YET from the THEATRES thefe penetrating Judges march to the Coffee, Chocolate, and

Eating-

Eating-Houfes; there pafs a learned Cenfure on every Air and Thought, while they prefide magifterially at a Table of Fools, where the Words of an abfolute Dictator make up for want of common Senfe.

A Family of this judicious Tribe, form Schemes of Judging (as an eminent Bard did his heroick Poems) in their Coaches; they drive from Houfe to Houfe; and, like a Shop-Keeper, only give you a fmall Pattern, by which you are to judge of the whole Piece.

THEY rife from Dinner about Seven, peep in at the *Hay-Market* for one Song; then get a Snap of the Third Act at *Drury-Lane,* and a Morfel of the Fourth at *Lincoln's-Inn-Fields*; then *Prefto-Pafs,* like a Juggler's Ball, they finifh with the *Opera:* You may ask their Sentiments of the *Three Entertainments,* they'll give them very freely and gravely; but you might be as well fatisfied of the Truth by their Coach-Horfes. Yet to the Drawing-Room or Affemblies they fly; there diffect, mathematically, every Scene; expatiate on the ill Tafte of fuch an Air, had not S——*no* exerted himfelf; and pity the Fate of two beautiful Songs murder'd by *C*——*oni*'s having a Cold, and *F*——*ina*'s being out of Tune; then tell you of the charmingeft PLAY, how fine, yet natural the Thoughts! —— how fublime, yet eafy the Diction! —— how furprizing and moral the Fable! —— Thus they decry or extol, as it pleafes the Weather they fhould be in, or out of Humour; thofe Barometers in POETRY and MUSICK, upon whofe Tempers being fair or foul, the Rife or Fall of Wit and Sounds depend.

I met one of thefe judging Gentlemen, after a New PLAY, at the Coffee-Houfe; fo ask'd Sir
William

3

William how he lik'd the new P L A Y? ─────
Extreamly well, Sir, a mighty full Houſe ────Did
Mrs. *Ol*───*ld's* Part become her? ────── *I ne-*
ver ſaw her look with better Red and White in my
Life─── *W*───*ks,* they ſay, appear'd to great Advantage in his── *Certainly, the prettieſt fancy'd*
Suit of Cloaths he ever wore! ──── Was not *M*───*lls*
prodigiouſly clapp'd? ──── *He ſpoke ſome fine things,*
and I muſt own, the Cock of his Hat and Dangle
of his Cane were not amiſs: But C──────r *is, ſure,*
the comicaleſt, impudenteſt Dog, that ever was born.

Bu t had I ask'd Sir *William,* whether it was
Tragedy or *Comedy* he ſaw, the Baronet would
have been mightily embaraſs'd for an Anſwer,
and thought it very abſurd to put ſuch a Queſtion to a fine Gentleman. Yet by ſuch Judges
muſt the beſt Compoſer's M u s i c k live or die,
though their Ears cannot diſtinguiſh betwixt *Ca-*
ſtruccio's Fiddle and *David's* Baſs.

U p o n this Foundation muſt the greateſt Poet's
Succeſs be rais'd; before ſuch Judges muſt he,
trembling, wait his Doom; and, as the Wind
blows, or according to the Time of the Moon,
meet with a Twenty Day's Run──── or, perhaps,
not a Third Night to recompence a Year's Labour, by paying his Waſhing and Garret-Rent.

C o u l d Time be recall'd, ſuch Judges would
let *Otway* ſtarve, and *Lee* run mad again; while
an *Italian* Singer, or *French* Dancer, would be
careſs'd, and loaded with Riches. Could the
Dead be rais'd, D R Y D E N would once more
be reduc'd by ſuch Judges, to the extreameſt Want,
and his immortal Genius vilify'd; while *Settle*
would grow fat, and *Shadwell* be crown'd with
Lawrel. Did Fate put it in our Power to reform
ſome paſt Errors, yet would ſuch Judges over
and over repeat their Follies; the ſecond Time

Damn

Damn *Phædra* and *Hippolitus*, and give the Author of *Ch---t Ch---t* a Thousand Pound. Such Judges would again drop the *Provok'd Husband* for the miserable low Scenes in the *B.---r's O----a*, and swallow greedily the wretched Dregs of M u s i c k, which have occasion'd this incredible Run ; while *Rhadamistus* and *Siroe* are perform'd to almost *Empty Benches:* An Infamy to the *English* Nation, not to be wip'd off by the greatest Length of Time, and a Crime against every thing polite, not to be expiated by the severest Repentance.

I f a Man is not qualify'd to be a Judge, what the D---l has he to do in medling with Affairs above his Capacity, and which concern him not ? Let him consider an Entertainment cooly, give his Opinion of it modestly, and in saying it pleases or displeases him, at least give a sort of a Reason for what he advances : A Judgment formed in this Light will be impartial, and proportioned to every Man's Abilities.

B u t it is not sufficient for some Mortals to be born Fools, to have their Friends and Acquaintance satisfied of the Truth, till by attempting Things out of their Sphere, the Fact is made publick, and, by Beat of Drum, and Sound of Trumpet, the Monster is shewn to the World.

A s no Law of the Land obliges these Gentlemen to commend what displeases them, so no Law of just Criticism obliges them to be pleas'd, whether they will or no ; but their Judgments in such Matters should never go beyond the Length of their own Noses, the Eyes of their Understanding seldom seeing farther.

I have at last, with much Difficulty, press'd through a Crowd of Judges, to the Seat of Judicature, where their elder Brothers, the Criticks, preside.

preſide. No Art is more frequently and publickly profeſs'd than *Criticiſm*, or leſs underſtood.
It was firſt deſign'd to illuſtrate the Works of
the POETS, by bringing forth hidden Beauties
to Light, and reſcuing ſome obſcure Paſſages
from falſe Interpretations; they ſounded loud the
modeſt Poet's Praiſe, and ſhielded his Name
from the Venom of the Cenſorious; ſuch as the
proper Criticks of this Age: How chang'd!---
how fallen now from what they originally were!

SOME People may wonder, that I ſhould thus
cenſure that Fraternity, of which I ſeem ambitious to be thought a Member. Did they keep
up to the genuine Behaviour of the antient Criticks, it would be my Pride to be eſteem'd the
leaſt meritorious of the Name; but as it is practis'd and underſtood at this Time of Day, I
diſclaim the Title. The true Critick is out of
the Queſtion; I only laſh the ignorant Pretender.

I look upon our preſent Race of Criticks to
be either formal, deep finiſh'd Blockheads by
Nature; or thoſe, who from tolerable natural
Parts, are made ſo by Art, wrong underſtood,
and Talents miſapply'd.

THE firſt ſtupid Set only criticiſe, becauſe
they will do ſo; they have juſt Senſe enough to
imagine, that Scandal is eaſier hit off than Praiſe;
and that Satyr will ſooner procure a Man the
Name of a Wit, than Panegyrick: Beſides, their
Tempers lean ſtrongly to Ill-Nature, while Envy
and Ignorance puſh them forward. Being incapable of penetrating into the Merit or Beauties of
any Work, they look at all with Jaundic'd Eyes,
and think them ſilly, becauſe they are ſo. Being
determin'd to find Fault, their critical Opinions
are quickly deliver'd, and, like Chain-ſhot, deſtroy all within their Reach: They examine no-

P 2   thing

thing Piece-meal; they judge by the Lump, and demolish all they judge.

THE Criticks of the second Class come into the World with tolerable natural Parts, and a Disposition for Instruction; but in Place of being improv'd by true Learning, they are sowr'd with Pedantry, and puff'd up with Pride. Thus their Judgments are thrown into a wrong Biass, while they have not a Stock of good Sense or good Nature to keep them steady, and ballance against opposite Imperfections. They immediately establish critical Rules, by which the World must be guided; the old Laws are refin'd upon, new made, and stated Limits fix'd, over which no enterprizing Genius must leap, tho' of ever so great Advantage to the Republick of Letters; if he does, the Fate attends him by which the *Roman* suffer'd, who conquer'd without Leave of the General. No POET is to be pardon'd, who in the least passes such Bounds, though in the God-like Heat of Fury and Inspiration; there's no Reprieve, once Sentence is given; nor are their Punishments made equal to the Crimes; but, like *Draco*, all Faults they punish with Death: Those *Turk* Criticks, who never give Quarter to a poor captive Bard.

THEY never take notice of the visible and real Beauties in any POET; that ridiculous Curiosity is banish'd the Province of their Enquiries; as if *Criticism* was invented only to spy Blemishes; and that it is a Crime in a Critick to be pleas'd. These ill-grounded, unjust Notions have so far infected their Judgments, and their Practice has had that Influence on the Generality of the World, that the Art and its Professors are become odious and shocking to all Men of common Sense. In short, the Name is now commonly

monly receiv'd, as a genteeler Conveyance to our Ears, of an ill-natur'd Blockhead.

THERE is another Branch of this flourishing Tree, who being bless'd with large Fortunes, and little Brains, think, like *Simon Magus*, that every thing is to be purchas'd with Money.

THESE Gentlemen, at the Expence of much Labour and Birch, are whipp'd at School into bad Translations, false *Latin* and dull Themes; from thence they run the Gantlope through all the pedantick Forms of an University-Education: There they grow familiar with the Title-Pages of antient and modern Authors, and will talk of *Aristotle, Longinus, Horace, Scaliger, Rapin, Bossu, Dacier*, as freely, as if bosom Acquaintance: Their Mouths are fill'd with the Fable, the Moral, Catastrophe, Unity, Probability, Poetick, Justice, true Sublime, Bombast, Simplicity, Magnificence, and all the critical Jargon, which is learn'd in a quarter of an Hour, and serves to talk of one's whole Life after.

WITH this Stock they set up as Overseers of *Parnassus*, and what then? ---- why then! ------ they criticise, and take Snuff --- and afterwards --- they take Snuff and criticise.

THESE Tinsel Criticks (who only shine with a false Glare of Learning, and whose Stings can but penetrate the Skin of the polite Arts) are very loud at the top Chocolate and Coffee-Houses, and teize Men of Sense to Death, with their Shew of Wit and false Reasoning. Yet I must confess, that of all bad Criticks, they are the best: For if a Poet is but communicative, submits his Works to their better Judgments, or begs a bad Copy of recommendatory Verses, he infallibly makes a Knot of them his best Friends: But if a Man of Merit neglects such nauseous Flattery, or scorns

P 3   such

such infamous Slavery, he's proclaimed an insig-
nificant, stupid Dog, to all Intents and Purposes.

ANOTHER large Tribe (the Spawn of the
last nam'd) fix the Standard of their Judgments
by the Name, Character, or Circumstances of an
Author: If he is of Rank in the Eyes of the
World, either as to Fame or Fortune, his Works
pass their critical Muster without Examination;
or if examin'd, they must be good; it is impossible for such a Man to err.

BUT if the young, or poor Poet, is unknown
in the Temple of Fame, or wanting in the Bles-
sings of Fortune, so must his Merit and Poverty
remain at a Stand; till perhaps, like *MILTON*,
he's found out to be worth looking into, some
forty Years after his Death.

No Part of *Criticism* is more absurd, unjust
or detestable, than where Censure or Praise is
implicitly founded upon the Name of any Author
dead or living. Every Man of sound Reason must
form to himself a strange Idea of that *Critick*,
who defers his Opinion of any Piece, till he is
satisfied whose it is. Such an Enquiry is foreign
to the Business in Hand, before our Judgment
is given, that Curiosity is very ill tim'd, and
but helps to expose our Weakness, and impose
on our Senses; for we are all (both *Poets* and
Criticks) sensible how Fame is generally acquir'd
in this Life; and we never ought to trust to that
as a Guide, to shew us the Road to what is beautiful or noble in POETRY, or measure Wit by its
Height.

IF any Gentleman is determin'd to criticise,
let him judge the Work, and not the Man; let
him try every Line and Thought, by the Standard
of those natural Graces and artful Proprieties
which should make one a *Poet*, and t'other a
                                         Critick,

Critick. If he proceeds by any other Rules, he will be eafily led, by an *Ignis Fatuus*, into the deepeft Pit of Error; he will not condemn Non-fenfe, but Obfcurity and Poverty; or extol Merit, but Fame and Fortune.

A natural Inclination to Idlenefs, or a real Want of Bufinefs in their feveral Vocations, force vaft Numbers into the critical Service, who elfe would never have dreamt of fuch an Employment.

THE Saunterers head this Troop, who lie a Bed one half of the Day, ftudying how to fpend the other, and that is doz'd away; but if rouz'd by any extraordinary Accident, from Sloth into the Spleen, their Venom is fpit at all, who, to make Life agreeable, choofe never to be idle.

PHYSICIANS without Patients, Lawyers without Clients, and Parfons without Parifhes, fwell this Body to a large Bulk; and with them may be joined feveral young Students of the Inns of Court, and both Univerfities, who are as much out of Humour, that other People can write, as that they are oblig'd to read.

CRITICISM is an open Port, all are free Traders there, and no Bufinefs lies more natural, or ready for thofe who have nothing to do: Any Man commences Mafter when he will, without ferving a Prenticefhip, and is fure of a Majority of Cuftomers againft a fair Dealer.

OF all Criticks, I acknowledge, that ill Writers are the moft fevere, efpecially where real Merit is found out and applauded: They greedily prey upon the fmalleft Faults in a great Genius; they'll turn and torture them a thoufand Ways, to pleafe their Malice, and fatisfy their Spite: They have no other Way of being reveng'd upon

the

the World, and, like the fallen Angels, curfe, and ftrive to blaft that Heaven they cannot climb.

I believe, under fome one of thefe general Heads, all Species of Criticks may be rank'd: And as every confiderate Author, Reader, or Spectator, muft be fatisfy'd of the Ufe, Beauty, and Merit of folid, unprejudic'd Criticifm; fo muft they be diftafted, when Ill-nature and Ignorance ufurp the Intendancy over the polite Arts, to the utter Deftruction of true Learning and juft Wit.

IF we place this Art and its Profeffors in a proper Light, we fhall quickly perceive, that the Criticifm of the Antients was an agreeable Dofe of Phyfick, given by a skilful regular Phyfician, which carry'd off infenfibly all noxious Humours, without any Injury to the Conftitution: But modern Criticifm is a rank Poifon, adminifter'd by an illiterate Quack, which indeed gets the better of the Diftemper; but the Operation deftroys Life.

A juft Critick, like an induftrious Bee in his unbounded Flights, ranges Gardens, Groves and Meads, tries every Flower, or Herb, or Shrub, taftes all their Sweets, and ranfacks all their odoriferous Stores; then culls what's excellent, preferves it from the rude Spoiler's Wafte, and Teeth of Time; loads his little Thighs with Nature's choiceft Gifts; then, in his artful Cell, out of them furnifhes a Banquet for a Prince: But the *Snarler*, like a fluggifh, wafpifh Drone, drags along a bloated Carcafs, dully, in the fame beaten Track; the faireft Fruit, and richeft Scents, he fhuns, or touches but to blaft; and, in the Midft of Nature's flowery Pride, fcorns all her Dainties, to fatten on a Dunghill.

BEFORE

Before I conclude this Essay, there remain two very material Points unobferv'd.

The firft is, That I am perfwaded the profefs'd Criticks of this Age have brought upon us, from Time to Time, thofe Showers of bad Plays, which have almoft wafh'd the Shadow of *Dramatick Poetry* from off the Earth. They adhere fo ftrictly to the fevereft Letter of Criticifm, and prefs fo earneftly the Obfervation of their Rules alone, that all our young Writers think nothing elfe but Art requir'd, and that a Heaven-born Genius (which breaks through all their Cob-web Fetters) is ufelefs in *Parnaffus*.

Upon this, any Gentleman that has nothing elfe to do, very gravely gets the critical Receipts by Rote for all Kinds of Poetry; he takes half a Dozen frefh Characters, and keeps what's for his Purpofe; a proper Quantity of new Fable, if to be got; if not, he fkims the beft of the old; of the true fublime, a handful, very fine fhred, that it may go the farther; Half a Pound of Terror, to a Quarter of Pity; he mixes them all very well together, and thickens the Plot with a Quarter of a Peck of fine Language, obferves nicely, Time, Place, and Action; then melts down a Pound of Rhime, with two Ounces of Similies diffolv'd in it, to fweeten the latter Ends of Acts, and fprinkles it over the Whole. Laftly, to give it a poignant and wholefome Relifh, he feafons it with about the Bignefs of a Nutmeg of Morality. He may add a Spoonful or two of Satyr, or Panegyrick (as his Tafte is) or let them alone.

Thus furnifh'd, he fits down with the fame Form and Serenity to write a *Tragedy*, that his Cook-Maid does to make a Plumb-pudding.

M r

My second Obfervation is, That whatever Difparity may be betwixt the antient and modern POETS, I am convinc'd, that in the Way of Comparifon of Merits, the Difference is as wide betwixt the Cricks of former Ages and this; nor will it be difputed, fhould I affert, that the Generality of late Bards, would have met with Applaufe and Encouragement more adequate to their Performances, had every Man of their Judges been an *ARISTOTLE*, and every Woman a *DACIER*.

BUT, at the fame Time, I beg Leave to hint, that by the modern POETS, I caft not an Eye towards the Majority of Verfe, or Play-wrights; nor can I allow, that the leaft Beam of that divine Art fhines upon, or appears in the Works of every Coxcomb, that tags a Song with Rhimes, fcribbles Lampoons, or prevails on the Actors to give the Town a thing call'd a PLAY, becaufe it is divided into Acts and Scenes, with, *Enter King,* and, *Exit firft Minifter.*

IF that Clafs of my Readers who form our Theatrical AUDIENCES, perfift in their Errors, as to Behaviour, when their Faults have been fo gently and plainly laid open, I have no means of Redrefs to hope for, but in humbly propofing to the P----t (as a Matter of the laft Confequence to the Publick) that our *Play-Houfes* may be enlarg'd after the Manner of the *Grecian* and *Roman* THEATRES, and feparate Lodges contrived for thofe who go there only to chat, intrigue, or eat and drink; that impertinent Mirth, publick Amours, or ill-tim'd Gluttony, may not break in upon the Amufements of thofe, who go there purely for the Sake of the Entertainment.

As

As I have been very copious on the Head of *Criticism*, I make no Doubt but this Essay will have the Original of every Copy drawn here, upon its Back; but Truth, Juſtice and Virtue can ſtand any Shock: I ſhall readily give up any Point here advanc'd, if the Objection is founded on ſolid Senſe and calm Reaſoning; but where Arguments are ſupported by Vehemence and Scurrility, I am not oblig'd to reply; that being only *Billingſgate* PLAY, where they who talk loudeſt and faſteſt, are certain of Victory; and where Wit and Learning proceed from the Lungs, not the Brain.

ESSAY

ESSAY VI.

OF MASQUERADES;

Their great Antiquity ; their Use and Abuse ; capable of being contriv'd so, as to prove of vast Advantage to the Publick : With an Examen of the bare-fac'd MASQUERADES, *call'd* RIDOTTOS, *and* PRIVATE ASSEMBLIES. *To which is added, A Proposal for the Encouragement of the* ORATORY.

 Have here ventur'd upon the moſt difficult Task in the World to ſucceed in ; the Subject is tickliſh, and muſt be manag'd with the greateſt Caution : It is the critical Moment, upon which depends the Fate of theſe ESSAYS ; it being impoſſible ſo to handle this Affair, as not to incur the Diſpleaſure of ſome conſiderable People : For
while

while I am engag'd in the Cause of *Virtue* and *Truth*, I shall of one Side or t'other innocently make the whole Nation my Enemies.

MASQUERADES have for some Years past made a vast Noise in this Kingdom, to the unspeakable Delight of most fine Gentlemen and Ladies; and with equal Dissatisfaction to many of his Majesty's well-meaning Subjects. They have divided us into two furious Factions, as opposite as *Whig* and *Tory*; neither Side admit of any *Medium*, to moderate their flaming Resentments: One Party in general Terms altogether approving of this Diversion, without limiting it to what is useful, or at least simply innocent; the other as absolutely condemning the Design and Consequences of such an Entertainment; and cursing by Bell, Book and Candle, all who frequent it, though with the most harmless Intentions.

BUT Justice (under whose Banner I fight) commands me to censure the Proceedings of both Parties: The first, for maintaining its Cause, where its Freedoms are unbounded, and its Errors manifest; the other, for blindly striking at the Foundation, without Regard to those Advantages which may be drawn from its Influence on the World.

WHO dreads the Viper's Poison, while indulging in a Mess of their envigorating Broth?—— or the Bee's Sting, with a Finger in the Honey-Pot?—— Remove the Evil, and enjoy what's good.

BUT thus the Frailties of human Nature will judge at Random, according to the darkened Notions we entertain of Things; the least Gratification, or Discontent, make us fly out into the Extreams of ungovern'd Passions: Nothing can

Q   please

pleafe or difpleafe, but it is Heaven or Hell; Lovers can fee no Blemifhes, and Foes no Beauties; fome will pull up a Tree by the Roots, upon account of one rotten Branch; and others let a dead Stump ftand in an improper Place, becaufe it once had green Leaves.

But, in this Essay, I propofe purfuing a Method widely different from this: What is Praifeworthy, I fhall encourage; what is blameable, remove, either by turning its Bent towards fomewhat perfectly harmlefs, or fubftituting in its Place, what may be render'd of Ufe to the World.

At firft View, and to fuperficial Underftandings, Masquerades may look with a very modern Face; and, indeed, fo they once appeared to me, their Agility of Motions, and Frefhnefs of Complexions induc'd me to be of this Opinion; till pulling off the Masque, by penetrating into the very Bowels of Antiquity, and fearching into the remoteft Records of Time, I found the Defign and Confequences of a Masquerade, to be of the oldeft Standing of any Miftery now in Being; and as antient as the very firft Ceremonies of the *Roman, Grecian, Perfian,* or *Egyptian* Religions.

From the very Beginning of *Paganifm,* the heathen Priefts acted always in Masquerade, and kept the Secrets of Religion appropriated to themfelves, or at leaft reftrain'd to a very few Members, what they thought the moft folemn or material Parts of their Devotion.

The Priefts of the fuperftitious *Egyptians* characteriz'd every thing religious, moral, or civil, by Hieroglyphicks; which Cuftom firft (I believe) introduc'd Masquerading into the World: No Deity was allow'd to appear to the People, but in the Difguife of an Ox, Dog, Ape, Onion, Cucum-

Cucumber: And thus the Notions of a supreme Power were convey'd to them in a familiar Dress, that they might seem less terrible.

THE *Persian Magi* in a manner retir'd from the Commerce of Mankind; they hid themselves and their Worship from the most piercing Eyes; they affected a religious Obscurity, in what they communicated to the Vulgar, either by Writings or Traditions; and the Sun, with them, was only a Cloak to veil their *Oromazes* from mortal View.

THE *Grecians*, above all Nations, envelop'd their most sacred Misteries with Darkness; the *Eleusina Sacra*, or Festival of *Ceres*, was the most celebrated of any in *Greece*; so careful were they to conceal their private Rites, that if a Person initiated dar'd to divulge the least Part of this secret Solemnity, he was treated as one sentenc'd by divine Judgment to suffer Death.

THEY had other Festivals of this Nature sacred to *Vesta*, *Diana*, *Cotys*, &c. observ'd all in the Night, and with the greatest Secrecy.

THE *Romans* made a Collection of all the Gods of other Nations, and solemniz'd their Misteries according to the Institutions of the different Countries they borrow'd them from: The religious Vizard was in great Request with their Priests; and, to their Piety, were owing several nocturnal misterious Sacrifices to *Venus* and *Adonis*, *Priapus*, *Bacchus*, &c. where MASQUERADING was absolutely essential to the Manner of Adoration.

HERE we may observe, that in the religious Ceremonies of the wisest, politest, and most powerful Empires, Secrecy, Night, and a Disguise were held necessary, both in the Initiation and Performance: Nor was the last of them confin'd to these private Solemnities alone; the most publick Festivals were celebrated both by Priests and

People

People muffled up in particular Dreffes : So that indeed, the whole of Religion with them, was a well-regulated MASQUERADE. And if Ignorance be the Mother of Devotion, what can fo powerfully promote that End, as being led blindfold into it.

THE Adverfaries to this well-intended Defign will readily object, that there were feveral Impurities acted, and fcandalous Liberties allow'd at thefe private, though feemingly religious Mifteries ; that, by my own Confeffion, they are the very Foundation of our modern MASQUERADES; and that the Enormities complain'd of in one, have been continued in the other, in Encouragement, if not in Action——— To all this heavy Charge, I plead, *Guilty*; nor fhall I, by any Evafion, recede from what I have urg'd, in relation to the Rife or Progrefs of this *Entertainment*. My Intention is not to vindicate the Errors in the prefent Management of it, but to indulge the greateft, wifeft, and beft-bred Part of the Nation in the Appearance of a Diverfion they are fo fond of ; yet turn the Current into quite a different Channel, while they enjoy only the Name. Let us refolve to difcountenance and lay afide whatever is really irregular in this Amufement ; which is not impoffible : And I fhall plainly demonftrate, that it may be render'd not only innocently agreeable in Speculation, but of the laft Confequence in Practice, to all Degrees of People ; nay, to a higher Pitch of folid Service, if not Inftruction, than any other publick Entertainment can pretend to : Nor fhall any Part be play'd in a MASQUE, but what conduces to the general Good, when fhewn forth *in Propria Perfona*.

BUT to proceed regularly with the Hiftory of MASQUERADING, and bring it down to the
present

prefent Times, it will be neceffary to obferve, Though Religion (after thefe dark idolatrous Ages) was refcued from the mifterious Juggles of their Priefts, and reftor'd to its primitive Luftre, and unadorn'd Beauty; yet where Superftition and Ignorance got any Footing, they kept their Ground ftifly; and of confequence, Religious MASQUE-RADES continued in as great Requeft as ever. To this Day they maintain the higheft Reputation in moft of the chief Kingdoms of *Europe*; where Religion is fo differently drefs'd, that, in the fame City, the Garbs it puts on are as various as its Profeffors. It remain'd in the fame Situation with us here in *England*, till towards the latter End of the Reign of K-—— H---y VIII. when People began to be afham'd, or tir'd of it; and tho' in Q---- M----y's Reign it rais'd its drooping Head a while, it was but the laft Blaze of Life, for it foon after languifh'd and dy'd. The Well-Wifhers to our Peace and Profperity, hop'd it for ever buried in Obfcurity; but fome reftlefs Spirits blew up a few neglected Sparks into general Flames, about the Year Forty One; when, in a frantick Fit, the whole Nation run a MASQUERADING, and all Affairs of Church and State were thrown into one Grand JUMBLE, or MASQUERADE, till People danc'd themfelves quite out of Breath, and then they came to their Senfes. In K ---
C———s the S———d's Reign, Religious and Political MASQUERADES were pretty much laid afide for thofe of another Complexion, and nearer a-kin to thofe now in Vogue at the H---y M--t. During his Time they flourifh'd, and with him they fell, or by Degrees dwindled to nothing, till reviv'd about the latter End of the late Q---'s Reign, by D ——— D——t, the F——h A——r; who, by that Means, cunningly introduc'd the

P———r,

P———r, about half a Dozen C———ls, and as
many Scores of J———ts and C———ns, all in their
proper Robes; which alone were Dresses sufficient to have form'd a large M A S Q U E R A D E in *G--t*
B———n. This threw the settled Nation into a
Ferment. My Friend Mr. *H———r* wisely took the
Hint, and has firmly establish'd that Amusement
by his exquisite *Gou,* in what is polite and diverting. But the sober Part of this Kingdom, who
wisely view things with both Eyes, carefully look
for something more in an Affair of so publick
a Nature, than a Supper or a Dance; which has
put me upon the following Regulation, not to
destroy, but refine upon *H———r's Entertainment*;
thus fix M A S Q U E R A D E S upon a more durable
Basis, by making it equally advantageous to him
and us; that we may at least enjoy the Shell of
Instruction, while he picks up the Kernel of Profit, which we throw away.

But to finish with the Historical Part of this
E S S A Y, I shall only make a small Remark here;
that religious *Masquerading,* at present with us, is
reduc'd to a large Band and short black Cloak,
disguis'd in the natural Vizard of Hypocrisy.

Having given my Readers a just Idea of
the Original of a M A S Q U E R A D E (which proves
not despicable) I shall next enquire into the more
immediate Usefulness, which may be reap'd from
this Amusement judiciously regulated; at the
same Time set Bounds to any licentious Extravagancies that may have been admitted there,
and display to my darkened Countrymen, who
oppose them, the mutual Benefits Nature and
Art must receive in Conjunction, from its Reception, with proper Restrictions; by which
Means it may be considered as a general Good,
either in publick or private Life.

N A Y,

NAY, fhould we join with thofe People, in decrying *Mafquerades* in general Terms, and act with all the ignorant Caution, and fimple Zeal, which compofe their Arguments; yet in anfwer to their moft material Objections, we might offer numberlefs Advantages arifing from fuch an Amufement, to the poor, or trading Part of any Nation.

ITS Confequences neceffarily occafion fo great an Expence, fuch a Circulation of ready Money (which elfe would lie dead in Bankers Hands, or Iron-Chefts) and fuch a Spirit of Bufinefs to all Callings, relating to every Branch of Trade, or *Mechanifm,* that this Plea in its Favour, might very well caft an agreeable Luftre upon the darkeft Side of this Diverfion, and make it pafs current with the moft fcrupuloufly prudent.

BUT thefe Topicks have been lately fo learnedly and copioufly handled in a wonderful Book, where *private Vices* are undoubtedly prov'd to be *publick Benefits*; and the fame Arguments being liable to be urg'd in Vindication of the moft notorious Crimes, I fhall wave making Ufe of a Rol'n or precarious Defence, in proving the Ufe and Innocence of a MASQUERADE: I fhall produce the moft fubftantial Evidences, back'd by undeniable Matters of Fact, to ftrengthen what I have afferted in the Title of this ESSAY.

NOT to dwell too long upon the *Preface,* but at once to ftrike into the Body of my Work, and let its Strength and Perfpicuity of Reafoning ftare my Opponents full in the Face, I pretend to demonftrate, that a well-regulated MASQUERADE, may be of infinite Service to any Kingdom or State, in feveral different Political, Oeconomical, and Moral Views; whether we confider the Support of the Government, the
Happi-

Happiness of each particular Family, or the Wit and Politeness of every individual Member, in respect to their several Stations in the Commonwealth.

FIRST then, and principally, a MASQUE-RADE should be encouraged by every Government, to the End that all Employments, Offices, Posts, E——l, C——l or M——y, in C——t, C——y, C——h, B —— h, or A——y, may be supply'd with proper and useful Members, in a juster and clearer Method of Choice, than has been yet preach'd or thought of.

I remember to have perus'd in the Original *Spanish*, a very valuable *Treatise*, call'd *Les examen des Ingenios*; where it is laid down as a fundamental Maxim in the Education of Youth, that by the Laws of Nature, Art, good Sense, and Oeconomy, Parents are oblig'd thoroughly to consider the Genius and Constitution of their Children, and nicely weigh Perfections, and Defects in every Capacity, before they attempt the throwing them into Business for Life.

IF they indiscreetly force tender Natures into those Callings, or Employments, Heaven never design'd them for; this blind, rash Choice will be generally attended with two very fatal Consequences; a private and publick: In the first, they render their Off-spring miserable in this Life, by putting them upon acting that Part which is entirely disagreeable to them. In the second, they are guilty of a manifest Injury to the Publick, in allowing their Children to fill those Offices, where they are incapable of discharging the Duty.

THE Reasons which may be justly alledg'd on this Head, as circumstantial Proofs, are so numerous and obvious, that to quote one, would
be

be impertinent: And it may be very modeftly urg'd, in behalf of any young Gentleman whipp'd into a Poft after this ill-concerted Manner, that he may fucceed by a very lucky Hit; but that the Odds are apparently againft him, without the Shadow of a Fault on his Side.

I fhall want but few Words then, to make it appear, that in this Cafe, the MASQUERADE, reduc'd to Order and Decency under the Eye and Wing of publick Authority, is the moft ready, natural and proper Trial of Wits and Difpofitions. This *Entertainment* in it felf being agreeable to moft youthful Inclinations, our bearded Boys and Infants of fix Foot high will be eafily cajol'd into fuch a School. Then the Variety of Habits allowing of as great a Latitude in the Characters of Life correfpondent to them, every Man of any Tafte will choofe that Drefs his Inclinations infenfibly prompt him to; and of Courfe he'll exert himfelf to act up to what it reprefents; ambitious to be thought what he only affects to perfonate; and thus we fhall penetrate into the Excellencies of every one's hidden Talent, and judge from thence what buftling, or quiet Scene of Life, Nature cut him out for.

FOR Example, Let us fuppofe a MASQUERADE conducted after this fober and polite Manner, eftablifh'd in P——nd, where their M——arch is Elective, as well as M——rs of S—te, B---ps, or other inferior Officers. All this might be tranfacted very much to the Purpofe, in a large Plain, finely illuminated with Flambeaus, and in the Space of a Summer's Night, all Vacancies might be fill'd up with the greateft Eafe, and to the entire Satisfaction of every individual, as well as the Reprefentatives of the People.

FOUR

FOUR Foot in the Shoulders, with a proportionable Height; a Voice like Thunder, always Fore-runner of a Storm; well-knit Arms and Legs, that in a common Method of walking, would mow down half the Company like so many Stalks of Wheat, would appear to vast Advantage in a *Turkish* Robe and Turban, and naturally speak the very Monarch; for who so proper to defend a Nation as he, who is most capable of offending them? according to the political Maxims of the *East.*

THE nimble *Arlequin* (who has his Nose at every Man's Ear, and a Slap at every Man's Rump; who, like the *Camelion,* can change to any Colour, and with *Proteus* assumes all Shapes) by the dexterous Management of a simple wooden Stick, would readily point out to us a first M——r.

THE sober Behaviour, grave Aspect, and venerable Garb of a *Scaramouch,* determine us in a worthy M——n.

THE subtil Innocence of an artful *Pierro,* who pries into all Secrets, yet keeps himself conceal'd, would decypher to us at once, a rare S——te,, S——y, or C——t J——r.

THE meddling *Punchinello's,* who are every Bodies humble Servants, always at Court, always busy, and nothing to do, would furnish us with a perpetual Fund of Gapers for Places, who are pleas'd with dancing over a daily C——t Attendance, and content to be Slaves, without the Name of an Employment.

THESE few Instances will quickly let People of any tolerable Degree of Penetration, into the Use and Beauty of my Design; and demonstrate with what Ease any P——ce might grace his C——t with C——ns, T——rs, C—— rs, S——ys,

S——ys, E——ys, S—— ds; by obferv-
ing, cautioufly, the proper Managementof a Key,
a white Switch, a Purfe, a Goofe-quill, a Spur,
a Stick of Wax, and fo on, to the fmalleft Officer of the Ex——fe.

But, in order to render this Scheme compleat, and not leave the leaft Cranny for the
Shadow of an Objection to creep in at, there
muft be eftablifh'd by R——l and P——ry Authority, a felect Number of Commiffioners to
to infpect this Entertainment, in the feveral
Branches of it, which particularly concern the
Publick; to fee that the Whole is carried on with
the ftricteft Decency and exacteft Order; that
all irregular Perfons are banifh'd the Place; that
every one behaves up to the Propriety and *Decorum* of that Habit which denotes his Characters, both in Action and Speech; from whence
they may judge of the Merit of every Performer,
as to Underftanding, Behaviour, Strength, &c,
by the Help of a refin'd Sagacity, quick Eye, and
ftaunch Nofe; which Qualifications are effential
to thofe dignify'd with fo laborious an Office.
Indeed thefe Commiffioners will have vaftly the
Advantage over thofe defign'd in the fecond Essay, to choofe Actors for the Stage, as to properly diftinguifhing different Talents; becaufe all
People appear at a MASQUERADE in Propriety of Drefs and Character. They affume what
is natural to them, and acting in Difguife, act
without Referve: They can add the Beauty of
an artificial Affectation to their borrow'd Perfons; whereas the others have no Oportunity
of fhewing but what is pure Nature. Tho' if
this my Project meets with due Encouragement,
where any Blemifh (as to Integrity, Honefty,
or other trifling Virtues) affects the Reputations
of

3

of thofe pick'd up at a MASQUERADE for great Employments, they'll ferve to fupply the *Play-houfe*, in perfonating thofe Offices; fo the Reality and Appearance of all Parts in Life be furnifh'd from the fame Shop. How juftly and acutely would fuch Gentlemen diftinguifh the aw-ful, filent Senator, in the folemn *Venetian* Robe! The uncorrupted Judge, in the fpotlefs *Ermin!* the invincible Hero, in Buff and Scarlet! The able Lawyer, in the learn'd Full-bottom! The mortify'd retir'd P---on, in the *Capuchin*'s Thread-bare Cowl! and the rough Sea - Captain, in the Skippers tarry Jacket! Nay, the fawning Cour-tier, formal Citizen, tricking Attorney, plodding Ufurer, thoughtful Merchant, or biting Stock-job-ber, will be manifefted in fome Particularity of Garb or Addrefs: Induftrious Nature, like Oil, will rife uppermoft, and make apparent each dif-fereat Quality fhe form'd.

A s I intend that this Project fhould be univer-fal in its Improvement, and diffufive in all Kinds of Benefits, the loweft Parts of Life need not be excluded from their Shares in a general Good : But to this prudent Method of Choice, I would truft the fixing on all civil Capacities, from the Juftice of Peace to the Petty-Conftable ; and the firft Magiftrate of a Corporation, to the Bell-man.

N o r would I put a Lad out to any Trade, from my *Lord Mayor*'s, to a Seller of Matches, till his Genius pafs'd Examination at a MASQUE-RADE; where it would certainly fhine out, though in a MASQUE, by turning its natural Bent, in an efpecial Manner, towards that Part of the Entertain-ment which it affected. A Devourer of Oranges and Apples will grow up to a Fruiterer; as he that fwallows Jellies, and pockets Sweet-meats, muft have a fine Tafte for a Confectioner. The
Fre-

Frequenter of the Side-Boards has undoubtedly a Turn to a Viatner; as the quick Difpatch of a cold Fowl or Lobfter will diftinguifh the Poulterer from the Fifhmonger: Moreover, the Expence of that MASQUERADE, by which their prevailing Inclinations are try'd, will fave the Trouble of giving them a Surfeit, at their Entrance into Bufinefs, in order to hinder them from eating out their Mafter's Profit; as Grocers ufe to ftuff their young Apprentices full of Plums.

LET us now turn my Propofal from what may ftill be done, to thofe Inconveniencies, which by our Prudence might have been remedy'd. Thus, by curioufly viewing it on both Sides, the Contraft will fix in a more affecting Point of View, both the Difeafe and Cure.

HAD this Manner of Choofing, and fitting young Gentlemen for all Employments, been obferv'd, then feveral ftrong-lung'd P---ns would have been excluded mounting a P——t, who might have made a bright Figure at the B——r; and inftead of deafening, or tiring a Congregation, have prattled Tautology and Nonfenfe by the Hour to fome Purpofe: And fome dull, heavy L——rs, who ftupidly dofe over their Clients Affairs, might have lovingly flept with their P——fh the whole Length of a S——on.

SOME graduate Doctors, that have had very bad Succefs as Phyficians, might have fupply'd our Markets with admirable Butchers; as feveral tender-hearted Butchers might, in Return, furnifh the Colledge with very clever Anatomifts.

MANY M——ates, whofe Behaviour and Underftanding difgrace the B——h, might fhine out in a Farm; and feveral fenfible Yeomen, who fatten Hogs, whiten Veal and grope Tur-

R   kies,

kies, make Generofity and Juftice the Ornaments of a C————rt.

SOME pretty, fmart Fellows would be whipp'd from the Plough-tail, as fad, idle Dogs, that would fparkle in the Side-box, or at the Head of a C————ny of G————ds; and many of our Lollers in Gilt-chariots whiftle over an OPERA Air, to a Team of Oxen or Horfes.

WHAT Numbers of fpruce, polite Journey-men might be remov'd from behind Counters, in order to fill feveral confiderable Vacancies at St. J————'s, with the weighty Forms of Good-breeding, and the material Nothingnefs of pro-per S————te Ceremonies; and feveral aukward, fimple C————t Of————rs be doom'd to their pa-ternal Bufinefs; caft Accounts, weigh Plums, and meafure Silks for Life.

THUS, in the dark Reign of old *Chaos*, a vaft Concourfe of unruly Atoms being jumbled to-gether, at laft danc'd themfelves all into their proper Places, and form'd this beautiful, regular Plan of the World, fo compleat in all its Parts.

THE Arguments and Examples I have here produc'd, fure muft prove fufficient to confute the moft prejudic'd and obftinate, in Relation to the Merits of a MASQUERADE.

IT is impoffible to fix upon any other Scheme fo perfect, or adapted to the Defign of worthily filling all Places, E————l, P————l, C————l or M————y: For every Genius would have Room and Oportunity to exert it felf in the Bufinefs of a Piece with its Nature; all would behave with Pleafure to themfelves, and with Alacrity dif-charge their Duty to the Publick. No Man would go unwillingly or ignorantly into his Office; but then we fhould fee the * * * * * * * * and our * * * * * * * * and fuch * * * * * nor would
* * * *

* * * * * * * nor fuch * * * * * * * * and
then * * * * * perhaps * * * * * * better fupply'd.

WE will fuppofe then MASQUERADES fettled upon fo lafting a Foundation, that the whole
Nation may be affur'd of their being continued,
protected and fupported by the higheft Powers;
that they fhall be the Touch-ftone of Capacity,
in all Pretenfions to Employments, of whatfo-
ever Dignity or Profit (if not hereditary to the
Fools of fome particular Families) that the fevereft Penalties fhall be inflicted upon all Of-
fenders, who fhall dare to difturb thefe Entertainments, or difobey Orders in Matters of Judgment, Election or Amufement.

THEN People would be proud of preferving
the Reputation that this political Diverfion would
claim from fuch Encouragement; nay, in a few
Years it would be common, to run to the Maf-
querade-houfe for every Man's Character, as to
Wifdom, Honefty, Courage, &c. — Nor am I
in the leaft folicitous about every Thing's being
tranfacted with the utmoft Decorums; being certain, that the moft diforderly Mortals upon Earth
will be kept in Awe, and reftrain'd to a Carriage
highly decent, by the Fear of being for ever banifh'd the MASQUERADE, fhould the leaft
Shock to Modefty be prov'd upon them: And I
am fatisfied, there needs no other Punifhment
be mention'd, to terrify licentious Riot it felf into Sobriety: For, as they would by this Means
be depriv'd of the moft delightful Entertainment
in the World; fo on the other Hand, they would
lofe the Profpect of being Candidates for any
honourable, or profitable Employment.

I here in the ftrongeft Terms infift, that all
Love Intrigues be utterly difcarded and forbid,

as Appendixes to this Diversion; excepting, where a Gentleman is desirous to penetrate gently, or pry into a Lady's Perfections, or she to experience his Abilities, with a full View to Matrimony; and that Vigour or Capacity are to be made manifest, in order to their becoming Man and Wife.

WHICH Thought naturally leads me to my second Assertion in Favour of MASQUERADES, *viz.* That they will be a great Promoter of pure and unspotted Wedlock Joys; and more especially aiding in the two principal Points of that holy State, --- a happy and fruitful Life.

UNSETTLED are the Desires, and as various the Fancies of Men in the Pursuit of a Wife: We expect a hundred Perfections in Woman, and often meet with a fair Female bless'd with one of the Number; but we cannot find the Ninety and Nine: The Passions of the other Sex are as changeable, and their Tempers as difficult to be pleas'd; so that in short, the Whole of Marriage, as to a well-judg'd Choice, consists in a lucky Hit. Or, if we are resolv'd to choose with Caution, and not trust to Fortune, I can only say to my Readers, what a wise *Presbyterian* Parson prudently hinted to a youthful Congregation, on this Head, in a bridal Sermon; when, after learnedly stating the whole Case he proceeded thus: *My beloved, it signifieth not, though your Wives be young, lovely, virtuous and religious, if they be not fit Wives; therefore look ye out with Care for fit Wives, and then ye will become as one Body.* Now where can any Man so properly try to catch a fit Wife, as at a MASQUERADE? ——— If he loves Reservedness, there are *Spanish Prudes:* Would he have Life and Air? there are *French Coquets:* Hunts he after Innocence? there are
Milk-

Milk-Maids, and Shepherdesses: Is ignorant Youth his Game? there are large Babies in Leading-Strings: Covets he Riches and Virtue? there are venerable Matrons, old and ugly: Does he think Knowledge convenient? there are Widows, just come from their Husbands Funerals: Seeks he the obedient Slave? there are *Turkish* Ladies just elop'd from a *Seraglio:* Is Religion alone his Aim? there are Nuns and Quakers: But would he have all Perfections in one Habit? there are *Domines.*

A proper Method of negotiating a matrimonial Conjunction, is allow'd to be a very nice Point, and apt to breed bad Blood betwixt the Parties concern'd, if not handled to the Purpose: Therefore what Project can be more *apropos*, to prevent the Consequences arising from the Animosities, Discontents, Heart-burnings, Jealousies, Elopements, Divorces, and separate Maintenances, which so often clog the married State, and are of infinite Prejudice to its Reputation, and Detriment to the publick Welfare; as but too few can boast of living altogether free from some of the Grievances just nam'd.

Let us then imagine a Gentleman in Pursuit of a Wife at a MASQUERADE; at last he springs his Game, to all Appearance she promises well; the Air, the Motion, the Wit of the Lady charm him; nor are his Person and Conversation disagreeable to her; so far of the Treaty proving satisfactory, it is necessary to push the Matter Home. They retire, Preliminaries are soon settled; the Congress is open'd; both Parties agree to go to the Bottom of the Affair in Hand: If all secret Articles are settled to their mutual Satisfaction, those that are publick, and of less Concern, follow of Course; but if some Allies are

deny'd

deny'd their Pretensions, or refuse to be Guarantees of the Treaty; Matters being at a Stand once, and not put in regular Motion, must drop: Thus either Way, all ends well. If those Things that are of a private Nature, are brought to bear to both their Contents, upon being produc'd, 'tis a Match; if not, the Familiarities that pass'd betwixt them must remain a Secret, the Parties being utter Strangers to one another.

THIS Method of proceeding in an Affair of so great Importance, is too well supported, to be treated as chimerical by any of my Adversaries. This discreet Trial of Tempers and Constitutions before Marriage, would prevent all those small Differences which too often attend it, and put to Silence those very civil Speeches that by way of Interjections lard connubial Love ——— *Very fine!* ——— *indeed!* ——— *is it possible?* ——— *Infinite Assurance!* ——— *had I known that* ——— *Horrid Creature!* ——— *before I'd have done it!* ———— *My G——·d!* ——— *I'd be burnt alive first!* ——— *Always foul Weather at Home!* ——— *Is this Matrimony?* ——— *Look ye, Madam!* ——— *Dem-me!* ——— *Fool, Fool!* ——— *Yes, I have it!* ——— *Devil! Catch me a second Time!* ———

WE all know, that but one happy Pair have ever yet claim'd the Flitch of Bacon, though the Custom is of several Centuries standing. But were due Encouragement given to what I have here propos'd, in a little Time every married Couple would at least put in for a Rasher.

THE seven wise Men of *Greece* would have approv'd of this Scheme, though none of them had the Head-piece to think of it; that being reserved as an eternal Monument of Glory, sacred to the Family of the *Primcocks*.

INDEED

INDEED the wifeft of the old *Grecian* Philo-fophers (in his Regulation of that Common-wealth, whofe Rules were the moft ftrictly fevere) fquinted a little this way, in eftablifhing a Sort of a political RIDOTTO, in which the young Men and Maidens promifcuoufly met, in order to pro-voke them into Matrimony.

BUT fo fhocking to all Modefty was this pru-dent Law-giver's State-Cookery, that it muft fur-feit any Stomach but that of the groffeft Feeder; he not only forbidding the Ufe of MASKS to conceal Names , and hide Blues; but even ftripp'd them of their Petticoats and Breeches, and left blind Nature to inftruct them.

MY decent Expedient, I hope, will be receiv'd fuitable to its Merit; its Conveniency, as well as Refervednefs, anfwering better to all Purpofes in the End : By this Means it will be in the Power of a Bride and Bridegroom to come together with fome Profpect of living happy, they being the laft confulted, if at all, in the matrimonial Bar-gain; becaufe they are moft deeply concern'd, Parents thinking it but juft that their Chil-dren fhould be pleas'd with the Perfon, if they are with the Fortune.

NO Man takes, upon the Judgment of another, a Pair of Shoes, or Gloves; he firft tries them on, then fays, whether they fit or not : Yet muft he, without the leaft Trial or Experience, be clapp'd into the Marriage-Doublet for Life, and fcarcely be allow'd to make a wry Face, when the Yoke pinches, or flip his Neck out of the Collar, when it is too wide for him.

IF a MASQUERADE, rightly difpos'd, can produce fuch wonderful Effects in filling all va-cant Employments with Perfons of Genius and Capacity for the Bufinefs (as has been fully

pro-

proved) I believe it may be fupported by Arguments as felf-evident, that it is the only Place in the World, where any Youth may be thoroughly qualify'd for all publick Affairs.

I may venture to affirm, that this *Entertainment* will form in thofe who frequent it, the trueft Judgments of all Part in polite Life ; fharpen them to the fineft Edge of Wit, properly fet for the genteeleft Converfation, and be the fureft Guide in conducting them to Perfection in all the liberal Arts : So that a MASQUERADE may be depended upon as a perpetual Fund of good Senfe ; the Whet-ftone of Repartee, and a real Academy of Sciences.

THE various Characters that are there feemingly reprefented ; the different Inclinations, Defires and Interefts that fill every Breaft, and that Medley of Nations, Languages and Judgments, muft form the moft agreeable Mixture of Converfation imaginable, giving every one a true Tafte of eafy Dialogue, and of confequence infpiring them with a fprightly Turn, and fixing the Standard of each Member's talking pertinently in his Character or Profeffion.

IN order to compleat this laudable Defign, every Perfon muft not only humour and ftrictly adhere, in the minuteft Particulars, to what he appears ; but where he finds a Body of People harping upon the fame String, and to the Tune of his Inclinations, he muft ftrike in there, and herd with them, as the fureft and eafieft Method of attaining to that Knowledge he thirfts after.

IN one Corner may be heard a Confultation of Phyficians, determining Life and Death ; their Heads full of Receipts , and Mouths of hard Words ; all agreeing in the Ends of their Patients, but differing in the Ways thither : In another, a
noify

noify Bench of Lawyers, torturing and comment-
ing upon old Charters, Statutes, Deeds, Records-
Wills, *&c.* and spitting at one another, *Judgments, Arrests, Scire Facias's, Noli-profequis, De-
murrers,* &c.

HERE they may spy a Tribe of Natural Philosophers weighing Air, making Experiments upon Kittens and Puppy-Dogs; boasting of their
Mummies, venemous Animals, and monstrous
Births; astonish'd at the wonderful Variety of
Nature in Minerals, Fossils, Shells, Feathers, *&c.*
There a Group of *Virtuosi,* poring their Eyes out
on Medals, Seals, Intaglias, Camæas, *&c.* prai-
sing every thing antique, damning every thing
modern, reducing what is beautiful in this World
to still Life, in Pictures, Statues, Bass-Relieves,
and other Curiosities of Art.

IN one Room they'll find a Circle of Mathematicians surrounded with Globes, Quadrants,
Sectors, Dials, Theodolites, Microscopes, Tele-
scopes, *&c.* demonstrating the Proportions, Lines,
Figures of Squares, Angles, Cones, Numbers,
Measures, Weights, *&c.* explaining the Problems
of *Euclid,* and making familiar, to the meanest
Capacity, the Difficulties of *Algebra;* talking more
in a Quarter of an Hour, than can be understood
in an Age : In another, they may reconnoitre
a Troop of military Men forming Camps, ordering
Battles, quartering Soldiers, laying Sieges, raising
Blockades; nothing to be heard but Thunder, Blood,
Fire, Batteries, Bombardments, and Great Guns.

IN this Apartment a Band of musical Gentlemen will be very loud, with Concords and Dis-
cords, Flats and Sharps, Crotchets and Quavers,
Times and Movements, Air and Composition;
chiming together as melodiously as a Set of Pack-
Horses, with each a Bell at his Ear, to keep him
in

in Tune: In that a double Line of Poets will be
no lefs noily in matching Crambos, weighing
Cadences, and trying Words, like Earthen Pip-
kins, by the Sound, to know if they are good for
any thing. Here a Man may learn to rhime,
fill Pocket-Books with Thoughts, for Ode, Paftoral Elegy, or Epigram; and perhaps fome Sen-
tences, proper for the Epick or Dramatick.

Thus in a few Masquerade Evenings, a
young Gentleman of tolerable natural Parts, by
applying himfelf to a particular Study, may either qualify himfelf for any Employment or Calling, and afterwards, by exerting thofe Talents
there, pop at once into good Bufinefs; or if he
is difpos'd for univerfal Knowledge, carry home
with him the Marrow of all Sciences, to fit him
for the brighteft Converfation, without the tedious
Forms of a Scholaftick Education.

If the Behaviour, Cuftoms and Languages of
all foreign Nations were punctually obferv'd in
a Masquerade, young Gentlemen need not
lofe Money and Time in travelling fo far from
Home, to admire one, and acquire t'other. Our
Infants of Q———y, that are willing to improve,
need go no farther than the *Hay-Market* to be
inftructed, where they dance beft, or fing fweet-
eft, or bow the genteeleft, or drefs the richeft,
or eat the niceft, or walk the ftatelieft; *Paris,
Rome, Venice, Naples, Vienna* and *Madrid* would
all be found in that inchanted Spot.

Nor fhould we forget the Advantages this would
bring to the *Englifh* Tongue, as our Speech is a
Purloiner from all Languages, antique and modern, daily getting, yet ftill wanting; where could
we hope for fo beautiful an Introduction of foreign Words and Phrafes, as from that Variety
of Characters and Reprefentations of different
Nations

Nations at a MASQUERADE? Then we need
not steal, but boldly use what we lik'd, as the
Properties of those Persons whose Habits we wear;
nor should an expressive Monosyllable escape being naturaliz'd, from the old *Greeks* to the present *Hottentots*.

THAT even the most barbarous Sounds add a
Greatness, or Grace to our Language, is evident
from a late Collection of Travels, where the most
uncouth and tramontane Expressions have been
greedily receiv'd, and universally us'd. If Captain *Gulliver* had never travell'd, our *Beaus* and
Belles would never have pronounc'd *Lilliput*, *Brob-
dinag*, *Blamerfescu*, or *Hoyhnms*; *Glumdalclish* might
have wept her Eyes out for us; our Ignorance
would never have dream'd of the Flying Island
of *Laputa*, nor profited by the wonderful Discoveries of the Natural Philosophers of *Balnibari*;
and we should have mistook a *Hoyhnm* for a Horse,
and a *Yahoo* for a rational Creature, to the End of
Time.

As nothing is more essential to the Growth of
all Arts (from their first springing up to their
Maturity) than Freedom, so a MASQUERADE
being a perfect Commonwealth (as every Body
is there upon the Level) is the very Country of
Liberty, in which they must flourish; and conse-
quently, by a well-judg'd Encouragement and
strictly-regulated Institution, this Entertainment
may prove the Root, from whence all Branches
of the Sciences may spread faster and farther,
than by any Method now practis'd in the known
World.

THE Reasons I have given, and the Proofs
made use of in supporting the general Use of a
MASQUERADE, being as clear as strong, I need
                                                    speak

speak no farther in Praife of Truths fo undeniable and felf-evident.

WHILE I am bufy with the Merits of this illuftrious Family, it may be expected, that fome
honourable Mention fhould be made of a near
Relation, call'd Sign*r.* *Ridotto*, which is indeed a
tolerable pretty Jumble of MUSICK, DANCING,
GAMING, &c. But at beft a bare-fac'd MAS-
QUERADE, where People are admitted difguis'd,
without a Vizard, and hide their Hearts by their
natural Faces.

As all the Members of this Society make their
Appearance in the fame Character, drefs'd in the
fame Habits, and acting in their proper Perfons,
they muft do every thing with Conftraint, and
cannot be fufceptible of the Advantages entail'd
upon a MASQUERADE; this its younger Brother
having the natural Tendency to all the Extravagancies and Irregularities of the elder, without the
Fortune to fupport them, or the Senfe to improve by
them. Therefore I may affirm, that all thofe Benefits
which may accrue to a Nation from a MASQUE-
RADE, cannot be acquir'd at this Amufement;
yet Vice and Folly fhine there in full Splendor.

IN fhort, a *Ridotto* is as ftupidly infipid, as the
other is wittily brillant; and as infignificant as
the other is neceffary: Where one may find Love
without Gallantry; a numerous Affembly, without Life or Gaiety; and Converfation without
Wit. It is indeed as different from a MASQUE-
RADE, as *Afh-Wednefday* from *Eafter-Holidays*,
and may ferve as a *Lenten Entertainment* in *Italy*,
but will not pleafe in *England*, where we keep
Carnival all the Year round.

How it is carry'd on Abroad, or why introduc'd here, I think is not very material, or worth
enqui-

enquiring into: I look upon it as an Interloper; nor will it ever be admitted as a Publick Diverfion amongft us, as long as we can meet with what is more agreeable, or inftructing.

SINCE I am got into this Road of Amufements, many of my Readers will be defirous, that I fhould not pafs by Drawing-rooms, Affemblies and Vifiting-days, without calling in: But as thefe *Entertainments* are at moft of a private Nature, and confin'd to particular Sets of People; to touch upon them would be taking me out of my Way.

THEREFORE I fhall only remark, they are upon as dull a Footing as *Ridottos,* if not worfe; where the Corner of a Room may do as much Mifchief as the Middle of a MASQUERADE; where Honour and Refpect are gain'd by a fortunate Card, or a lucky Caft; where good Senfe and good Breeding are meafur'd by the Sounds of Titles, and Shew of Fortune; where Scandal and a Grin are taken for Wit and genteel Behaviour; where Brocade and Embroidery make the fine Lady and fine Gentleman: And where a common Sharper, with a long Purfe of Gold, is admitted as an Equal to the firft Peer in the Kingdom.

As I began this ESSAY with the Article of R —— n; fo I muft return to the fame Topick, before I take my final Leave of the Amufements of People of the biggeft Fafhion, and confider how far they ought to be indulg'd, in going to C —— h meerly as a Diverfion; then clofe with a modeft Propofal.

I own this is look'd upon as an Affair of that Confequence (efpecially one Day of the Week) that it would be abfurd to let it pafs unregarded:

S   ed:

ed: Tho' I know it will be immediately objected, This is not my Province, to infpect Matters
of fo high, folemn, and grave a Nature. I own,
the Charge, and dare only touch upon it here,
as they have drefs'd it up to my Hands: And,
as they have turn'd the moſt ferious Part of Life
into a trifling Amufement, none of the publick *Entertainments* is frequented with fo little
Profpect of Improvement, or Defign to be
inftructed. The P——t is more neglected than
the Stage, and the P——r than the *Opera-book*. Had
they not turn'd the Service of the C———h into a bare Amufement, and made it to confiſt of
a Smile or Frown, a Whiſper or Ogle, a Bow,
or Curtefy, to fee and be feen, I fhould not
have prefum'd to mention it here as fuch. I have
no Warrant to infpect C- - -hes (*quatenus* C—hes;)
but am at Liberty to animadvert upon the Behaviour of the greateſt and fineſt Part of the Congregation, who turn them into T H E A T R E S, or
Idolatrous Temples, while they do nothing but
worfhip one another: Nor will it be held Prefumption in me, to fay, that the Whole of their
Duty might be better difcharg'd by keeping at
Home, than coming there to fet ill Examples in
Devo---n, and by their Forms and Grimaces, divert the Eyes of the ill-bred, ill-drefs'd Part of
the Affembly, from the Bufineſs of the Place.

But as the Genius of the polite Part of this
Nation has a prodigious Tendency to every thing
mighty new, I hope they'll meet at the Or---ry
in N——rt---m---t, with thofe Novelties that may
tempt them thither, amufe them while there, and
fix their Attention to what is then fpoken or acted; nor fickly change, till the Bloom of Youth

at

at leaſt is gone, and the ripening Fruit is ready
to be thrown away.

I hope, tho' this *Entertainment* boaſts a little
of the Face of R——n, that will be no Objection to the ingenious Inventor and Founder of
the *Oratorians,* whom I recommend to the Quality and Gentry of both Sexes, in the moſt particular Manner.

His Academical P——t has form'd the moſt
happy Alliance betwixt R——n, Morality, and
the *Belles-Lettres :* And as he inculcates the Quinteſſence of all Arts and Sciences with his
Div——ty, there is this particular Benefit to be
reap'd from his Doctrine, that we go to C——h
and School at the ſame Time.

If any Thing that has the Appearance of a
Ch——pel can pleaſe, this muſt; where a polite Variety quickens our Dev———n, inſpires
Zeal, and furniſhes our Libraries with a new Li-
turgy.

It would be wonderful, if ſo bold, ſo diſin-
tereſted, ſo publick-ſpirited an Undertaking ſhould
fail of Succeſs, where R——n is ſtripp'd of all
ſuperfluous Ornaments, and only allow'd a few
neceſſary Furbeloes, to hide what may prove
diſagreeable to the Squeamiſh and Ignorant; yet
light and eaſy to the Wearer.

It ſounds well of this Gentleman's Side, and
ſhews the Solidity of his Principles, that the
Cl——gy are in general averſe to his Deſign,
and are to a Man join'd to decry the H——ly-
niſts.

But we are ſenſible that they hate Improve-
ment, for fear of Reformation ; and under the
Pretence of avoiding Innovations, would give us
R——n as it was about Eighteen Hundred Years

S 2 ago,

ago, without allowing for thofe Amendments, or Additions, which particular Humours or Occafions may require.

I could not forbear touching lightly in this Place, thefe two laft mention'd Heads; which are of greater Moment than moft People at firft fight imagine: Nor can I think Affairs of this Nature improperly tack'd to the Tail of an Essay upon MASQUERADES.

ESSAY

E S S A Y VII.

Of the GYMNASIA, THEATRES, AMPHITHEATRES, NAUMACHIÆ *and* STADIA *of the Antients; but particularly of the antique* CIRCUS, *and modern* BEAR-GARDEN: *A Comparison between the* GLADIATORS *and our* PRIZE-FIGHTERS; *The* Italian STROLERS, *and our Mountebank* STAGES: *With a small Sketch of our* COCK-PITS, PUPPET-SHEWS, FAIRS, *and* PUBLICK AUCTIONS.

I SO far profess my self a bigotted Admirer of the *Antients,* and all their Performances, that every Thing which bears the Authentick Mark, or boasts the least Resemblance of Antiquity, touches me with Veneration, Surprize, or Pleasure: Of Consequence, when we narrow-soul'd, half-witted

Mortals,

Mortals, the Moderns, follow, tho' at the greateft Diſtance, or imitate in the aukwardeſt Manner, any Cuſtom, Amuſement, or Work of theirs,
I own my ſelf ſecretly prepoſſeſſed in Favour of
that Affair, even to a Degree of Partiality.

H A V I N G in the Six former E ſ ſ a y s, gone
thro' moſt of the Publick *Entertainments*, (at leaſt
thoſe reſorted to by the *Beau-monde*) this ſmall
I N T R O D U C T I O N was occaſion'd by my re-
collecting a Diverſion truly *Engliſh*, the laſt mention'd, becauſe ſupported moſtly by the Commonalty; but which I look upon with Veneration,
and frequent with Delight: Nor can the rude,
vulgar Apellation of the *Bear-garden* give any
Diſtaſte to my Ears, ſince it was certainly deſign'd with a clear View to the *Antique Circus*.

A s our *Bear-garden* may be juſtly eſteem'd no
bad Copy of the *Antient Circus*, it plainly de-
monſtrates, that the Souls of the loweſt of our
People are inſpir'd with a natural Propenſity to
the greateſt and fineſt *Entertainments* of Antiquity; and ſhould be accordingly diſtinguiſh'd, by a
particular Politeneſs in their *Gou* from all other
Nations.

T o ſet this Matter in a true Light, and give
my Readers a juſt Notion of the Reaſons for
this Compariſon betwixt two Places, which may
ſeem at firſt View widely different, it will be
abſolutely neceſſary to run over, in an hiſtorical
Manner, the various Shews which gave firſt Birth
to ſo ſpacious a Building, and trace them Step
by Step, thro' the ſeveral Ages and Parts of the
World, where theſe Spectacles have been exhibited with greateſt Splendor and Applauſe.

T h e Original Inſtitution of a *Circus* was undoubtedly *Grecian*, whether we conſider the Place,
or the general *Entertainment*, at leaſt upon the
Foun-

Foundation they had laid. The *Romans* erected their Superstructure, and furnish'd it likewise with proper Materials for the Inside, as shall be easily made manifest.

THE Design, Use, and Exercises of the *Grecian* GYMNASIA and STADIA, were in most Particulars the same, as to Building and Games, with the CIRCUS and AMPHITHEATRES of the *Romans :* And as for all the other Sports made use of in the latter, and wanting in the first, they were, without Dispute, borrow'd from the sacred Solemnities of the *Pythian, Nemean, Isthmian ;* but particularly from the Trials of Skill, in all Feats of Activity, at the celebrated *Olympick Games.*

BUT in Order to qualify my Readers to be competent Judges of what I have here advanc'd, I'll as briefly as possible recapitulate what Authors of Antiquity and greatest Credit have handed down to us on each Head, without canvassing different Opinions, as to Time, Place, Etymology, or Institution of every Particular ; then leave the Parallel to their Discretion.

THE GYMNASIA were common in every City of *Greece,* but first Founded at *Lacedemon :* They consisted of several different Piles of Building united together ; each of which serv'd for a several Purpose. They were properly a Kind of *Academy ;* and all Sciences for the Improvement of the Mind, as well as all Exercises for strengthening the Body, were cultivated here with the greatest Assiduity. The *Porticos* were fill'd with Seats for the Conveniency of the Scholars, who study'd, discours'd, or attended the Lectures of the Philosophers, Rhetoricians, Grammarians, or other Professors. The other Parts were particularly fitted up for exercising their Youth in all
those

thofe bodily Arts which ennur'd them to Hard-
fhips, knit their Limbs, confirm'd their Healths,
and train'd them up to appear in the Lifts of
Fame, at the Games of their greateft Feftivals.
In one they Wreftled, Run, Leap'd, Box'd, &c.
in another, play'd at Ball, in a third, Danc'd : Nor
were they without their feparate and convenient
Apartments for Bathing, Anointing Dufting,
Dreffing, and for making their Matches, fixing
what Sport they would contend in, and the Prize
of Conqueft. Thefe were fo order'd, that the
Whole of the Affair was tranfacted without any
Confufion, or Interruption to one another; tho'
the chief *Gymnafium* was generally capable of
accomodating feveral Thoufands of Spectators at
once, befides Numbers of Students and Combatants.

THE *Stadium* was either that Part of the *Gymnafium*, of a large femicircular Form, in which
all the fore-mention'd Exercifes were perform'd;
and where Seats were rais'd above one another,
for the Convenience of Multitudes, who flock'd
thither to fee thofe Practices in Skill and Strength;
or elfe were built apart from all other publick
Edifices, in the Form of a *Circus*, and for the
fame Ufes; of which the moft remarkable was
at *Athens*, built all of white Marble, being very
long, with two parallel Sides clos'd up circularly
to the Eaft End, and open towards the other. So
far the *Stadium* of the *Grecians* anfwers to the CIR-
CUS and AMPHITHEATRES of the *Romans*,
as being the undoubted Foundation of them, both
as to Building and Ufe. Let us now infpect the
folemn Feftivals of *Greece*, and fee what Materials were borrow'd from them for fupplying the
Circus with Variety of Amufements. The moft
noted of thefe publick, facred Games, were the
Olym-

Olympian, dedicated to *Jupiter Olympius,* for his Conqueſt over the Sons of *Titan,* which was the moſt celebrated Meeting in *Greece,* all States in general crowding thither: They were ſolemniz'd every fifth Year, and laſted five Days; no Woman, upon Pain of Death, was ſuffer'd to appear at this Solemnity. The *Pythian* Games were conſecrated to *Apollo,* in Memory of his deſtroying the Serpent *Python;* they were held near *Delphi,* and perform'd every Ninth, or afterwards, every fifth Year. The *Nemean* Games were inſtituted by *Hercules,* in Honour of *Jupiter,* after he had overcome the *Nemean* Lion, and were celebrated every third Year, near the Village of *Nemea,* where *Jupiter* had a Magnificent Temple.

THE *Iſthmian Games* were ſo call'd from the *Iſthmus* of *Corinth,* where they were ſolemniz'd. They were inſtituted in Honour of *Melicertes,* by *Siſyphus,* King of *Corinth,* or *Neptune,* by *Theſeus.* They were obſerved every third or fifth Year, and held inviolable.

Now let us take a ſhort View of the principal Exerciſes us'd in theſe ſacred *Games,* and the Honours paid to the Conquerors in thoſe Glorious Contentions.

THE principal Exerciſes made uſe of in theſe ſacred *Games,* conſiſted of Leaping, Running, Boxing, Darting, Throwing, Dancing, Wreſtling, and Racing. Leaping was perform'd with heavy Weights upon their Heads and Shoulders, and ſometimes carry'd in their Hands: They were uſually of an Oval Figure, with Holes in them to put their Fingers through, or Thongs to faſten them by. Running was in the higheſt Eſteem with the antient *Grecians;* Swiftneſs being thought a great Qualification in a Warrior, either as to a ſudden Onſet, or nimble Retreat.
The

The Courfe they ran was call'd the *Stadium*, being of the fame Number of Paces with that Meafure; tho' the Extent of the Race very often varied. Boxing was perform'd by the Combatants having great Balls of Iron, or Lead, in their Hands, to add Weight to their Blows. Their Hands, Wrifts, and Arms were bound round with Thongs of Leather, as high as the Shoulder. This fmall Armour was call'd *Ceftus*, and help'd to defend themfelves, and annoy their Antagonifts. In Darting, they went feveral Ways to work; they fometimes threw a Javelin, Rod, or other long Infrument out of their naked Hands, or by the Help of a Thong tied round its Middle; at other times, they fent out of a Bow, or caft out of a Sling, an Arrow, fmall Spear, or Dart.

In Throwing, the *Difcus* was made ufe of, being a *Quoit* of Brafs, Iron, or Stone, which they threw, by the Help of a Thong put thro' a Hole in the Middle of it. This was hurl'd in the Manner of a Bowl; not with the Hands lifted up and extended, as in Darting. Some of thefe *Difci* were of a Spherical Figure, others fourfquare. If Agility of Body was in fo great Requeft at thefe Games, DANCING could not be forgot. This was always perform'd in Armour; nor did the Weight of fo cumberfome a Drefs hinder them from fhewing the lighteft, nimbleft Motions. The chief Dance of this Kind was the *Pyrrhica Saltatio*. In Wreftling, they firft contended only, by Strength of Nature, to throw their Antagonifts; but afterwards the Art was introduc'd, by which the Weaker were enabled to foil thofe Superior in Strength. They never Wreftled till all their Joints and Members were well rubb'd and fomented with Oil; and

three

three Falls were requir'd to claim a Prize. *Racing* confifted either in running fingle Horfe againft Horfe, or by two Horfes; one for the Race, the other to leap on at the Goal; or by Chariots, in which were two, three, four or more Horfes, coupled together; not Pair after Pair, as we put Sets in a Coach, but all a-row in one Front. The greateft Skill in this Exercife was fhewn, in dextroufly avoiding the touching the Goal; in which if they fail'd, the Danger was as imminent as the Difgrace. Befides thefe Exercifes already mention'd, often *Poets, Muficians, Orators,* and *Hiftorians,* by repeating their Works, fpeaking *extempore* on any Subject, or by comparing Notes, contended for the Victory: But generally thofe Sports which moft conduc'd to fitting Mankind for warlike Exploits, were regarded with a favourable Eye, and look'd upon as the greateft Accomplifhments. Thus we fee that the Games practis'd at thefe publick Solemnities, were the fame with the Sports of the GYMNASIA; the Youth exercifing themfelves in the latter, to ripen them to Manhood, and qualify them for Victory in the former. The Honours paid to the Conquerors at any of thefe folemn Feftivals, were of the higheft Order allow'd to Mortals, and wanted but little of Divine Adoration to the principal Deities. They enter'd the City in a triumphal Chariot, the Walls being broke down, to make them a free Entrance; the greateft Pofts in the Army were affign'd them, and the firft Places at all publick Shews; magnificent Prefents were offer'd them by their Native Cities, and they were ever after maintain'd at the publick Charge. A fingle, or repeated Conqueft, was look'd upon as a prodigious Happinefs, and equal to the greateft Triumph,

umph, in Point of Fame: But to come off Victor in all the Exercises, was thought attaining to the highest Pitch of Felicity, and Merit, that human Nature could be capable of: Nay, being exalted to a Degree above the State of Men. Nor was this wonderful Respect confin'd to themselves alone; it extended to every Thing that related to them; it render'd the Place which gave them Birth, noted; their whole Family fortunate, and their Parents thrice happy, in the Eyes of the World. Fame indeed was what they all contended for; the Prizes adjudg'd the Conquerors at any of the Games, being in their intrinsick Value inconsiderable, being generally Crowns, Garlands, or Wreaths of Laurel, Palm, Beech-leaves, Parsly, Pine-leaves; which were thought sufficient to distinguish the Hero, and give him Immortality.

HAVING drawn this little Sketch of the *Grecian* Exercises, Games and Diversions, let us in the same concise Manner inspect those of the *Roman* State; then observe where they agree, or differ, upon the Parallel.

No Nation upon Earth ever so much delighted in all publick Spectacles as the *Romans*, or exhibited Shews with that expensive Magnificence, or diversify'd them with that agreeable Variety: Especially after being establish'd some Centuries, their primitive Rudeness was a little worn off; and by their frequent Recesses from War, and Intercourse with other Nations, they became insensibly softened, and of Consequence, easily moulded into all the politest Customs of the *East*.

THEY had THEATRES and AMPHITHEATRES erected at a vast Expence, and design'd with an Air of Grandeur; but indeed, all their

2　　　　　　　　　　　　　　publick

publick Buildings diftinguifh'd them as Mafters of the World. Thefe Edifices are often mention'd by Authors thro' Miftake, as *Synonomous* Terms; yet differ'd very much both in Form and Ufe. The THEATRES were entirely appropriated to all Kinds of *Dramatick* Poetry; the AMPHITHEATRES were referv'd as particularly for the Combats of the *Gladiators,* or thofe of Beaft againft Beaft, or Men and Beafts. The firft were of a *Semicircular* Form, or rather half of an Oval; the laft was made up of two of thefe exactly join'd. In the firft rude Ages of that Republick, thefe Structures were like the People, plain and ordinary; generally made of Wood, to ferve a prefent Occafion: But with the Empire their Magnificence rofe; as thofe of *Pompey, Marcellus, Tiberius, Claudius, Cornelius, Balbus, Titus,* &c. ---as the Defcriptions of their jufteft Writers, and the Remains of fome of them to this Day, teftify.

THERE were likewife feveral *Xyfti* in *Rome,* which were large *Porticos* for Wreftlers, and the Performers of the other Exercifes to practife in, when the extream Heat of the Sun, or wet Weather hinder'd their performing in open Air.

OF their *Odeum,* I can give but an imperfect Account, as I have already hinted in the fecond ESSAY. I meet with it often in Authors, call'd a Mufick THEATRE, and defcrib'd much in the common Form of other THEATRES; but as to their fatisfying us in the particular *Entertainments* there ufually exhibited, they might talk as much to the Purpofe, in telling us what a *Mufick-houfe* is at *Amfterdam.*

BUT of all publick Amufements, none were fo much the Favourites with the *Roman* People in general, from the Emperor to the Lictor, as

thofe

thofe call'd the *Circenfian* Shews; under which Title I comprehend all Reprefentations in the *Circus*, the *Naumachiæ*, the *Stadia*, or the AMPHITHEATRES; they differing more in the Name, than the Defign, or Application.

THE Shews exhibited in the *Circus*, or the AMPHITHEATRES, were much the fame; the latter only being erected for the more convenient Celebration of fome particular Sports or Exercifes, which were before prefented in the former. All the Paftimes, or Feats of Strength and Activity in Vogue there, were an exact Copy of thofe us'd at the *Grecian* Games, and juft now defcrib'd, and were generally comprehended under the Title of the *Pentathlum*, or *Quinquertium*, which included Running, Leaping, Wreftling, Throwing, Boxing, Darting, &c. The Manner of contending, the Laws for regulating the Victory, and the Prizes of Conqueft were in Effect the fame with thofe of *Greece*.

THE *Chariot-Races* were in as high Efteem with the *Romans* as any of the *Circenfian Sports*. The *Charioteers* were divided into four Companies, and all *Rome* into as many Factions, in Favour each of his darling Colour, which diftinguifh'd them. They made ufe in their Chariots of two, four, fix or feven Horfes. And *Suetonius* fays, That *Nero* drove a Chariot drawn with ten Horfes coupled together, at the publick Games: Nay, the fame Emperor at leaft oblig'd Pairs of Camels to perform in the fame Service: And *Heliogabalus* refin'd upon him, and introduc'd Elephants.

THE Extent of the Races, and the Number of Matches perform'd at once, was uncertain, being vary'd upon extraordinary Occafions, or at the Pleafure of the Emperor. The Conquerors

rors in this Sport were rewarded with Crowns, Coronets, and Garlands, as was cuſtomary in *Greece*; or ſometimes with very conſiderable Sums of Money.

The *Trojæ Ludus* was ſaid to be invented by *Aſcanius,* and was celebrated by Companies of noble Youths, neatly fitted out with proper Armour and Weapons, and headed either by the next Heir of the Empire, or the Son of ſome eminent Senator, who was ſtil'd, *Princeps juventutis.* This Game was perform'd on Horſe-back, in which all Motions of a warlike Onſet or Retreat were made uſe of, in order to inſtruct them in Martial Exerciſes, and anſwers to the *Pyrrhica Saltatio* of the *Greeks*; only the latter was exhibited on Foot.

The Shews of wild Beaſts were in general deſign'd to the Honour of *Diana,* Patroneſs of Hunting; and to anſwer that Inſtitution, all Species of them were, at an immenſe Expence, brought from the moſt remote and moſt different Parts of the World.

Some of theſe Creatures were preſented meerly to gratify the Curioſity of the People, who doated on ſuch ſtrange Sights, as Crocodiles, Unicorns, and Flying-dragons: Others were produc'd for the Combat; as Lions, Tygers, Leopards, Lynxes, Rhinoceros; others purely for the Delight and Uſe of the Spectators, who were allow'd to catch what Deer, Hares, or Rabbits they pleas'd.

A Shew of Beaſts then may be reduc'd to three Heads; the firſt, when the People were thus allow'd to carry off what Boars, Oxen, or Sheep they could catch for their own private Uſe; the ſecond, when Beaſts fought againſt Beaſts; as a Lion match'd with a Tyger, a wild Bull with

T 2   an

an Elephant; a Rhinoceros with a Bear, or Deer hunted by a Pack of Dogs: The third, when the Combat was betwixt Man and Beaft. The Men engag'd in this Enterprize had the general Name of *Beſtiarii*, and were either condemn'd Perſons, or thoſe who hired themſelves out, like the *Gladiators*, for a ſet Pay; and at laſt the Nobility, Gentry, and even their Women, had the Bravery to engage voluntarily in theſe glorious Encounters.

B u t of all the *Circenſian* Shews, that of *Gladiators* was the Favourite *Entertainment* of the *Roman* People in general. Their Riſe was owing to the very antient Cuſtom of ſacrificing Captives or Slaves at the Funerals or Tombs of eminent Men; the old Heathens fanſying the Ghoſts of the Deceas'd to be pleas'd with the ſpilling human Blood. Then finding the People highly delighted with ſuch cruel Diverſions, it grew into a Cuſtom, not only for the Heirs of the principal Magiſtrates, but even of the wealthy Citizens, to preſent them with theſe bloody *Entertainments*: Nay, even the Prieſts themſelves were often Exhibitors of ſuch ſanguinary Amuſements.

A t laſt the *Conſuls*, *Dictators* and *Emperors*, in order to ingratiate themſelves with the Commonalty, made a Birth-day, a Triumph, or a Conſecration of any publick Edifice, a Pretence for exhibiting a Shew of *Gladiators*: And, as their Return grew more frequent, ſo did the Number of Combatants, and Days of the Solemnity encreaſe; the firſt riſing from three Pair to three Hundred and twenty; and the latter, from one Day to One Hundred and twenty three.

T h e ſeveral Kinds of *Gladiators* are not neceſſary to be mention'd here; as to their Condi-
tion.

tion, they were at firſt, either Captives of War, condemn'd to that Life, or Slaves bought, inſtructed by able Maſters, and let out to hire for that Purpoſe.

But in a little time the Freemen themſelves claim'd the Priviledge of being kill'd, to divert their Fellow Citizens, and took Pay for ſo doing at the AMPHITHEATRES; nay, the Knights, Senators, and Ladies of Quality, bluſh'd not to enter the Liſts, and own the Profeſſion, till reſtrain'd by a publick Edict of *Auguſtus.*

The *Naumachiæ,* as to their Form, are no where particularly deſcrib'd, but are ſuppos'd to differ very little in that from the *Circos,* or AMPHITHEATRES, only the lower Part, or Groundplat, was fill'd with Water for the Repreſentation of Naval Fights, or a Contention of Rowing for Victory. They were at firſt deſign'd to initiate their Men in a Knowledge of Sea-Affairs, in their Wars againſt the *Carthaginians,* and were afterwards improv'd into one of their ſolemn Shews, as well to gratify the People, as to encreaſe Naval Experience and Diſcipline: And ſome of the Emperors affecting Popularity, were at vaſt Trouble and Expence to court the People by *Entertainments* of this Nature.

The Emperor *Claudius* made Uſe of the *Fucine* Lake; on which he preſented a moſt magnificent Sea-Engagement, to an infinite Multitude of Spectators. *Domitian* form'd by Art a Sea of Waters; then produc'd a Number of Veſſels on either Side, ſufficient to have furniſh'd out two compleat Navies for a real Fight: But *Heliogabalus,* in his Repreſentation of a *Naumachia,* fill'd the Channel with Wine in place of Water, and thus *out-did* all his other *Out-doings.* The *Stadia* were Places in Form of a *Circus,* ap-

propri-

propriated entirely to the Running of Men and Horses; the moſt noble of which was built by *Domitian*.

THE *Campus Martius*, conſecrated to the God *Mars*, was mightily reſorted to by the *Romans*, on Account of the Sports and Exerciſes perform'd there. Here the young Nobility practiſ'd all Feats of Activity, and learn'd the Uſe of Arms, and Rudiments of War. Here, often, the Races for Chariots, or ſingle Horſes, were undertaken; which pleaſing Variety of Sights, made it one of the moſt agreeable Places in or about the City.

I have been as conciſe as poſſible on this Head; but in an Affair of this Conſequence, Obſcurity is more to be avoided than Prolixity: Therefore I ſhall at once proceed to conſider the Diverſions of our *Bear-garden*, upon a Parallel with thoſe of the *Antique Circus*, as ſuccinctly as a neceſſary Perſpicuity will admit of.

I muſt here caution my Readers to remember, that under the general Title of the Shews of the *Circus*, or *Bear-garden*, I comprehend all thoſe *Entertainments* I have ſpoke to in this ESSAY, as far as they related to the *Antients*, or that I ſhall ſpeak to, as copied from them by the Moderns: And when I talk of either of theſe Places in the ſingular Number, that repreſents the reſt of the Brotherhood in *Athens*, *Rome* or *London*. It will be altogether foreign to the Buſineſs in Hand, to recapitulate, or enlarge upon the Part the *Grecians* play'd at all *Entertainments* of this Nature. What I have already advanc'd on this Subject, is ſufficient to ſhew, that the publick Exerciſes to which they train'd up their Youth, in order to appear as Candidates for

Fame

Fame at all their Games, were undoubtedly the Noble Original of the *Roman Circus* and *British Bear-garden.*

THE Great *Circus* in *Rome,* was a very large Oblong Square, with Noble Galleries, of the finest Architecture and Materials for the Spectators of the Games, according to their several Degrees; and under them, the Caves and Dungeons for the Beasts and Malefactors, who furnish'd out the *Entertainments.* In the Middle were several Ornamental Pillars, Altars, *&c.* with the *Meta,* round which the Chariots in their Races turn'd; where they set out, and where the Race concluded. In the *Arena* (which was strew'd with Sand, to suck up the Combatant's Blood, and hinder their Feet from slipping) were all the usual Exercises perform'd.

To this, in Use, if not in Grandeur and Beauty, answers our *Bear garden*; the same the Design, End and Form, tho' I cannot say much as to the Buildings, Ornaments, or Encouragement which the other boasted: Tho' I will venture to affirm, that our Copy is upon an equal Foot of Merit with their Original. We have indeed some sorry Balconies and wooden Galleries for the Use of the Spectators, and a Pit for the exhibiting our Shews; but all conformable to the Appearance of those who are the chief Support of these Amusements, the lowest of the Vulgar; which as it is a Shame, it is a pity, and as it is a Pity, it is a Shame.

IN the *Circus,* the chief Spectacles were Men against Men; —— Men against Beasts —— and Beasts against Beasts: Chariot, or Horse-races, Leaping, Wrestling, and other Exercises of the like Nature.

IN

IN the *Bear-garden*, our *Prize-fighters* Tally with their *Gladiators*, shewing as much Sport, and spilling less Blood; our Courage being made manifest thus to the World, without their Cruelty.

MEN indeed seldom enter our Lists against Beasts, unless Butchers against Bull-dogs, in brotherly Alliance with their own Curs; whose Preservation and Honour are justly as dear to them as those of their Wife and Children.

BUT as for Beasts against Beasts —— I think we may modestly say, we equal, if not exceed any Thing they ever produc'd on that Head; our charming Bears, our noble Bulls, and nobler Mastiffs, must give those Spectators (who have Sense enough to frequent all publick Amusements, to be instructed as well as delighted) the truest Notions of an invincible Bravery, join'd to the most sagacious Conduct. On the other Hand, the Tygers, Leopards, Rhinoceros, Lions and Elephants of the *Antients*, never afforded that Variety of Diversion; the whole of that Affair being the same brutal Fierceness repeated, void of all just Courage and fine Contrivance.

THEN our teizing of a tame Ass into Madness, with Dogs at his Heels, and lighted Squibs and Crackers all round him——the baiting a wild Bear with Wheel-barrows, and teaching Horses to Dance, play at Cards, and tell Fortunes —— are *Entertainments* of that Novelty, Beauty and Grandeur, as never were known to the most Expensive and Luxurious of the Old *Roman* Emperors.

IF we cannot boast of their Chariot-races, we can, to the Immortal Honour of our Country shew, that the Noble Sports of Wrestling, Cudgel-playing, Fisty-cuffs, Leaping, *&c.* flourish

rifh in *Britain,* more, perhaps, than ever they
did in *Greece :* Diverfions that have more Humanity and Difcipline in them, than the well-tim'd
Crack of a Whip, or the nice Turning of a
Poft.

THESE fhould have been the principal Foundation of their *Circus,* as they were of the *Grecian* Games, and are of our *Bear-garden :* And
tho' they have been the Admiration of Antiquity, not a Shadow of them now remains, but as
happily preferv'd in their Original Purity by the
Britifh Nation.

As thefe publick Games were the Delight of
Greece for many Ages; on which principally depended the Education of their Youth, and the
Amufements of the Old, being maintain'd by
the joint Confent of all the feparate States, tho'
ever fo much difunited on other Accounts; and
this at a Time, when at their Height for Power,
Learning and Magnificence.

So with the *Romans,* the Reprefentations of
the *Circus* were the Darlings of their People,
when their Wit was clear, their Studies folid,
their Pleafures polite, and their Sway univerfal.
And in either Empire with thefe they flourifh'd,
and with them fell; bravely furmounting all Difficulties, and withftanding all Shocks, till fwal-
low'd up in that of a general Ruin.

PEOPLE of Genius and Spirit may fhew a
reafonable Surprize, that the Amufements of the
Bear-gardens are fo ftrangely neglected by People
of Senfe and Diftinction; efpecially, as they are
prov'd juft Copies of fuch Glorious Originals:
But what will they fay? when I fhall plainly
demonftrate, that they may be render'd of the
utmoft Importance to this Nation, by keeping
up the true Old *Englifh* Spirit, and training up
every

every individual *Briton* to be a General! ———a Hero!

I f the vaſt Diſparity betwixt the *Circus* and *Bear-garden*, in the Articles of Grandeur and Expence, is objected to us, let us but conſider the prodigious Encouragement given to their S H E W S by *Senators, Conſuls, Dictators, Emperors*, and their whole State : Nay, the World in Conjunction with them, ſtrove who ſhould add greateſt Luſtre to their Games.

A n d as we can boaſt the ſame Foundation, I think our People of Quality, Fortune, and publick Spirit, ſhould with the greateſt Zeal promote theſe Diverſions, if not with a View of pleaſing or inſtructing themſelves, yet with a due Regard to the Delight and Improvement of the *Populace*, and the Honour of their Country.

T h u s will the In-bred Valour and Martial Genius of this Nation be rous'd up and fix'd : Thus will the loweſt of the People be inur'd to behold with Raptures, gaſh'd Faces, ſpouting Veins, goary Sculls, hack'd Limbs, *&c.* Thus will they be harden'd to the moſt fearleſs Contempt of Danger and Death : Thus will our Bulldogs, thoſe Noble Creatures, our other ſelves (Beaſts by Nature appropriated to this Nation) be kept in perfect Order, and that valuable Race preſerv'd : Thus will ſuch Spectacles add to the Native Fierceneſs of both, and breath a new Soul into the whole Kingdom.

A n d indeed, if we enter'd a little more particularly into the real Merits of the *Circus* and *Bear-garden*, we ſhall find, that in Variety, the Original Deſign, and deſir'd End, they differ not widely, however we fall ſhort in Point of Luxury and Magnificence.

F i r s t,

FIRST, then, let us examine the antient State of the *Gladiators,* upon the Parallel with our Modern *Prize-fighters,* they being the main Pillars of the *Circus* and *Bear-garden.*

I have already shewn, that the Rise of the *Gladiators* was owing to that barbarous Custom practis'd in all Ages of Antiquity, of sacrificing Captives, or Slaves, at the Funerals and Tombs of great Men. The *Romans,* who exceeded in Humanity most other Nations, scorning such mean Butchery, commanded them to kill one another like Men. Their first *Gladiators,* tho' they were of the same Rank with those who grac'd the foreign Funeral Altars, being either Slaves by Birth, Captives of War, or Malefactors condemn'd by Justice to Death. The first fought for Liberty, the others for Life. As they came more into Reputation, People voluntarily enter'd themselves into the Service for Pay, were regularly enlisted as Soldiers, and an *Academy* establish'd for instructing them in the Art of cutting Throats cleverly and decently. At last, to oblige some of the Emperors, Persons of Figure and Distinction enter'd the *Circus* as *Gladiators,* greedy of Immortal ¦Fame: And *Nero* once compell'd a Thousand *Knights* and *Senators* in one Day, to grace his SHEWS, and cut, flash and slay one another in the most beautiful Manner, for the Good of their Country.

THE Combats were attended with Freedom to the Conquerors, if Slaves; or Donatives from the Emperor and People, if hir'd Persons: But Death to the Vanquish'd, if Life was not granted upon imploring Mercy from the Spectators; and this happen'd just as their Fingers and Thumbs chanc'd to be in Humour.

THO'

Tho' during the whole Courfe of the *Roman* Empire, all the *Circenfian Shews* were the Delight of the People; yet this of the *Gladiators* was look'd on with the moft favourable Eye, always receiv'd with uncommon Raptures; and, at all Triumphs, Feftivals, Funerals, or any publick Demonftration of Joy, or Grief, the Solemnity was counted imperfect without it.

Thus with fome fmall Intermiffions (and vifible Tokens of Decay, as the Empire it felf grew feeble and aged) the *Gladiators* ftood their Ground till the Year Five Hundred, that a King of the *Oftrogoths* totally banifh'd them from *Italy*: And, certainly, nothing but a *Goth* could have been fo barbarous as to have thus rudely deftroy'd a Diverfion, which for fo many Ages charm'd the wifeft, politeft, and moft powerful State upon Earth! But in my poor Judgment, the Manner of their Deftruction is an undeniable Proof of the Merit and Politenefs of the *Entertainment*.

Thus in *Italy* the *Gladiators* rofe, flourifh'd, fell, and for feveral Centuries lay bury'd, till luckily reviv'd in *England*: The only Nation upon Earth that can boaft the raifing from the Dead an Amufement in it felf equally ufeful and genteel; an Amufement, which from its intrinfick Worth fo long claim'd a due Refpect from the Mafters of the World.

This my laft Affertion may meet with fome Oppofers, who will readily object to me the *Jufts* and *Tournaments* fo much in Vogue for feveral Centuries, and which have been altogether dropp'd for thefe two Hundred Years paft; as likewife the Bull-Feafts that are held in fo great Requeft, at prefent, all over *Spain* and *Portugal*.

I

As

As to the firſt of theſe, I cannot in the leaſt Feature find out a Reſemblance betwixt them and the old *Gladiators*, either in the Deſign, the Conduct, or the Conſequence of the Combat; but am more apt to think them rather an Imition of the *Pyrrhica-Saltatio*, or *Trojæ-Ludus* before deſcrib'd; only in theſe, there never was any Blood ſhed, which but too often happen'd in their *Juſts* and *Tilts*.

As to the latter, the *Spaniſh* Cavaliers indeed ſet forth in dreadful Array to encounter their wild Bulls, come very near one material Article of the SHEWS of the *Circus*, that of Men a-gainſt Beaſts: But I am inclinable to think, that with the *Romans* the *Beſtiarii* were not allow'd to be mounted ſo compleatly arm'd, or well at-tended to defeat, in an apparent Danger, the furi-ous Onſet of a Villainous-minded Bull, as the bold-ſpirited Dons are.

IT remains for me now to ſpeak to our Mo-dern *Prize-Fighters* in a way of Compariſon with the Antient *Gladiators*; and at the ſame time come to the material Deſign of this ESSAY, and ſhew that we can carry this *Entertainment* to a greater Height, both as to Pleaſure and Profit, than has been known to former Ages; where there ſhould no Cruelty appear but in the Way of Juſtice; no Blood ſhed but for Inſtruction; and Life or Death only conſider'd, as every Man is devoted to the Good of his Country.

OUR Modern *Prize Fighters*, thoſe happy Co-pies of the Old *Gladiators*, ſhew a Spirit ſuperi-or to the boaſted Bravery of the *Romans*: For as they are not Slaves, of Conſequence not oblig'd to Fight; they only Fight for Fighting's ſake.

U BUT

But as I would embellish the *Bear-garden* Scene with the greatest Variety of *Actors*; and have always in Reserve a Number sufficient, not only to amuse the People, but to answer the unexpected Exigencies of the State, in Case of a Rebellion, Invasion, &c. So we must not too far trust barely to Hirelings for that Service. All Ages and Nations have experienc'd that Supply to be precarious; and especially in a Country of Liberty and Property, will altogether depend upon Whim and Humour. Therefore I propose, as a Matter of the last Importance to this Nation, and as the greatest Promoter of beautiful Justice—First—That all our Malefactorscondemned to Death, be forc'd to stab, hack and hew themselves to Pieces for the Good of their Fellow Subjects; then their Deaths will infallibly prove of a more general Use to their Country, than their Lives could have been pernicious. By this Means the most profligate Wretches may die the truest Patriots; and every *Blueskin*, or *Sheppard*, go off the Stage, a *Curtius*, or *Murtius-Scavola*. Thus argued *Tully* himself, when the Charge of Barbarity was laid to the Shews of Gladiators. —— *These* Shews, says he, *may seem to some People very inhuman; but where only guilty Persons compose the Number of the Combatants, 'tis impossible that any Thing should fortify us with more Success, against the Assaults of Grief or Death.* And he might have added —— *or more effectually instill a warlike Disposition into the Minds of the People.*

Secondly, —— I would oblige all State Criminals adjug'd to Transportation, or other corporal Punishments, to List themselves in the Service of the Bear-Garden, in order, by small Play, to be instructed themselves in the Ru-

3   diments

diments of War. Thus a little Gaſh, Cut, or Thruſt, will inure them to the bearing of greater Wounds; be a Puniſhment in ſome Reſpect adequate to their paſt Crimes, and at the ſame time delight the *Populace*; train them up to Martial Exerciſes, and arm them againſt all cowardly Ideas.

THIRDLY, —— to encourage Spectators to come there with a ſincere Deſign to improve, the Go————nt ſhould allow any Man that is willing to be enroll'd as an Out-penſioner, to be call'd upon in Caſes of Neceſſity, to be free of the BEAR-GARDEN, both as to Diverſion and Inſtruction; and that he ſhould be abſolutely at Liberty to have a crack'd Skull, a Thump on the Ribs, or broken Shins, whenever he demanded them, *gratis*.

I have already ſhewn what particular Influences this Propoſal, well executed, may have on the Minds of the Commonalty of *England* in general. I now beg Leave to hint at the principal Advantage to which the whole Scheme muſt naturally tend.

As the Scituation of this Kingdom, the fundamental Conſtitution of our State, and the Temper of our People require not a great Number of Standing Forces, kept in conſtant Pay; ſo if, upon any Emergency, our Affairs ſhould ſtand in Need of a larger Supply than is uſually kept on Foot, where ſhall we find Recruits to anſwer the preſſing Neceſſities of the State, and form, in a Hurry, a large Army? All Ages and Nations have experienc'd, and ſmarted for the Folly of truſting too far, to raw and undiſciplin'd Troops: —— Where then can we hope for a ſeaſonable Relief in ſuch a Scene of Diſtreſs, but from a well-regulated BEAR-GARDEN, whoſe

U 2　　　　　　　　　Auxili-

Auxiliaries may prove new-rais'd Troops, but veteran Heroes? 'Tis evident, that it may be brought to that Pass, as to form an *Academy* for the Army, a Nursery for Infant-Warriors, as *Chelsea-College* is for the Old. Let but our Encouragement rise to an equal Height with that of the *Romans*, in the SHEWS of their GLADIATORS, and we should never be reduc'd to so low an Ebb as to beat up for Voluntiers: Several Regiments, at a short Warning, might be borrow'd from the BEAR-GARDEN UNIVERSITY; every Man at least a Batchelor of Arts in the Sciences offensive and defensive, and a sufficient Number always kept in *petto*, as a *Corps de Reserve.*

SOME People may sneer at my Project, as absurd or chimerical; but let those merry Gentlemen consider, how often the *Romans* were oblig'd to Lift their GLADIATORS, when their Legions out-stretch'd *Arithmetick*, and they were Masters of the World.

LET any Man but read over attentively the Bills of Defiance from any of our BEAR-GARDENS, or AMPHITHEATRES, and the brave Replies of their Antagonists; if there be the smallest Spark of Courage *latent* in his Soul, such intrepid Terms of Honour must blow it up to a Flame of Glory. The World may talk of *Alexander*, *Scipio*, *Hannibal*, and *Julius Cæsar*, whilst I set fearless in their View, *Kned Sutton*, *Jack Fig*, *Tim Buck*, and *Bob Stokes.*

As I have before provided the Army with Of———rs from the *Mas*———*de*; so I have now furnish'd it with private Men from the BEAR-GARDEN, which will be a certain Fund upon all Emergencies, without any real Expence to the Nation.

WERE

WERE it thought neceffary to cultivate the Genius of thofe defign'd for Sea Affairs, in the fame Method of Education, 'tis but turning our Eyes towards the *Naumachia* of the *Antients*, and obferving nicely all the Rules eftablifh'd in the BEAR-GARDEN only with Refpect to the Difference between Sea and Land-fervice. I fancy we may then produce fomething on the *Thames*, which could not have been fo well executed on the *Tiber*.

I muft own, all the other *Entertainments* of the BEAR-GARDEN, are prudently imagin'd, and becoming the Bent of a brave People; and all conduce to the great Defign, of mixing Inftruction with our Amufements: And, that Men may be inftructed by Brutes, *Æfop, Lemuel Guliver*, and *Hockly in the Hole* fhew us. Who can view Dogs tearing Bulls, Bulls goaring Dogs, or Maftiffs throtling Bears, without being animated with their daring Spirits! And what is brutal Fiercenefs in them, may produce true human Courage in us. Were the BEAR-GARDEN once rightly eftablifh'd, the Managers of it might venture to introduce Lions, Tygers, Unicorns and Rhinocero's in formal Combat: This, with an Elephant or two to fhew Poftures, and a Flying-dragon for the high Ropes, would give the jufteft Notions of, and put us upon a Level with Antiquity, in the Articles of Grandeur and Variety.

BUT not to dwell altogether on the Merits of the BEAR-GARDEN, or our AMPHITHEATRES for PRIZE-FIGHTERS, as founded on the *Entertainments* of the antique CIRCUS, before I entirely quit the Regions of fighting Men, and fighting Beafts, I muft not pafs by, unregarded, our fighting Fowls.

U 3 THE

THE Diverfions of our COCK PITS are really *Englifh*, as to the Invention, Excellency, and Application: And as no Nation can pretend to match us in a Sprightly, Noble, Martial Race of *Cocks*; fo I think, the Amufement they give us, may vie with any thing Antique or Modern, as to Humanity and Politenefs. Our Tafte on that Head is fo refin'd, fo adapted to People of the firft Quality, and moft elegant Education, that the Affurance of fome Countries is to me amazing, where they would be diftinguifh'd by a *picquant Gou*, and an univerfal Knowledge in every Thing polite, as to our killing Time in the moft agreeable Manner; ——— yet have not the leaft Notion of COCK-FIGHTING.

THE Pride, the Life, the Courage of thefe little Creatures, would inflame a Coward, and fpur him on to the moft daring Attempts. Who could, unmov'd, behold thefe feemingly infignificant Birds, cut, flafh, and tear one another to Pieces! It muft animate a *Therfites* with the Soul of *Hector*, to view them all over one gaping Wound, yet difdaining to yield their Hold or Ground, tho' in the Pangs of Death! No Spectacle can be more becoming a Man, except the Refinement upon this Diverfion, as practis'd on Shrove-Tuefday, *the bravely knocking them on the Head with Clubs*; an Amufement parallel to which no Time, or Nation of Antiquity can boaft of.

I am fo elevated with this Subject, that when once I am fairly enter'd, I could talk of it without ceafing; and, perhaps, in my Fury be tranfported to fay fomething not over much to the Purpofe: But fuch a World of Matter crowds this ESSAY, that I am oblig'd to proceed in examining the Merits of another *Entertainment*,
which

which indeed difgraces the BEAR-GARDEN, in being mention'd in fuch bad Company, as our *Italian* Strolers.

IN the third ESSAY upon DANCING, I took fome fmall Notice of the Original and Conduct of the true *Italian Stage*, which always appear'd to me a tolerable Copy of the Old *Mimes*; as thefe travelling Stagers feem to be only proper Appendixes to the Retinue of a *Mountebank*.

WE have been often promis'd the Top Company of *Europe* in their Way, and as often deceiv'd, being ftill forc'd to take up with the Refufe which foreign Stages had caft away : Nay, thofe merry Gentlemen who lately engrofs'd the *Opera-Houfe*, in fo magnificent a Manner, were but the Gleanings of thofe Rabble Sets, who had the Honour of entertaining the *French* Nobility in the Neighbourhood of *Soho*, at the *Ginger-bread* THEATRE, on the other fide the *Hay-market*.

TO form a true Idea of thefe itinerant Players, and undeceive that Part of the World which may expect mighty Matters from them, I am inclinable to think, that moft of them were got under Hedges, born in Barns, and brought up in Houfes of Correction : Nor fhould they ever dare to fhew their Faces in any Place but a wooden Booth.

FOR, undoubtedly, the buskind *Ragamuffins* that *Thefpis* firft carted about the World, muft have been *Demi-gods* and *Heroes*, to thefe Pedlars in Poetry, and Gipfies of the Stage.

IT is impoffible to enter into a regular Criticifm, either on their Action, or *Drama*, to get thro' fuch Heaps of Rubbifh, would require more than *Herculean* Help : The Confufion of fuch Nonfenfical Scenes cannot be view'd forwards,

wards, they will not bear the least Light; nor have they the Merit even of a Witch's Prayer, to be read backwards.

THEREFORE to set them off to the best Advantage, let us only consider them as deck'd out in the most glaring Ornaments, and painted in the gayest Colours, in their own publick Bills; --- of which the following is but a Specimen ———— This Evening *Argentina will represent a particular Fatigue, call'd the* Hobgoblin; *with a Prologue by all the Devils in Hell: A* Comedy *of that Variety of Incidents, that she personates all Nations upon Earth, with Singing and Dancing in all their different Manners.* —— Another Evening, Pantalon *undertakes his particular Fatigue, by performing a* Comedy *in a* Comedy; *where he's engag'd by Honour,* Argentia *suppos'd a Countess by Mistake of a Picture;* Diana, *a cheated Lady;* Arlequin, *a mistaken Eunuch; in which Signior* Franchelino *danc'd with a Machine on his Head, the Favourite of the King of* Morocco. —— Arlequin *in the* Proteo Novello, *personated a* French *Officer, a Chimny-sweeper, a walking Statue, a Blackmoor Stand, an Astrologer, an Infant, a* Diana; *to which was added, the comical Scene of a stuttering Musick-master, by* Brighella. Argentina *went thro' another very particular Fatigue, in the Affectation of a new Title, wherein the Doctor, by the Name of* Tabarin, *perform'd a new Character, both very comical and jocose, never yet seen on any Stage. Then* Brighella, *in the surprizing Disguises of* Cartouche, *counterfeited the Personages of a* Turk, *a petit-maitre, a Merchant, a* Swiss, *an* Armenian, *a* Florentine, *a* Venetian *Gondolier, an* English *Water-man, a* French *Dwarf, and a fine Lady; in which Signior* Grimaldo *of* Malta *danc'd a wonderful Dance within a dark Lanthorn, never*
yet

yet seen; with the diverting Humour of the Mistress Devil, and the Maid Devil.

Let any Pretender to common Sense judge of the Merit of their Performances, from this Theatrical *Gallimafry* of Poetry, Musick and Dancing, as ingeniously express'd in *Phrases* peculiar to themselves.

Did they strictly adhere, in any Point, to the Old Institution and Art of the *Pantomimes*, they might be introduc'd in most *Stage-Entertainments*, by Way of an Interlude, with great Success; particularly, they might with Propriety fill up the Vacancies betwixt the Acts in the *Italian Operas*, which would prove an agreeable Variety to most of the *Audience*.

But in the Manner their *Dramatical* Jumbles are conducted, they are a Scandal to any Stage, an Encroachment upon our Theatres, and a Banter on all Kinds of *Poetry*. As the Affair of Theatrical *Dancing* is carry'd far beyond their weak Attempts in our own *Play-houses*; so there is nothing else left for them, in which they dare pretend to please.

We having once fairly got rid of them, It may be thought unnecessary, even to have condescended to mention them; but having formerly found several Patrons, it is necessarily proper to prepare People to receive them suitable to their Merits, in case of a second Visit.

While I am engag'd in this stroling Family, I cannot in Conscience neglect the most valuable Branch of it, a *Mountebank*'s Travelling-Stage; which we shall readily perceive to be in all Respects superior to their Relations from Abroad.

For, if we nicely and impartially examine the Conduct of these Gentlemen (from Doctor *Smith*, who

who keeps his Coach and Six, to the Old Pim-
ple-fac'd *Quack*, who paces from Market to Market on his py-ball'd Pad) we muſt be convinc'd,
that they are the moſt publick-ſpirited Men upon
Earth; that they only profeſs *Phyſick* for the
Good of their Country, and throw *gratis* their
Labour, Tumblers, Rope-dancers, and Jack-pud-
dings into the Bargain.

THIS is honourable; this is acting without
Reſerve, for the Benefit of Mankind: Nay, they
are often ſo generous of the Fruits of their Labour, that in order to provoke People to rectify
what is amiſs in their Conſtitutions, they part
with their *Phyſick* for leſs than what it coſt them.

NOTHING can be more judiciouſly imagin'd
than their additional Stage-Amuſements, nor more
apropos to the Affair in Hand. They prudently
conſider, that *Phyſick* never operates ſo well,
as when the Patient is in good Humour. Thus
with every Medicine they give you an equal Doſe
of Mirth, to prepare you by proper Motions for
its working. A *Merry-Andrew* will whip out
your Tooth, as he catches you laughing at his
dry Jeſt; or whilſt a Country-fellow is gaping at
the Rope-dancer, he may have a Paper of Pills,
or a black Potion thrown down his Throat.

THEN the Doctor's Solemnity of Addreſs,
Gravity of Countenance, and Rich Clothes, give
the Vulgar ſo juſt an Idea of his profound Capacity, that they muſt at leaſt prove the better
half of the Cure in any Diſeaſe: For, undoubtedly an implicit Faith in our Phyſician, is the
moſt valuable Part of his Pacquet, or Preſcription.

WERE we to enter into a formal Compariſon
of theſe Rival Twins, we ſhould find that the
Mountebank-Stage, in every Particular, exceeds the
Itinerant

Itinerant Italian. The Defign, the Conduct, the End propos'd in all publick Amufements, are judg'd with greater Propriety, and executed more to the Purpofe, in the firft than the laft; they aim at fomething, and feldom mifs the Mark.

One acts always in Cover, the other in open Air; a ftrong Argument in Favour of them whofe Deeds and Words can bear the niceft Scrutiny in Day-light, and ftand the publick Teft of the World.

Some People may affert, that there is no effential Difference betwixt them; the Action and Expreffion of both being extravagantly low and ridiculous, confifting altogether of Grimace and Nonfenfe: But even here the *Mountebank* triumphs, he executes what he defigns; his Pretences to Wit and Action, are calculated to be upon the Level with the Underftandings of the Mob; and all their Tricks and Jokes are fo many Baits artfully difpos'd for the catching greedy Gudgeons.

Therefore as I have been often a Spectator of both Performances, and confider'd them in a juft, critical Light, I will maintain, that the *Mountebank* Drollery is in all Points more natural, genteeler, and better hit off than that of their fcurvy Imitators, the *Italian Farce-Actors.*

There remains nothing now for me to add to what has been advanc'd on this Subject, but wifhing thofe Gentlemen Strolers fo much Bufinefs at Home, that they may never have Leifure, or Inclination, to favour us with another Vifit.

I am of Opinion, That from fome fmall Hints fcatter'd up and down this Essay, and fome of the former, moft of my Readers will be convinc'd, that no Man can be in a worfe Scituation,

tion, as to a polite Taste in publick Amusements, than an Admirer of *Operas* at *L———n's-I———n-F———ds, Grotesque* Dancing at *D———y--L———ne,* and *Italian* Plays in the *H---y---M———t.*

IN the whole Course of my Travels, nothing ever excited my Curiosity in a higher Degree, or gave me more sensible Delight, than taking particular Notice of the several Diversions of every Country, in order from thence to form a Judgment of the various Dispositions of different Nations.

THE Mechanical Genius of the *English* is obvious to every body in many Cases, but in none more properly, than in the Contrivance and Conduct of our PUPPET-SHEWS: The Improvement of which is certainly owing to us, if not the Invention; and, indeed, it has often prov'd our Province to refine upon the first Thoughts of others, in Works of Art and Ingenuity.

I confess, I cannot view a well-executed PUP-PET-SHEW, without extravagant Emotions of Pleasure: To see our Artists, like so many *Prometheus's,* animate a Bit of Wood, and give Life, Speech and Motion, perhaps, to what was the Leg of a Joint-stool, strikes me with a pleasing Surprize, and prepossesses me wonderfully in Favour of these little wooden Actors, and their *Primum-mobile.*

THESE portable Stages are of infinite Advantage to most Country Towns, where *Play-houses* cannot be maintain'd; and, in my Mind, superior to any Company of Strolers: The Amusement is innocent and instructive, the Expence is moderate, and the whole Equipage easily carry'd about; as I have seen some Couples of Kings and Queens, with a suitable Retinue of Courtiers and Guards, very well accommodated in a

single

single Band-box, with Room for *Punch* and his Family, in the same Machine. The Plans of their little Pieces do not barely aim at Morality, but enforce even Religion: And, it is impossible to view their Representations of *Bateman*'s Ghost, *Doctor Faustus*'s Death, or Mother *Shipton*'s Tragical End, but that the bravest Body alive must be terribly afraid of going to the D——l.

IT is necessary to observe here, That the Plans upon which these little *Tragi-Comedies* are form'd, are generally borrow'd from those Subjects I recommended in the first ESSAY to the *Opera-house*. Those Domestick Matters of Fact always prove the Favourites of the People; which induc'd me to believe, that they might appear with equal Success on the Stage of the great PUPPET-SHEW in the *H——y-m——t*.

I have already hinted at the beautiful Imitation of an *Antique-Chorus*, so justly executed by the Prompter of the PUPPET SHEW, in the Person of *Punch*; who, exactly in the Manner of the *Coryphæus* of the *Antients*, has something to say in every Scene, and makes every bodies Business his own.

AS I have particularly taken Notice of *Rope-dancers, Strolers, Mountebanks, Puppet-shews,* &c. and mention'd them with all the Respect due to their Merits; it would be look'd upon as the highest Ingratitude, carelessly to pass unregarded those Places where they oftenest shine, and in greatest Splendor; I mean our publick *Fairs*.

HAVING only profess'd to reform the Errors, or point out the Beauties in our publick Diversions, no Man will expect, that I should in the least touch upon the Article of Trade, it being quite foreign to my Design, and the *Fairs* I speak of, commonly of a Nature opposite to it; tho'

X   even

even in that Point, they may be render'd very advantagious, by bringing of well-difpos'd People together, for their mutual Profit and Amufement: For where fuch Meetings are prudently, and conveniently contriv'd, there will be Trades of fome Sort or other continually going forward. Nor do I intend to infpect the yearly *Rendezvous* at *Sturbridge*, *Bury*, or other large Towns; they not falling naturally within the Precincts of my Enquiries: Nor, indeed, dare I venture fo far out of my Depth, as to go beyond the Limits of the Bills of Mortality.

I have in my Days feen *May-Fair*, that Favourite of *Nobility* and *Mobility*, quite demolifh'd, to the general Regret of all, but thofe Powers to whom, with Patience, we muft fubmit. Nay, my Old Friend *Bartholomew*'s Wings are clofe -lipp'd; his Liberties retrench'd, and Priviledges invaded. How alter'd! —— how funk from his former Golden State! —— Thofe merry, drunken, whoring Days! —— when immortal *Ben* thought it no mean Subject for his comick *Mufe*. We live in Hopes, the Loffes there fuftain'd will be made up to us t'other fide the *Thames*, and that *Southwark* may be what *May* and *Bartholomew Fairs* have been. It happens at that dead Time of Year, when Bufinefs and Diverfions in *London* fink under the Weight of a long Vacation, when Trade lies dead, and Pleafure languifhes; whilft there they raife their drooping autumnal Heads, and revive to charm us with new budding Delights, as in the Spring.

THERE Scepter'd Kings, and Long-tail'd Queens fill the capacious Stage, to awe with their tinfel Grandeur, the admiring Populace. There Love-fick Heroes, and fighing Princeffes too, in friendly Murmurs, to break the Hearts of

amorous

amorous Prentices, and draw Floods of Tears from good-natur'd Chamber-maids. There the humorous Clowns and cunning Sharpers display their Talents of Joke and Trick, till tickell'd Cockneys stretch their Sides with immoderate Laughter. There the Beaus and Belles (who have only breath'd the dusty Air of *Hide-Park,* all Summer) may find themselves lost in the Middle of the *Fair,* and not discover where they are, or what they have been about, till the Mist is clear'd from before their Eyes, and the agreeable Vision vanish'd.

To enter into a curious Detail of every particular Amusement to be met with in these *Fairs,* would swell this pigmy Volume to an enormous Bulk. Therefore I shall close this Scene with observing, that from my nicest Remarks upon these publick Meetings, and the Variety of Spectators and Amusements that attend them, I cannot avoid saying, that they nearly resemble the *Secular Games* of the *Romans,* and the *Jubilees* of their modern Successors; only what they enjoy'd in the Revolution of every Hundred, Fifty, or Twenty five Years, we can command at different Places and Seasons, often in the Compass of twelve Months, whilst we can justly laugh at the pompous Proclamation of their Shews, which no Man could hope to live to see a second Time.

Just as I had resolv'd to shut up this my last Essay upon our publick Diversions, I recollected, that I was about disobliging five Parts in Six of the numerous Inhabitants of this *Metropolis,* by neglecting to make honourable Mention of our *Publick Auctions;* which of late Years are become one of the principal Amuse-

ments

ments of all Ranks, from the Duke and Dutch-
efs to the Pick-pocket and Street-walker.

I am fenfible that many People (whofe Judgments are actuated by Prejudice, or their private
Intereft) will immediately object to the Progrefs
thefe *Auctions* have made, and call loudly for a
Stop to be put to fo growing an Evil. They'll
affert, That in Time, their irregular Motions will
caufe a Stagnation in Trade, hinder Money to
circulate juftly, and ruin even thofe of large
Fortunes, by buying fo many good Bargains.

They'll pretend to argue, That the Notion of
Oeconomy, wrong underftood, has fo far infected all Degrees of People with the Hopes of
buying every thing immoderately cheap, that
they crowd to *Auctions* to purchafe what they
do not want, rather than mifs of a charming
Pennyworth. That fine Ladies go there only
to get the better of fome idle Hours, and that
fine Gentlemen will follow them: Both are o-
blig'd in Honour to bid for fomething, tho' e-
ver fo unneceffary; and when they are fo happy as to meet with a delicious Bargain, they do
not know what to do with their Purchafe, and
would give Fifty *per Cent.* to have this Piece of
good Fortune taken off their Hands.

THESE Foes to our publick *Auctions* infinuate, that the *Virtuofi* go there to part with their
old Curiofities at a dear Rate, and pick up o-
thers more valuable for a Trifle; breaking
Tradefmen to get ready Money for ftale Goods:
The Setters to bid for every Thing and buy
nothing; and the *Auctioneer*———— to be the only
gaining Perfon: Nay, they add, that the Infatuation is now fo general, there is no Way left
of opening the Eyes of the World in this Le-
thargick

thargick State, till the Smart of their Follies a-wakens them.

THUS will some Mortals rail at, or ridicule every thing that is carry'd on successfully for the publick Good : Critick-like they live by finding Fault; ill Nature works in them, as Poison does in a Toad; they must spit their Venom, or they swell,——they burst,——they die.

FOR my Part, how they can be thought prejudicial to Trade, is to me miraculous; when the Furniture of our Houses (which generally consists of our own Manufactures) is bought up in such Profusion, that the Frequenters of *Auctions*, not only over-stock all their Apartments, but lay up whole Magazines, and turn every Garret into a Lumber-room. If the Buyers at *Actions* merit not the Title of *Oeconomists,* as to the Article of laying out their Money; yet they certainly may claim it, as to the Management of their Time, which is abundantly more precious. These *Entertainments* are so calculated for the Use of the *Idle* and *Indolent*; that Morning, Noon and Night, they may know where to be most agreeably busy.

WHETHER the Sticklers for, or against publick *Auctions* prevail, I care not, but think my self oblig'd in Honour to do Justice to a near Relation of our Family, before I drop this Subject; the worthy Mr. *Cock* of *Broad-street,* near *Golden square.* He is allow'd by all the World, to be a very clever Gentleman in his Business, and manages his little Hammer as much to the Purpose as any Instrument can possibly attain to : His Flourishes are genteel, yet significant; his Manner of Address easy and well-bred, but intrepid; his Phrases manly without Rudeness, and expressive without Obscurity, or Circumlocution. Not *Tully* himself could fill a *Rostrum* with more

X 3   Grace

Grace, or Eloquence. And we may venture to affirm, for the Glory of this Age, and our own Nation, that if affifted by the Endeavours of the Reverend Mr. *H——ly,* Reftorer of the antient Elocution and Action; that the Induftry and Capacity of thefe two Gentlemen will raife *Pulpit-Oratory* to a higher Pitch of Fame than Mankind yet has known.

I fear moft of my Readers will feem fhock'd, when after this copious Lift of Town Diverfions I muft confefs, that I have not touch'd upon the moft material Part of all, which gives the greateft Delight to the Majority of Audiences, or Affemblies of every Kind: And without which, the moft perfect *Entertainment* is look'd upon as ridiculous and infipid: But I hope their Surprize will readily abate, when I fet full in their View the Beauty of a Crowd: —— A Crowd! ——— which never fails to give Harmony to flat O P E-R A S Spirit, to dull Plays, and Life, to heavy Dances. Nothing could be added more *apropos* to the Nature and Defign of thefe E S S A Y S: For even with thofe who would be efteem'd the principal Judges of all publick Amufements, a Crowd is generally the Touch-ftone of Merit.

W H A T would our fine Ladies fay to an *Af-fembly,* or *Opera,* where they are not crowded to Death? *Lard!* —— *'tis fo agreeable to be joftled, and fqueez'd, and pufh'd, and pull'd to Pieces.* In what a filly Light would *Cato* appear to our genteel Criticks, with vacant Benches!——How dull the brighteft Preacher, with a thin Congregation?——and how ugly a reigning Toaft in an empty Drawing-room?

A Crowd is the Soul of *Mufick* and *Poetry;* the Quinteffence of good Senfe, and the Wit of a *Mafquerade.* In fhort, it is the *Je ne fçay quoy*

in

in every thing that pretends to the Name of a polite Amufement, and the *tout enfemble* of Perfections in all publick *Entertainments*.

I think it altogether needlefs, to canvafs any farther thofe Diverfions of the Town .which I have already touch'd upon, or hunt out for others, which are not of Confequence enough to be look'd into. I hope that every Part (of thofe which are moft frequented) have their Beauties, Defects and Amendments made fufficiently manifeft; and every Point fo fupported by undeniable Circumftances and Examples, that no Proof can be more felf-evident.

I make no Doubt, but feveral of my Readers will look upon my Method of handling this Topick as too circumftantial and prolix, while others will think me too concife, and perhaps very defective, in omitting what they call a publick Amufement. I have, in thefe Essays, furnifh'd out a Magnificent Banquet, to which the whole Town is invited: Every Man will either barely commend the Difh he likes, and find fault with all the reft; or if his fingular Palate is not touch'd with fome particular Kickfhaw, damn the whole Treat.

The wife Cabals of our *News-mongers* (who feed upon our publick Papers, and gravely hold forth in the principal Corners of our Top Coffee and Chocolate-Houfes) will be ftruck with Amazement, that in the prefent Pofture of Affairs, the State of *Europe* is not look'd into, War and Peace never mention'd, and the Ballance of Power forgot; when thefe Points, artfully vary'd, ferve to amufe four Parts in five of the deepeft Heads in *Great-Britain*.

Our natural Philofophers will fneer at my total Neglect of *Mary* of *Godliman*, and the whole

whole Rabbit-scene. *What! not a Page of his Book set aside, to inspect the Affairs of the wonderful Rabbit-woman?* — *No Notice taken of D---r M——in's Physical, or Monsieur St. A——e's Anatomical Discoveries?* —— *Stupid Creature!* —— *He writes* Essays *upon publick Diversions, and never names* Cunny Moll; *who, like the B——r's O——ra, engross'd all Conversation for six Months; after whom all Degrees of People ran so fast and so long, that both the* Entertainment *and they were quite out of Breath.*

The *Literati* and *Politicians* will expect a full Detection of the artificial, natural, and political Mysteries in *Gulliver's* Travels. They undoubtedly will be astonish'd at my so negligently touching an Affair of that Moment to Mankind in general, and to this Nation in particular; or that I should in so careless a Manner, only throw in a few loose Hints, in Relation to that wonderful Book, which has in some Measure surpriz'd, diverted, or instructed every *Briton* great and small, rich and poor, young and old, whether they understood it or no.

Nay, Fawks's *Dexterity of Hand, the moving Pictures, Musical-Clocks,* Solomon's *Temple,* the *Wax-work, all alive,* the *High-german Artist, born without Hands or Feet,* the *Cow with five Legs,* the *Hare that beats a Drum,* the *Savoyard's Rareshow,* and all other Curiosities of Art and Nature, will find their Admirers, who would demand a formal Essay in their Favour, to illustrate their Beauties, and make manifest their Use and Instruction.

But were I to canvass the Merits of such Trifles, what I propos'd as a necessary Pocket-companion, would soon fill a Folio Shelf in a Library. My Design was, to animadvert upon
the

the Standard *Entertainments* of the present Age, in Comparison with those of Antiquity; not to take Notice of every Mushroom Amusement in my Way, which dies, perhaps, the Day it springs up; or if set fairly a going, yet can't outlive its first Run.

Having, to the utmost of my weak Endeavours, strove to execute so laudable a Design; I shall conclude here, preferring an expressive Brevity to an unmeaning Circumlocution. The World, by this rude Sketch, may readily guess at the absolute Necessity of a Work of this Nature, and, perhaps, the Out-lines I have here so unskilfully drawn, may tempt a masterly Hand to touch up these Figures with some finishing Strokes. It is Honour sufficient for me to have led the Way in so great an Undertaking, in Hopes that those who have Power and Capacity, may one Day fix our publick *Entertainments* upon a Basis as lasting, as beneficial to Mankind.

F I N I S.